CLEAN CLOTHES

A Global Movement to End Sweatshops

Liesbeth Sluiter

PlutoPress
www.plutobooks.com

First published 2009 by Pluto Press
345 Archway Road, London N6 5AA and
175 Fifth Avenue, New York, NY 10010

www.plutobooks.com

Distributed in the United States of America exclusively by
Palgrave Macmillan, a division of St. Martin's Press LLC,
175 Fifth Avenue, New York, NY 10010

British Library Cataloguing in Publication Data
A catalogue record for this book is available from the British Library

ISBN   978 0 7453 2769 3   Hardback
ISBN   978 0 7453 2768 6   Paperback

Library of Congress Cataloging in Publication Data applied for

This book is printed on paper suitable for recycling and made from fully managed
and sustained forest sources. Logging, pulping and manufacturing processes are
expected to conform to the environmental standards of the country of origin.
The paper may contain up to 70 per cent post consumer waste.

10   9   8   7   6   5   4   3   2   1

Designed and produced for Pluto Press by
Chase Publishing Services Ltd, 33 Livonia Road, Sidmouth, EX10 9JB, England
Typeset from disk by Stanford DTP Services, Northampton, England
Printed and bound in the European Union by
CPI Antony Rowe, Chippenham and Eastbourne

Contents

Photographs

For my mother,
who loved to make clothes for her ungrateful daughter

Acknowledgements

Like the clean clothes movement, this book would not have seen the light of day without the collaboration, enthusiasm and stamina of many people. I am grateful to all those who gave generously of their time and were willing to share their knowledge and experience with me. In the Clean Clothes Campaign, I would especially like to thank Marieke Eyskoot, always in high spirits and an invaluable source of information and support, and Ton de Heij, who never once failed to answer my requests for data, photos and figures. Editor Charles Peyton polished and strengthened this text with great consideration. Guus de Klein has not only been my rock, but also my rock & roll.

This book has been written with support of the Stichting Democratie en Media, Le Fondation de Droit de l'Homme au Travail, the FNV, the ASN Bank, and the Stichting Brandnetel.

Essential Abbreviations

BSCI   Business Social Compliance Initiative: a business-driven organisation for code of conduct compliance in the garment industry. It has no multiple stakeholders, and audit reports are not published.

CCC   Clean Clothes Campaign: a global network for the improvement of labour conditions in the garment industry.

CSR   Corporate Social Responsibility: a form of voluntary self-regulation whereby businesses monitor their adherence to a set of standards in the realms of environment, consumers, employees, communities and other public stakeholders.

ETI   Ethical Trading Initiative: a UK-based multi-stakeholder initiative of businesses, trade unions and NGOs that executes pilot projects and exchanges best practices.

EPZ   Export processing zone: industrial area in a developing country that produces for export; taxes, tariffs and regulations are minimised and infrastructure optimised in the hope of attracting foreign investment.

FLA   Fair Labor Association: a US-based multi-stakeholder initiative of businesses, trade unions and NGOs that holds participant companies accountable to its code of conduct through a system of internal monitoring and external verification.

FTZ   Free trade zone: see EPZ.

FWF   Fair Wear Foundation: a Netherlands-based multi-stakeholder initiative of businesses, trade unions and NGOs that holds participant companies accountable to its code of conduct through a system of internal monitoring and external verification.

GSCP   Global Social Compliance Programme: a business-driven organisation for code of conduct compliance in the garment industry. It has no multiple stakeholders, and audit reports are not published.

ILO   International Labour Organisation: the UN agency for
           the promotion of social justice and human and labour
           rights.
ITGLWF   International Textile, Garment and Leather Workers'
           Federation: a global union federation.
IS   International Secretariat of the Clean Clothes
           Campaign.
ITUC   International Trade Union Federation: a global union
           federation.
MFA   Multi-Fibre Arrangement: a system of quota
           restrictions established in 1974 under the World Trade
           Organisation, intended to give the industry in
           developed countries the chance to adapt to cheap
           imports from developing countries.
MSI   Multi-stakeholder initiative of businesses, trade unions
           and NGOs that aims for corporate responsibility with
           regard to labour-rights standards along the supply
           chain.
NCPs   National contact points of the OECD, responsible for
           publicising its Guidelines, promoting the adherence of
           affiliated states, and reviewing complaints against
           companies.
NGO   Non-governmental organisation: civil society
           organisation.
OECD   Organisation for Economic Cooperation and
           Development: an organisation that promotes the
           interests of 30 countries committed to democracy and
           the market economy.
OPT   Outward Processing Trade: a trade and investment
           mechanism whereby clothes are made in eastern
           European countries with materials from EU countries.
SAI   Social Accountability International: US multi-
           stakeholder initiative of businesses, trade unions and
           NGOs that aims to bring global consistency to code of
           conduct standards and third-party verification
           procedures.
Socam   Service Organisation for Compliance Audit
           Management: C&A's organisation for code of conduct
           compliance in the supply chain. It has no multiple
           stakeholders, and audit reports are not published.

TNC   Transnational corporation: a corporation that manages production and/or delivers services in more than one country.

WRAP   Worldwide Responsible Apparel Production: a business-driven organisation for code of conduct compliance in the garment industry. It has no multiple stakeholders, and audit reports are not published.

WTO   World Trade Organisation: global organisation designed to liberalise and regulate trade.

Preface

Since the mid nineteenth century, garment industry employees have been among the most exploited workers on the planet. The inhuman working conditions in the early sweatshops of London and New York have been well documented. Less well known is the fact that today famous high street fashion brands and big-box retailers have their clothes made under those inhuman conditions in Bangladesh, China, Madagascar, Romania and Nicaragua – any place, in fact, where wages are low and workers are unable to organise themselves.

In the garment industry, globalisation has come to mean that fashion brands and big-box retailers seduce customers in the world's shopping centres with prices that seem too good to be true – and are in fact too good to be fair to the sweatshop workers in the world's production centres. But the misery behind our fashionable clothes has become invisible. One of the purposes of this book is exposing the injustices of this industry and the mechanisms behind them; the other is to show that something can be done. Everybody wears clothes; everybody is involved.

The Clean Clothes Campaign is a worldwide network that supports garment workers in their struggle for a better life, traces the industry's supply chains, and urges those in charge to respect labour rights. But, while in the past 20 years the campaign has successfully turned the spotlight on rights violations and contributed to the acceptance of corporate social responsibility among businesses, sweatshop labour still disgraces the global garment industry. The fight for clean clothes is not over yet.

Introduction

The Clean Clothes Campaign office is established in a former school building in Amsterdam. Visitors pass through a corridor lined with publications in several languages to find a cluster of rooms full of people who peer at computer screens, tap keyboards, dig into stacks of paper, confer in groups around tables, or shout into a telephone in the hope of being understood in an office on the other side of the world. Most of them are women. The atmosphere is informal and easy-going, but there is always a sense of urgency in the air.

This office is the nerve centre of a network that communicates with corporate directors in London and migrant workers in China's Pearl River Delta, and that connects shopping teenagers in Stockholm to home-workers in Delhi, fashion designers in Warsaw to seamstresses in Madagascar, housewives in Madrid to union leaders in Sri Lanka. It is a 'system of information, protest and planning, a system already coursing with activity and ideas crossing many national borders and several generations', as Naomi Klein puts it in the introduction to *No Logo*, her book that describes the birth of a movement that fights the adverse effects of globalisation.[1] The Clean Clothes Campaign is part of this movement and, after 20 years of protest and planning, it is no longer in its infancy.

The campaign got off the ground on 29 September 1988, when 50 women picketed in front of a C&A clothes store in Amsterdam. They were members of feminist groups, Third World solidarity groups, squatting communities and consumer organisations. They were angry because they had discovered that the clothes they wore had been made in sweatshops – places where people at the wrong end of economic development work long hours for little pay, under harsh conditions.

Their action was one in a long line of protest dating back to the nineteenth century. Around 1850 Charles Kingsley, a British Christian Socialist, wrote the pamphlet *Cheap Clothes and Nasty*, a diatribe against the 'sweating system' in London's clothing trade of the time. Its most amazing feature is that so many of the characteristics it describes still apply to the sweatshops of today.[2]

At the time, the production of ready-made, mass-produced garments was underway. In London's West and East Ends, contractors or 'sweaters' transformed the 'honourable tailoring trade'. In the past, craftsmen had made clothes in workshops where a master had paid them daily wages; now the work was let out to contractors who hired workers for a piece-wage. Facilitated by a progressive division of labour, the work was let out again and again. The competition between contractors and subcontractors ground wages and working conditions down to the lowest possible level: whoever delivered the clothes fastest and cheapest got the order. When the last drop of sweat had been wrung out of a worker, the next one was waiting, fresh from a countryside village or off the boat from Ireland. Because the work on a piece of clothing was split up, little learning was needed. Hand-sewing was still the norm; the newly invented sewing machines were expensive and unreliable. The workers, increasingly female, often lived in or above the 'sweatshop', usually the contractor's house. They worked long hours for so little money that they had to pawn their coats to be able to eat. Workers covered themselves with the clothes they were sewing to protect themselves against the cold. Sometimes they were out of work, sometimes there was so much that children had to help out. Sarcastically, Kingsley wrote:

> Sweet competition! Heavenly maid! Nowadays hymned alike by penny-a-liners and philosophers as the ground of all society, the only real preserver of the earth! Why not of heaven, too? ... All classes, though by their own confession they are ashamed, are yet not afraid to profit by the system ... What can be done? It is so hard to deprive the public of the luxury of cheap clothes ... if civilisation is to benefit everyone except the producing class – then this world is truly the devil's world, and the sooner so ill-constructed and infernal a machine is destroyed, the better.[3]

The first improvements occurred in large-scale manufacture. As early as 1860, some factories operated with modern technology which, together with an ongoing subdivision of tasks, allowed for lower production costs without 'sweating' labour, and in the second half of the nineteenth century, factories appeared with better working conditions and secure employment. The Factory Act of 1878 regulated hours and conditions of work in factories with more than 50 workers, and in some workshops. The textiles and garment industry became one of the engines behind Britain's economic development, and brought progress and prosperity for parts of the population. But sweatshops continued to exist at the market's low end, and legislative intervention passed them by. In the years to follow, trade unions and progressive political parties joined forces to combat degrading working conditions. But so strong is the combination of a competitive industry and a destitute labour force that, even today, migrant women sew clothes for poverty wages in the backyards of Britain's high streets.[4]

In the late nineteenth century, the rest of Europe and the US became acquainted with garment sweatshops, and the blueprint reads much the same: a combination of subcontracted orders, steep competition, lack of government regulation and unschooled, often migrant labour led to exploitation of workers and inhumane working conditions.

Where trade unions, labour law and socio-political movements had managed to narrow the margins of exploitation in industrialised countries, producers began to cast their nets in wider arcs, all the way to the developing world, to countries where no labour laws or trade unions would put a spoke in the wheels that drove production costs to the bottom. Sweatshops, after having served the industrial revolution in the western world, continue to cater to the needs of the present-day global economy. Subcontracting, untraceable supply chains, cheap labour, child labour, gender discrimination, migration, repression of worker organisation – more than 150 years after Charles Kingsley's call to arms, these practices continue to shape the landscape of sweated labour, albeit across much wider zones of time and space. Today it is possible to find Chinese women in a Swiss factory in Romania, making clothes for the luxury Italian brand Prada and the giant French retailer Carrefour.[5] Welcome to globalisation!

From its inception in the nineteenth century, the garment industry has led a footloose life. As a relatively 'lightweight' industry that does not need a lot of investment in heavy machinery or land, it is well equipped for travel, and travel it did – first within cities, then within countries, and finally stopped only by the natural borders of earth itself. Wherever workers succeeded in organising themselves and in raising wages and working conditions, the industry packed and moved on, in search of cheaper production sites. Relocation is one of its persistent characteristics, and a mechanism that defeats trade union organising time and again.

Towards the end of the last millennium, a new type of movement took up the gauntlet. It adapted to the flexibility of industry by being flexible itself. It took the form of a network that followed the industry's tracks all over the globe, mainly by making connections. Connections are its strong point, as befits a network. It connects people making clothes with people who wear them. It connects fashion designers in Warsaw to seamstresses in Madagascar ... and yes, after a detour in time and space, we return to the Clean Clothes Campaign.

After the Dutch organisation was formally established in 1989, it sprouted twelve more Clean Clothes Campaigns in eleven European countries. They are coalitions of development NGOs, unions, women's and youth groups, religious and consumer groups. Globally, they have built a partner network that in 2009 unites at least 250 organisations, from trade unions in Indonesian factories to workers' assistance centres in the Philippines and China. They concentrate on the countries where European clothes are made, and cooperate closely with anti-sweatshop groups in the United States and Canada that focus on their 'own' production countries. The people in this movement are determined to eradicate sweatshops, because their existence insults their sense of justice and equality or, as one campaigner puts it: 'We work towards a society that upholds the principles that all human beings are equal and that human rights must be enforced.' (See Part 3, Interlude.)

Clean Clothes is the story of that work, jumping back and forth between continents and decades, describing successes and defeats, street actions and European parliament resolutions, the worldwide partner network and its principles. It is based on interviews, archives, reports, newspapers, strategy papers and eyewitness accounts, and in this it mirrors the mosaic of the movement itself.

Chapters 1–6 concentrate on the globalising industry and on the network that globalises in the industry's wake. Chapter 1 discusses the Netherlands, where the movement began its campaign for clean clothes on the pavement outside C&A, the largest Dutch garment retailer. Chapter 2 describes the mechanisms and processes of relocation of the industry. Chapters 3–5 deal with Asian and African countries, with those of eastern Europe, and with Turkey – countries where the bulk of European clothes are made. The development of the garment sector in these countries is described, and members of the Campaign's local partner network relate their struggles and their hopes. Chapter 6 and the Interlude describe the development of the European network. Chapters 7–11 take up the debates about goals and strategies that began in 1989 and are still on the agenda in 2009. They focus on the four mainstays of the Campaign's work: support for workers, the role of consumers, legal reform, and the role of companies.

By exporting exploitation, globalisation has made it possible for prosperous world citizens to turn a blind eye to the people at the suffering end. We hope this book will open some eyes.

Part 1

A Globalising Industry

1
A Footloose Enterprise

THE QUIET GIANT AWAKENS

The Clean Clothes Campaign (CCC) was born on the pavement in front of the Dutch garment store C&A in Amsterdam, where on an autumn day in 1988 some 50 women protested against the fact that the clothes sold inside were made under sweatshop conditions. In the words of Ineke Zeldennrust, a pioneer 'clean clothes' activist:

> The action fitted into the general political atmosphere of those days. Internationalism was the buzzword, whether you were involved in the squatters' movement, the anti-apartheid struggle, or feminism. Many organisations targeted multinationals. I thought – and still think – that every strategy that is blind to the exploitation of women would ultimately fail.
>
> When the link between consumption in rich countries and production in poor countries dawned upon us, it became clear that solidarity with women worldwide meant that we should begin to put pressure on multinationals at home. The garment industry was and is possibly the most widespread example of a global commodity chain with western buyers in the driving seat. We decided to focus on C&A. It was Dutch, it was big, and we already had information about its use of sweatshop labour in the Netherlands and abroad. Targeting one company allowed us to focus our energy and use our resources efficiently.[1]

In the Netherlands, mass production of garments in workshops and factories began in the second decade of the twentieth century, between the First and the Second World Wars. At the time, producers and retailers were not competing on skirt length or autumn colours – fashion in the modern sense did not yet exist. Most important was price. When the first machine operators, recruited from the large cities' poor, began to organise and demand better wages, production moved partly to the provinces – an early example of industrial mobility. In the 1950s and 1960s, more than 100,000 people worked in the Dutch garment industry, and C&A was one of the star players.

C&A stands for Clemens and August, the two German brothers Brenninkmeijer. In the first half of the nineteenth century they regularly crossed the German–Dutch border to mow grass and cast peat. It proved rewarding to smuggle shirts and haberdashery as well, so rewarding that in 1841 the brothers were able to open a linen warehouse in the northern Dutch city of Sneek, and, 20 years later, the first C&A store.[2] It sold ready-made clothes in differing sizes, originally for the better-off classes and later for all the world and his wife – a huge success. In 1893 the company established itself in Amsterdam, and after that many Dutch cities became acquainted with the new clothes and the new way of buying them.

In 1911 the Brenninkmeijer family crossed the Dutch–German border again, in reverse this time, and carrying more weight than a few smuggled shirts, and opened their first German stores. In 1922 the first C&A was established in London's Oxford Street. After the Second World War, international expansion took off on a large scale. Between 1963 and 1995, eight more European countries were introduced to the red-and-blue logo and to C&A's concept of cheap clothes for the masses. In 1963 C&A crossed the Atlantic Ocean to establish itself in America by buying Ohrbach, a chain of garment stores, and in 1976 it arrived in Brazil. In the early 1970s the company had a 15 per cent market share in the Netherlands and in Germany, and employed 34,000 people worldwide. It was and remains a limited partnership, and the only owners and directors are members of the Brenninkmeijer family, which grew at the same speed as the company.[3]

C&A proved good at competing on price. Its large orders allowed it to put pressure on manufacturers, and business thrived. In the early 1980s, the return on investment in Germany (Germany being the only country where C&A was forced by law to publish its company books) was more than 50 per cent. With a worldwide turnover of equivalent to almost 7 billion euros (at 2002 values – and with an added 36-billion-euro turnover of investment companies owned by C&A), the Brenninkmeijers were shaping one of the biggest corporations in the Netherlands, and even in the world, on a par with Shell and Philips.[4]

But while C&A was going at full speed, manufacturers were struggling. They had to find ways to cut prices. In this labour-intensive industry, an effective way to achieve this is employing cheap and flexible labour. When in the 1970s the Dutch government enacted a minimum wage, a youth minimum wage and equal pay for women and men, garment producers had a hard time meeting these obligations. With rising wages on the one hand, and the sharp buying practices of C&A and other large companies on the other, profit margins were reduced to the extent that manufacturers began to look around for cheaper labour.[5]

Technological innovation in transport and communications had made the earth smaller; now it was possible to tap the reservoir of the Third World poor, and subsequently production was moved to low-wage countries like Tunisia, Taiwan and South Korea. Only design, packaging and quality control – the so-called 'head and tail' of production – stayed in the Netherlands. Between 1972 and 1974, Dutch employment in garment-production dropped by a clear 36 per cent.[6] This was the first wave of the so-called 'runaway production'.

Turnover, in the meantime, increased. Fashion, that powerful engine of sales, was on the march. Branding and marketing began to define the success of companies, and advertising budgets soared. At the beginning of the 1980s, C&A was by far the biggest advertiser in Dutch newspapers.[7] Management decided to diversify the clothes collection. No longer just a cheap store for the masses, C&A now positioned itself more upmarket, with separate labels for different ages and styles. In the late 1970s and 1980s, production was spread all over the world. Large lots of mass-produced 'ever-sellers', for which delivery schedules were not that tight, were ordered from distant Asia, where people worked one month for a Dutch daily wage. Fashion was produced closer to home – in Portugal, eastern Europe, Turkey and Tunisia. Production of the most fashion-sensitive clothes, which were on the racks for just a couple of months and needed a fast turnaround, was brought back home – not to the old factories in the provinces, but to sweatshops in the larger cities of Great Britain and the Netherlands, served by mostly immigrant workers. Following the 'runaway' production of the early 1970s, this was the so-called 're-runaway' production that moved production partly to other low-wage countries, partly back home.

DUTCH SWEATSHOPS

In the 1980s, in a climate of economic stagnation with high unemployment, Dutch sweatshops thrived. At the end of that decade an estimated 800–1,000 sweatshops existed in Holland, employing between 5,000 and 8,000 workers.[8] Home-workers, usually women without contracts or social security, were on standby for busy times. Many sweatshop owners were Turkish immigrants who had lost their jobs when the large Amsterdam shipyards folded. The garment branch suffered all the ills of fast work for little pay: excessive overtime, irregular work, piece-wages, unhealthy and unsafe working conditions in cellars or sheds. Owners paid neither taxes nor social security. They did not invest in workplace improvements because disclosure of their illegal practices was always around the corner. When they felt the heat they shut down, only to open up again a few streets away. The work took a heavy toll on the workers, but 'the worst thing is that we're always afraid to be caught. At work, on the bus, in a pub or in the street. You never know where and when. It is a stressful existence', said a Turkish illegal garment worker.[9]

Most of the workers, often trained stitchers, arrived in the Netherlands indebted, because they had paid heavily for fraudulent passports and visas. In fear of losing their jobs, they were forced to undergo hardship without protest. The sweatshops supplied their handmade, high-quality, cheap garments to the large brands and to 'boutiques' that ordered small lots of exclusive clothes. Sweatshop prices were low, because the competition was murderous. Between 1980 and 1990, market prices plunged by 60–70 per cent, paid for by wage reduction and tax evasion.[10]

The media, the public and the government pointed the finger at the owners, but they maintained that the brands, buying at the sweatshops through intermediary suppliers, left them with little choice. 'For a quarter less they go elsewhere', a Turkish sweatshop owner supplying C&A was reported saying. Another said that the piece price had fallen sharply since the early 1980s, and reckoned that C&A always made a profit of between 100 and 120 per cent on clothes made in his sweatshop.[11] Complaints also focused on the sometimes extremely short delivery times, giving rise to irregular and long working hours. The garment sector was not pleased with the negative publicity. To clean up its image, it sought cooperation with the government to try and eradicate illegal sweatshops. In 1993, the existing Law on Chain Responsibility was adapted to apply to garment sweatshops. C&A stated that this would 'solve the problem of buyer responsibility'.[12]

In the words of Ineke Zeldenrust:

In many respects the Law on Chain Responsibility was a good thing. Skika, the organisation of immigrant sweatshop workers and part of the Clean Clothes Campaign coalition that had formed by that time, contributed to the development of that law. But because legalisation relating to workers and workplaces was not part of the deal, the Law did not improve conditions in the workshops. Instead they were closed and workers lost their jobs.[13]

In 1989, SOMO, a Dutch NGO that researches transnational companies and the effects of their policies, had published the book *C&A: de Stille Gigant* (*C&A: The Quiet Giant*). It unravelled C&A's corporate structure, and described the company, a limited partnership and family business, as extremely secretive. It concluded that C&A's denial of 'multinational status' served to evade transparency regulation for multinationals, and to keep its books closed to external scrutiny.[14]

The Quiet Giant traced C&A's involvement in sweatshop labour in the Netherlands, in Great Britain and in Third World countries. The company in return published a booklet in which it professed its horror at the exploitation of vulnerable people and rejected the use of sweatshops. It maintained that contracts with suppliers always involved a clause that local law and social rules were to be respected, that buyers were instructed to oversee this, and that infringements were sanctioned by withdrawal of orders.[15] But eight years later, in the weekly branch magazine *Textilia*, C&A spokesman Jaap Bosman admitted that the company had sourced from illegal sweatshops in the past. 'But we definitely weren't the only ones', he added. 'We just had the bad luck to be targeted.' Regarding Asian sweatshop labour, he said:

> We belonged to the first group that went to the Far East; do you really think anybody was thinking about labour conditions at the time? I think we didn't even perform so badly, considering the times. We had a conduct code of sorts, the so-called General Delivery Instructions, in which the supplier promised to uphold the laws of the country. Of course the system wasn't watertight. The laws of those countries often do not match western standards. In Syria for example it was possible for twelve-year-old children to work. But at least we had something. Another problem was that we couldn't always check subcontractors. You weren't told. It happens that journalists discover miserable labour conditions in factories where we don't even know that they produce for us. That is bad for our image; we have learned from it.[16]

THE OTHER SIDE OF THE WORLD

In the meantime, the Clean Clothes Campaign in Amsterdam was gaining a grip on the complicated subject of the globalising garment industry. *C&A: The Quiet Giant* and further research had widened the scope of the campaign. The garment industry appeared to be like water; it headed for the lowest level – of both wages and worker organisation. In order to fight this, it was going to be necessary to follow the industry and cross borders. This idea was reinforced during the second action involving C&A.

In 1989, women from a Manchester trade union had taken up the case of a group of Philippine garment workers. In May, after a nationwide strike, the Philippines had embraced that milestone of civilisation: a minimum wage. But the management of the Intercontinental Garment Manufacturing Corporation (IGMC) had gone its own way. IGMC was situated in Bataan, a so-called export processing zone (EPZ) or free trade zone (FTZ).[17] When the women workers of IGMC in Bataan had demanded to be paid the minimum wage, they had been fired – all 1000 of them – and the factory had closed down. The machinery had stayed put, which had given the women reason to suspect that IGMC would reopen with new personnel. They had set up camp in front of the factory and begun a 24-hour picket that they kept up for months on end. Since IGMC was a subsidiary company of the UK-based multinational William Baird, the Manchester women supported their struggle.[18] When it was discovered that C&A, through William Baird, was a large buyer at IGMC, Dutch women joined the protest and targeted C&A. Ineke Zeldenrust said:

Although international solidarity was 'hot', the international division of labour and corporate responsibility were uncool subjects, reserved for a few academics, some radicals and a couple of anti-imperialist diehards. There was virtually no knowledge then about the way consumer products were made. The notion that Dutch companies had their products manufactured under bad conditions in faraway countries was unheard of, and it was unthinkable that one could hold a retailer such as C&A responsible. After all, what did C&A have to do with what was happening in the Philippines? The company simply washed its hands of all responsibility. Remember, this was long before globalisation became a household word and before the internet. It was in the midst of an economic crisis in the West when people couldn't care less about other people's jobs, especially on the other side of the world.[19]

With the second C&A action, the CCC intended to burst that bubble of ignorance. The date was 8 March 1990 – International Women's Day, a celebration of women's emancipation originating in 1908, when 15,000 women had marched in New York to demand shorter working hours, better pay and voting rights. In this spirit the Dutch women occupied Dam Square in the middle of Amsterdam, and climbed lampposts in front of the Royal Palace to hang a giant orange banner comparing the income of the queen to the income of a garment worker – the House of Orange has always been a favourite punch-bag for all kinds of protest. A public burning of clothes in front of the nearby C&A store led to fights between activists and police.

Esther de Haan, an early clean clothes activist and until 2009 a CCC staff-member, remarked: 'It wasn't an aggressive or very provocative action, so we were very surprised when the mounted police charged and even broke one girl's foot.' And Ineke Zeldenrust said: 'The same happened at the "fashion show" on Dam Square. A civilised, friendly action, involving 20 people and a small stage – and all of a sudden we see ten platoons of riot police around the corner.'[20]

The company publicly denied responsibility for what was happening at IGMC. Legally this was correct: C&A Great Britain bought from William Baird, and since the company was not a multinational, what did Dutch management have to do with it? Nevertheless, C&A asked William Baird to settle with IGMC, one way or another. Various organisations – including a trade union and a development organisation, feminist groups, consumer and Third World solidarity groups – jointly asked C&A to stop buying from William Baird because of its violations of Philippine labour law. In the meantime, research on C&A revealed new cases of sweatshop exploitation in Bangladesh, India, and in the Netherlands.[21] In Great Britain the spotlight was kept on the case by a coalition of the fair trade initiative Traidcraft, the NGO Women Working Worldwide, trade unions, and the Philippines Support Group. They urged the public to ask retailers 'how clean their clothes are'. Lucy Salao, a Philippine worker, toured Great Britain to disclose her and her colleagues' working conditions. The media attention led to a libel writ against a magazine reporting on the case, causing it to fold. The Philippine picketers consequently refused to accept the settlement until the libel writ was lifted. The garment company Littlewoods withdrew orders from William Baird and drafted a code of conduct, citing compliance with minimum labour standards as essential for suppliers. It was one of the first adopted by British companies.

After a year-long picket, IGMC management and the workers reached an agreement that provided for compensation and back-pay up to the minimum-wage level. The Philippine trade union asked for an end to the protests against William Baird. During the lockout, IGMC had continued as a trade export organisation, buying from small producers. In early 1990 it reportedly opened a new factory under the name of Prego Corporation, where workers were paid 25–30 per cent less than the former workers would have earned under the agreement reached.[22] For the budding CCC, the Philippine campaign opened up doors to new forms of cooperation, internationally as well as between groups of different backgrounds on the national level.

CAMPAIGN LAUNCH

At the beginning of the 1990s a permanent campaign on the garment industry was underway in the Netherlands. In its first publications, the group announced that it targeted this industry because of the consequences of its mobility.[23] It stated that large brands were moving to and fro between poor Third World countries and the rich industrialised nations, and did as they liked. The industry was a prime example of capitalist exploitation – the thinking in these days still exhaled some of the staunch educational socialism of former activist generations. A second argument for targeting the garment industry was found on the gender battlefield. For the largely female campaigners, the fact that most garment workers were women was in itself a reason to support them. More importantly, it accounted for the level of exploitation in the industry. Poor women were even more vulnerable than poor men. They were unskilled, and the money they earned was considered an extra to the breadwinner's income, which was an excuse for low wages. Many women were home-workers, that most deprived and outlawed division of the labour force. The gender issue would be important throughout the development of the movement.

Although socialist, feminist and anti-imperialist theories resounded in the background, the aim of the campaign was thoroughly practical: to improve labour conditions in the garment industry. As Ineke Zeldenrust put it,

We have always been involved in research and analysis, but action was an indispensable part of our work from the beginning. You might even say that putting theory into practice is one of our ideological principles. Also, the coalition model implied that partners could cooperate on a practical level, even if they had different ideological agendas. In the Clean Clothes Campaign you work to achieve a particular goal.[24]

In its campaign strategy, the CCC outlined four areas of work: brands and retailers, consumers, government, and garment workers.[25] Brands and retailers would be held responsible for the way their merchandise was produced, all along the supply line. There was a first mention of a 'Fair Trade Charter', a set of rules that retailers would be asked to adhere to, and that would guarantee that the clothes they sold were 'clean'. This concept would be hotly debated in the following years, and it would take a decade for an international Charter to materialise in the form of the CCC 'Code of Conduct'.

Consumers would be educated and persuaded to change their buying behaviour. A fair trade label on the shop window could show which ones sold clothes that guaranteed their producers an honest wage. If coffee and bananas could have a fair trade label, why not clothes? This would turn out to be a question that persisted until today.

Government and politicians, the third area of work, would be asked to develop laws and regulations concerning production, pricing and company transparency, nationally as well as on a European level.

Finally, garment workers would be supported both financially and through solidarity actions.[26] A 'founding principle' was that garment workers themselves must define the demands that the campaign would lay at the doorstep of western companies.

In November 1990, the loose coalition of various groups solidified into the Clean Clothes Campaign – in Dutch, Schone Kleren Kampagne.[27] Ineke Zeldenrust explained:

Cooperation between women's groups, the solidarity movement and the labour movement was unusual at the time, and coalitions were not long lived. We thought a foundation with its own secretariat was a feasible way to coordinate the actions of the groups involved. Every group could use its own methods, as long as the goal was clear.

And Esther de Haan commented:

> We modelled the organisation on the anti-apartheid campaign
> that put pressure on Shell to withdraw from South Africa: a neat
> campaign with a broad support base, targeting one company, and
> with a coalition structure. While the participating groups formed
> a legal body, the campaign as such was collective property, open
> to everybody. It was a common model in those days. It built
> upon the notion that everybody has the right to fight abuses,
> without first having to secure the approval of a *politburo*. It had
> the added advantage of safeguarding the organisation from the
> legal consequences of radical action.[28]

Although the FNV, the largest Dutch trade union federation,
participated in discussions and campaigns, it did not join the
coalition at that time.

> The FNV has always been supportive, especially on a practical
> level. A union is of course not an action group, and vice versa;
> we had to get used to one another. It took time to establish our
> relative positions. Now trade unions are active in CCC campaigns
> in European and developing countries, either as a member of a
> CCC coalition or cooperating to achieve a common goal.[29]

C&A, the company the CCC had decided to focus on, was the
Dutch market leader, with a 20 per cent share. A national magazine
described C&A as thoroughly anti-union, both in its supply line and
in its own stores. Its buying practices were reported to be tough,
with buyers receiving military-style training.[30] The CCC organised
a national day of protest against C&A's buying practices. In eleven
cities, including one in Belgium, C&A stores were picketed. Some
demonstrations were small; some went all-out with fashion shows,
fire-eaters and street orchestras. 'Clean clothes' seemed to strike a
nerve. The campaign, so the organisers thought, provided people
with a practical way to express solidarity with women and labour
organisations in the South, while challenging the power of the
multinationals of the western world.

C&A was worried. It threatened to sue the authors of *The Quiet
Giant*, and did in fact sue a consumer organisation that had printed
the findings from the book. The dispute was settled in court.[31]
Proposed negotiations foundered on C&A's demand that all talks
should remain unpublished. The CCC argued that informing

the public was one of its goals. In a newspaper interview, C&A spokesman P. Remarque said that the company complied with local law and brought employment to low-wage countries. He called it a sign of 'heart-warming naivety' to ask C&A to open up about purchasing practices. 'In our branch, competition is won or lost by purchasing policies.'[32]

NAMING AND SHAMING

In its own and in other magazines, the CCC regularly published news and research on Bangladesh, the Philippines and India, revealing the explosive development of the export-oriented garment industry and new cases of sweatshop exploitation, some of them involving C&A.[33]

After the first 'runaway' production, Asia had become one of the destinations of the 're-runaway' production. The Philippines was highly prized as a production zone in the 1990s by large brands such as Levi Strauss, Sara Lee, Wrangler, Triumph and William Baird. Most factories were small. According to government statistics for 1987, out of a total of 969 garment factories, only 20 (of which 19 were foreign-owned) had more than 1,000 employees. But these 20 ordered from 254 workshops with 45 or fewer employees, and from about 150 agents who employed 450,000 home-workers – two-and-a-half times the number of factory workers. Total production was worth over US$1 billion (at 1987 values), and was mostly shipped out to the US and Europe. In the larger factories worker organisation was on the rise, as illustrated by the IGMC case described above. Workers in smaller workshops and home-workers, all non-unionised, were at the mercy of whoever provided work.

In Bangladesh, small garment workshops had proliferated since the first ones had opened in 1976; by 1989 there were about 700. Many were joint ventures between local businessmen and companies from countries that, because of their fast economic growth over the preceding years, had been known as the 'Asian Tigers': Taiwan, South Korea, Hong Kong and Singapore. In 1985, the US and Europe introduced import restrictions on clothes from Bangladesh to protect their own industries. Nevertheless, in 1987 imports from Bangladesh to the Netherlands amounted to 10 million euros (at 2002 values). While labour accounted for 60 per cent of production costs in the West, in Bangladesh this figure stood at 8 per cent. Wages were generally below the legal minimum, and 80 per cent of the workers were women. For the first time in this country, where traditionally a woman's work was strictly in the home, women worked in factories. Unions were barred from the workplace, 10 per cent of the workers were under-age, and health and safety measures were below standard. In December 1991, 25 women and children died in the infamous Saraca factory fire near Dhaka. All factory doors had been locked. It led to a march by 20,000 garment workers, a sector-wide strike, and the foundation of a trade union of garment workers.

India differed from Bangladesh only in terms of scale. New Delhi had at least 20,000 sweatshops. Even larger concentrations were found in Mumbai, and especially in southern Tirupur, where wages were lowest. Textiles and textile products accounted for 30 per cent of total exports.[34]

In 1993, Marijke Smit, one of the authors of *The Silent Giant*, visited five 'model factories' in Hong Kong, China and Indonesia, on the invitation of Dutch brands supplied by these factories. In the local context, she reported, labour conditions were reasonable, but still left much to be desired. She recorded forced overwork of up to 77 hours a week and an absence of legal contracts while the minimum wage, if there was one and the factory complied with it, was usually not enough for a decent living. Freedom of association was nonexistent. In Indonesia, a rising star in the low-wage race, women had to pay more than an hour's wage to visit the toilet. Hong Kong, where wages were on the rise, was giving way to China's much cheaper Shenzhen export processing zones.[35]

At the end of 1994, a scandal erupted when the British newspaper, the *Mail on Sunday*, made headlines around the world with a series of articles about child labour in sweatshops in Bangladesh and India.[36] The Clean Clothes Campaign had never singled out child labour as an issue. In the words of Marieke Eyskoot, CCC's European coordinator:

Of course it happens, of course it is horrible, and of course we fight it. But child labour is part of a broader system of injustice and abuse. It is much harder to interest an audience in that broader context, but child labour will never be eradicated unless that system has been abolished.[37]

Nevertheless, the CCC provided the *Mail on Sunday* with background information in the research stage, as well as in the legal battle that followed publication.[38] In Dhaka, the journalists visited two factories and discovered children at work in pitiful conditions.

Levi Strauss and C&A were among the main buyers. C&A Great Britain reacted immediately by investigating the situation and, finding the allegations to be true, cancelled a £5 million annual deal. John Greene, head of corporate communications, said: '[The article] serves as a reminder that even if you have the finest code [of conduct], unless you have a rigorous inspection system, the code does not have much meaning.' He promised that all other suppliers in Bangladesh would be audited.

Mail on Sunday reporter Nick Fielding was then approached by a C&A buyer who said that in Tirupur, south India, children were stitching clothes for C&A as well. He headed south and, posing as a company buyer, found a shed where clothes were made for a C&A supplier. His article described the sweatshop, where workers were not paid the minimum wage and toiled for long hours – and among whom he claimed to find children. C&A protested to the Press Complaints Commission. It offered photographs and doctors' statements to contradict the charges, and stated:

> C&A do not for a moment pretend that the conditions in which factory workers in the Indian sub-continent often work are anything other than very basic compared with those prevalent in the West. They also fully accept that the wages paid to employees like Patma and Mahendran are low. In all probability, moreover, there are, outside the Medonna factory, numerous instances in which child labour is used in Tirupur and beyond. What C&A do say, however, is that by their Code of Conduct they show a firm stance against child labour, and that their efforts have not ended there. Wherever resources have allowed, they have arranged for spot checks of suppliers and sub-contractors of the kind performed at the Medonna factory.[39]

Nick Fielding argued that C&A ignored the role that buyers played in suppliers' practices:

> Several buyers I have since spoken to have told me that it is impossible for factory owners in Tirupur to compete on price unless they use child labour. It is endemic in the town and with such tremendous competition, most factory owners choose to turn a blind eye.[40]

In the end, the Press Complaints Commission found for the *Mail on Sunday*, arguing that the parties had presented contradictory evidence, that the Commission itself was not able to verify it, and that in such a situation publication was in the public interest.[41]

A CODE OF CONDUCT

In 1991 C&A Europe had introduced its Code of Conduct for Suppliers.[42] This was a set of guidelines designed to prevent supplier companies from violating workers' rights and endangering their health. It encompassed eleven items, the most stringent being the fourth, which demanded that suppliers adhere to local law and be alert to any signs of exploitation, risks to health and safety, or environmental hazards, with special attention to child labour. Suppliers were to ensure that subcontractors also complied with these ground rules; transgressions were to be sanctioned by the cancellation of contracts. According to the CCC, the wording of the Code was vague – it had no provision for its distribution among suppliers, nor for the enforcement of compliance.

In 1996 C&A Europe moved forward on the path of Corporate Social Responsibility (CSR). It announced a restructuring of its buying policy and revised its Code into a 'Code of Conduct for the Supply of Merchandise', which now included basic criteria on the issues of child labour, forced labour, wages, health and safety, and the environment. It expressed the intention to develop long-term relations with suppliers, and required that C&A operate on the principle of 'fair and honest dealing' with suppliers. C&A Europe also set up its own control mechanism: the Service Organisation for Compliance Audit Management (Socam).

Socam was put in charge of auditing factories supplying C&A. The first Annual Report, a handsome but rather fact-starved booklet, stated that Socam made unannounced inspection visits to over 1000 production units each year.[43] As a result, it had warned 50 suppliers and suspended contracts with 80, of which 30 were reinstated after a corrective plan had been put in place. It concentrated particularly on child labour and 'basic working conditions', and violations of these standards had been the main cause for suspension of business. An audit typically lasted between one and two hours, reported a C&A paper for a conference in 1997, which also mentioned that it was not always possible to check the truth of the information auditors received about working hours and wages.[44] All information obtained by Socam is deemed confidential, because of the relationship of trust with manufacturers that 'outweighs the advantages of complete transparency'. The public demand for 'some form of public audit' is recognised, but, according to the Report, no organisation existed with either the experience or capacity to do this. While expressing the wish to be part of the discussion about a universal code of conduct, C&A would 'continue to develop its own objective operation'.[45]

Socam and the new Code were the subject of a lively debate between the company and the CCC groups that had been launched in the 1990s in several European countries.[46] In 1996 and 1997, there were communications between C&A and the CCC in Belgium, the Netherlands, France, Switzerland and the United Kingdom. In 1996 Oxfam UK, platform member of the British Labour Behind the Label campaign, asked six large retailers, including C&A, to do something about the abusive practices in small garment factories in the Midlands, where Asian women worked a 50-hour week for £80. Home-workers were even worse off. In the factories fire doors were found locked, and some had no toilets. C&A took the lead in publicly committing itself to send investigators and shine some light into the industrial underworld.[47]

This was a sign that the days were over when C&A would deny all responsibility, and when it saw the CCC as no more than an obnoxious moth in the clothes closet. In a 1999 newspaper interview, Socam director Winfried Sternemann said: 'We have been really affected by the accusations of various campaign groups, who are saying that we conduct an unethical business.' The CCC in turn was happy to announce in 1997 that C&A was now the best among the bad guys.[48] 'It didn't mean that we were hobnobbing with C&A, or any other company for that matter', says Ineke Zeldenrust.

> We've never done that. Companies think they are having a communication problem with us and want to talk. But what we see is a production problem, and we want them to talk about that to people at the local level. We are not the negotiating partners, we are the microphone.[49]

The opening up of communications had not silenced the campaign's criticism. At the occasion of its International Forum in May 1998, the CCC presented a case file on C&A in which Socam and the new Code were scrutinised.[50] C&A's new Code, the case file said, lacked precise criteria. If, for example, child labour was to be banned, an age limit should be set. The local minimum wage that the Code set as a standard was seldom sufficient for a decent living. Basic human rights were missing in the Code – notably freedom of association, which would enable workers to negotiate for themselves. The Code prescribed no maximum working hours, and did not mention social security. In a sector with so many women workers, a provision for paid maternity leave would have been no luxury.

While the Code, despite its shortcomings, was seen as a step forward, the CCC did not see Socam as a credible tool for the control of working conditions in the supply chain. It did not believe that an office paid for and mandated by C&A could be independent. There were no signs that Socam inspectors interviewed workers in such a way that they could speak freely, without fear for retaliation by factory owners if they were to disclose unfavourable information.

A RARE INSIDE VIEW

In May 1998, C&A revised its Code of Conduct. It clearly defined child labour: workers must not be younger than the legal minimum age for working in any specific country, and in any case be 14 or older. Freedom of association was recognised, and suppliers were obliged not to obstruct it. The leash on suppliers was pulled tighter: they were obliged to make subcontractors aware of the Code and to comply with it, and had to admit Socam inspectors at any time. Sometimes, said spokesman Jaap Bosman, ten Socam officials entered a city simultaneously because factory owners had been known to warn each other: 'Watch it, C&A is in town. Sweep the children under the carpet.'[51]

Socam's 1998 Annual Report testified to the growing level of communication between C&A, the CCC, other NGOs and trade unions. It describes how the debate with NGOs led to the adoption of the freedom of association clause. Not included in the Code, however, was the right to collective bargaining, which, together with freedom of association, makes up International Labour Organisation (ILO) convention no. 154.[52] On this subject C&A said:

> In a number of countries such a requirement is in conflict with local law and established practice. We prefer to move steadily to improve conditions without imposing unrealistic requirements ... We believe that cooperating with our suppliers to improve their practices, rather than adopting an extremist position from the outset, will most help vulnerable employees in the long run.[53]

Calling an ILO convention 'an extremist position' was going a bit far, and labour rights advocates argue that the right to collective bargaining is a human right, to be supported as much as the abolition of child labour. But until today, collective bargaining is not included in C&A's code of conduct. Still, C&A's views had changed since the late 1980s, when the company, answering allegations of selling sweatshop-made clothes, had distributed a pamphlet in its stores saying: 'Nobody is helped by false incriminations. We want to hear names and addresses; we must be provided with documents that are not falsified. In the meantime we continue to offer you legally bought and sharply priced fashion.'[54]

That the problems were endemic in the sector was illustrated once more by C&A itself, when in 1999 Socam director Winfried Sternemann reported 'a lot of problems with illegal shops in Great Britain's Midlands, in cities like Birmingham and Bradford, and in the suburbs of Paris where many illegal immigrants live'.[55]

In that same year the British *Sunday Times* published an article headed 'Top shops use Europe's "gulag" labour'. In eastern Europe, which after the fall of the communist regimes became a new hunting ground for cheap labour and had the added advantage of relatively short delivery times, four undercover journalists had investigated factories producing for western brands, among them Marks & Spencer, Debenhams, Levi Strauss, Laura Ashley and C&A. A British businessman ran a sweatshop in the Latvian town of Jelgava that produced for C&A. He had been fined for failing to give his employees proper contracts. A local doctor reported that in the past summer, she had regularly had to resuscitate women who had fainted at their sewing machines. Others suffered from spinal diseases caused by malnutrition and by the long hours spent hunched over their work. In the small town of Hirlau in Romania, 900 women making clothes for C&A were paid 20p an hour. Daniela Stavarache, 31, worked 48–60 hours a week, but could not afford medical treatment. She was grateful for the work, but unable to feed or clothe her children properly.[56]

Some of the mechanisms behind these endemic problems are laid bare in *Clemens and August*, a documentary about C&A made for Dutch television in 2000.[57] In this film, C&A allows the public a rare inside view of its buying and monitoring work. At this time the company had hit a low point. In Great Britain, where C&A had been dubbed Cheap&Awful, it had just been forced to close down all of its 119 stores, having lost big chunks of the market to brands like Hennes & Mauritz, Gap, Mango, and Zara. In the Netherlands, where C&A had acquired the nickname 'Polyester Palace', three stores were closed, while others were being modernised. In Germany – the only country where C&A is obligated to publish its company figures – profits had plummeted from 196 million euros in 1990 to 27 million in 1996. Apparently, this has forced the company to open the windows and let a fresh breeze in. Several Brenninkmeijer family members have left the organisation, and a European holding has replaced the former nationally based structure. Although the company has retained the legal form of the limited partnership that allows it to safeguard its secrecy, communications with the outside world have become less cramped than before, as several Dutch media outlets enthusiastically reported.[58]

'We have always been number one, but not anymore', says a managing director in the opening scene of *Clemens and August*, in the middle of a strikingly empty store in Amersfoort, a provincial Dutch town. On the wall of his office are the portraits of Clemens and August Brenninkmeijer, opposite a crucifix. They have adorned every C&A managing director's office since the beginning in 1841. The managing director sighs that C&A's image has become stuffy, old-fashioned and middle-of-the-road, while the public is asking for youth and dynamism. Tom Brenninkmeijer, a young family member and head of marketing in the Netherlands, works on a new advertising campaign called *Affection in Interaction*. C&A must become more fashion-conscious, he says, while at the same time staying in the lower price range.

The second part of the documentary is all about that lower price range. In the Philippines, a C&A buyer of men's fashion meets the owner of Jenny's Garments, a company with which C&A has been in business for 25 years. They negotiate over winter coats, 35,000 of them. It is clear that the owner is losing ground. 'There's no way we can hit that price. We'll drop it.' Back in the car, the buyer says that the Philippines are more expensive every year. 'It's because of the trade unions. They have grown strong here – wages go up, we have to go elsewhere.' He has already carried out comparative research in China, where wages are lower, 'and even in Thailand, which used to be more expensive than the Philippines, factories are offering a lower price. They are producing in North Thailand now, where wages are lower.' When asked about C&A's social responsibility and the possibility of paying a little more, he says, 'Western people are wealthy but spend their money on houses, vacations and cars. Not on clothes.'

Jenny's Garments gets an announced visit from two Socam inspectors. They ask the manager about exits, toilets, ventilation, first aid, and freedom of association, and are generally satisfied with the answers. But do they believe the owner when he says that workers are free to join or start up unions? One inspector hesitates, then answers: 'I would accept his word for it.' A local union representative is interviewed. She is glad that companies are opening up and introducing codes of conduct, but she is not happy with results so far. 'Workers get paid a minimum wage but not a living wage; and as for admission of trade unions, these factories have a bad reputation.'[59]

Finally, the camera follows a buyer of young fashion into A.S. Garments, a sweatshop in an unidentified British city. Since collections change fast in the fashion market, rapid delivery is important and producers are sought close to home. Whereas Asian goods are in transit for months, Great Britain can deliver in six weeks. The camera pans the dingy, crowded workplace where sewing machines rattle away under mostly migrant women's hands. 'These conditions are on the edge of unacceptable', says the buyer. 'But we give them a big order, and if we want low prices they cannot work in luxury marble towers on the High Street, can they?' In the car on the way back, he says: 'My priority is buying a bestseller and selling it fast. It means I'm not going to check every order for its origins. But I know that I have to meet certain standards, because negative publicity can cost you your head.'[60]

By 2004, C&A had regained its leading market position in the Netherlands. Not only had it succeeded in adjusting its clothes collection and company culture to the spirit of the times, it had also moved forward on the road of corporate responsibility. Although it still did not commit to transparency through collaboration with unions and NGOs, it proclaimed itself ready for dialogue, and the concerns of the CCC and trade unions appeared to find their way into the Socam annual reports. The company expanded the scope and impact of the auditing process. The 2006 C&A Corporate Social Responsibility Report analysed the challenges facing the auditors: the volatility of a technically simple, highly subdivided and subcontracted industry, a workforce vulnerable to exploitation. It pointed out that C&A sourced from EPZs in Bangladesh, where trade unions were banned, but justified its presence there by stating that 'a pull-out would likely not lead to an improvement of the situation for those employed. Furthermore, with intensive auditing we contribute to ensuring adherence to the fundamental interests and work safety of the employee.'[61] But in 2006, Bangladeshi workers were not asking for a pullout. In fierce protests against starvation wages and repression of unions, they set 200 of their own factories on fire.[62]

Child labour was foremost on C&A's agenda. Ever since the first public outrage at pictures of children in harsh labour conditions, corporations were anxious to avoid those associations like the plague. C&A required suppliers who appeared to employ children illegally to continue paying the children their salary as agreed, while financing professional or vocational training. The report mentions that the company supports projects against child labour, together with local partners.[63] On wages, it says:

> However, should a fair wage not considerably exceed basic material needs? Many non-governmental organisations frequently pose this question under the keyword 'living wages'. The implementation of appropriate requirements in concrete guidelines and agreements, however, is still pending. C&A is monitoring current discussions on the topic with great interest and is prepared to actively participate in the framework of stakeholder dialogues … The more intense competitive conditions on the worldwide supply markets contribute to [low wages], as does the transfer of international trade to regions and countries whose social and production standards lie considerably behind the requirements of C&A. These are problems that C&A and Socam actively tackle in order to solve them. Constructive dialogue with other trading companies, auditing organisations and NGOs is gaining in importance and is continuously enlarged.[64]

AND THE BEAT GOES ON

That same year, a Brazilian magazine landed in the CCC mailbox with a loud thud. It revealed C&A's involvement with sweatshop labour in São Paulo, Brazil, where the company had been established since 1976 and was very successful, with 113 stores in 57 cities. With Brazilian Gisele Bündchen, one of the world's highest-paid fashion models, as its advertising figurehead, it aimed for a high-class profile, while selling clothes for an average of 20 per cent less than its main competitors.

Que moda é essa?, What kind of fashion is this? asked the lead article in the *Observatório Social Em Revista*, a publication of the Brazilian labour research group that disclosed the affair.[65] It described the slave-like lives of illegal Bolivian migrant workers, mostly women, in São Paulo sweatshops producing for C&A subcontractors. Working conditions were inhumane and not much different from the first sweatshops of the nineteenth century. The workplaces were overcrowded, noisy, dusty and hot, and the workers had been smuggled into the country by the infamous 'coyotes'. They did piecework and sat behind sewing machines for up to 16 hours a day. Some had no choice but to keep their small children with them; they played on the ground in the noise and dust. At night they slept on a piece of foam alongside their sewing machine.

The facts were indisputable, and C&A Brazil had been aware of them since October 2005 at the latest, when the Public Labour Ministry and a city council committee had investigated and formally confronted the company with hundreds of C&A labels found by the federal police in clandestine shops. As many as 80 suppliers were suspected of using clandestine workshops. The Brazilian C&A representative denied all responsibility. He explained to the committee that if, during visits to suppliers to check technical conditions, illegal workers were identified, this might be an obstacle to further orders. But the company was not in the habit of checking subcontracted work. 'Our business is with the supplier who was chosen.'[66] He maintained that C&A demanded a formal commitment from all suppliers to refrain from using illegal labour, and to affirm that they were unaware of any subcontractors operating this way. 'C&A cannot take on the role of the government and thus exercise a police role, but it can and should be, and is, an assistant to them', C&A Brazil wrote in answer to questions from the NGO Observatório Social. The president of the Sewers Unions of São Paulo and Osasco, representing 70,000 workers, said: 'Businesses in the formal sector complain considerably that C&A does everything but take their blood. At times, they can barely produce ... If they don't [give in], C&A goes somewhere else.' And that, she said, was where the clandestine shops came in. In a Dutch newspaper, Marques Casara of Observatorio Social explained how it worked:

> C&A ... orders at a legal supplier. It cannot make the clothes itself because C&A's price is too low. Instead the supplier subcontracts the order to an illegal sweatshop, where people work day and night for less than one Real (35 euro cents) per piece. The workers, who have entered the country illegally through people traffickers, have no rights whatsoever.[67]

On learning about the Brazilian sweatshops, the Dutch trade union federation FNV and the CCC immediately contacted

C&A Europe. Its head of corporate social affairs responded that headquarters were shocked and devastated by the report, and called the situation unacceptable. C&A Europe had been informed about it in December 2005. Relations with one supplier had been ended, and there had been a meeting with all 500 suppliers to find out more about subcontracting. A migrant workers' organisation had been asked to help C&A support the illegal migrants. C&A Brazil's management had expressed a willingness to change its course. A Socam office had been established.

A meeting took place between representatives of C&A, the CCC, FNV, and the Belgian trade union LBC. On the agenda were the credibility of code monitoring by Socam (owned by the organisation it was supposed to monitor); the question of why C&A did not join existing cooperative efforts of businesses, unions and NGOs to monitor codes; C&A's complaint procedure; the absence of the right to collective bargaining from the C&A code; and the connection between the purchasing practices of the company and excessive overtime and low wages in factories. Apparently C&A, unions and the CCC were now on speaking terms, but decent wages and working conditions in the industry were still beyond the horizon.

At the beginning of 2009, C&A seems to be performing well commercially. There are over 1,200 C&A stores in 16 European countries. In 2007 the company's turnover in the Netherlands had grown by 6.6 per cent compared to 2005, which was 5.6 per cent more than the sector average of 1 per cent. European turnover stood at 5.65 billion euros. The company changes some of its collections nine times a year, and has started selling on the internet through the mail-order company Wehkamp. It is expanding into shoes and financial services. The first C&A store in Russia opened in 2006, and in 2007 Turkey and China got their first taste of Brenninkmeijer basics. While the organic cotton collection is being expanded, newspapers report that C&A is repositioning itself by joining the price fighters at the low end of the clothes market, firstly in Germany. To that end the Avanti chain has been set up. Avanti manager Hans-Peter Stadler wants to 'cover Germany with a matrix' of stores, on prime locations in large cities. The clothes do not look cheap, but they are: 3 euros for a T shirt, 6 euros for Bermuda shorts. The Brenninkmeijers continue to be the richest family of the Netherlands.[68]

At the end of 2008, C&A's head of corporate social affairs, Frank Hoendervangers, was asked if he was willing to enter into dialogue with Ineke Zeldenrust of the CCC for this book. After 20 years of common history, it seemed that it would be interesting to hear both organisations' reflections on that past, and maybe try to glimpse the future together. Unfortunately, Hoendervangers was not prepared to do this. He symbolically met the CCC halfway by agreeing to an interview with the author of this book. Also present was Chief Operations Officer of C&A Netherlands, Edwin Fafié. The text of that interview follows.

In 'Acting responsible: C&A report 2008',[69] *C&A states that it feels responsible for working conditions in the supply line. It seems C&A has changed since 1990.*

FH: Standards and values have always been important to us. But it's true that in the sector awareness has grown that companies must take responsibility for working conditions in supplying factories. The question is: What can be expected of us? What is the extent of our influence? C&A has a code of conduct, and Socam to monitor the process of corporate responsibility. Corporate social responsibility is not a separate department; it must pervade every C&A activity in every one of the 16 countries where we are established.

Buyers negotiating with a supplier need to score on price. Is it not difficult then to keep social responsibility demands in the picture?

FH: Our buyers know what we want and communicate this clearly to suppliers. We sometimes have to take decisions that are difficult for the buying departments – for example, when we want to discontinue a relationship with a supplier who repeatedly violates our standards, or when we exclude entire countries like Uzbekistan, where children are forced to work in the cotton harvest. Most suppliers know the drill; they have been C&A partners for years. But violations will happen. To a large extent, clothes are produced in countries where working conditions are not always up to standard.

How does C&A perceive its own power to improve working conditions in the supply chain?

FH: A supplier using as much as 60 per cent of his capacity for C&A orders won't hesitate to get out of bed at six o'clock for a nine o'clock appointment with us. That is why we have moved from a portfolio of thousands of often small suppliers towards fewer suppliers with a more intensive business relationship. Now we have better control and more influence.

Can you give an example of a case where C&A has succeeded in improving working conditions in a production location?

FH: An immensely important issue for us is how to avoid child labour. We obtain many products from Tirupur in India. Over the past ten years, we've been able to contribute substantially to a decline in child labour in this area through controls, discussions with suppliers, collaboration with local organisations, and support for social projects.

Organisations fighting child labour say that low adult wages are a major cause; in other words, child labour is a symptom.

FH: I think there is a combination of causes. Lack of schooling, culture, and poverty too. Creating employment is one of the solutions.

Only if it is good employment.

FH: Yes, certainly. In many countries garment industry jobs are sought after, but of course I've seen often enough that they do not qualify as good employment.

Can the company help suppliers to comply with C&A's conditions for social responsibility?

FH: Violations of overtime standards are a big problem. We tell our buyers to plan orders in such a way that a supplier is not forced to do all the work in a few weeks. This is not just an ethical issue – everybody benefits by it.

Can C&A also contribute to suppliers' compliance through pricing? Pay more to allow for higher wages?

FH: It's not that simple – be assured that suppliers are also tough negotiators! Maybe we could dictate prices 20 years ago, but not anymore.

EF: And do not underestimate the impact on pricing of large retailers like Wal-Mart. Their buying power is so huge, they are in another league.

Is a living wage for garment workers something C&A would support?

FH: If there was a universally accepted definition of a living wage, if it was laid down in national laws ... As things stand, only the minimum wage is a legal obligation. C&A demands that suppliers pay at least the minimum wage, for the right amount of working hours. We often see that employees earn a minimum wage, but their overtime hours are not calculated accordingly and correctly, in the way we request.

The 2008 report showed more violations of overtime and wage regulations than in 2006. How is that possible, with adequate control?

FH: We're continually improving our methods of detection, and we increasingly buy in countries where conditions are not up to standard.

Did the Clean Clothes Campaign influence C&A's stance regarding responsibility for working conditions in the supply line?

FH: They have pointed out violations of labour rights standards in specific production locations that we were not aware of; we find that useful. We don't need the CCC or similar groups to tell us what is wrong in general, because we see that for ourselves. Maybe we can also work together in problem solving, but I think their main task is calling attention to concrete complaints.

I think the CCC would agree to the watchdog role, but they also plead for structural change, for a sector-wide approach to labour rights violations. Did you know that?

FH: Of course! We see everything they publish; we must know what is going on in the field of corporate social responsibility.

And what is your opinion on this? The CCC maintains that labour rights violations in the garment sector can't be eradicated unless enterprises work together. Even Nike and Gap say that cooperation is needed to create the 'level playing field' that will prevent laggard companies from undercutting measures that responsible companies want to undertake.

FH: In the past ten years there have been several initiatives to cooperate on corporate social responsibility. We have only become a member of Global Social Compliance Programme.[70] Until now, we have preferred to continue our own work with Socam. It is tailor-made for C&A. Communication channels between Socam and C&A are short and wide open, allowing for fast reactions.

But that doesn't solve the problem of the level playing field.

EF: In the Netherlands, but also in France and Germany, we are asked to join business associations that unite small- and medium-sized enterprises that are now beginning to get involved in social responsibility – they can no longer escape it. Because we are way ahead, we're asked to share our knowledge and experience, which we do. But the gap is huge, and we also need to move forward; it's up to them to catch up.

What you are saying supports the idea that it's especially the large companies that need to work together to achieve decent wages and working conditions.

EF: But the players in the field differ enormously! Take the very large companies that position themselves as discounters on the European market. The goods enter Rotterdam harbour vacuum-packed. When you unpack them, suddenly you have an awful lot for awfully little money. Society apparently appreciates this, but it is an alarming development. We have to deal with it.

Is C&A with its Avanti brand not one of those players?

FH: Yes, but our code of conduct also applies to Avanti clothes, and Socam controls are the same. If there were a system to represent the various branches of this sector, we would gladly be part of it.

Does C&A not see the Fair Wear Foundation (FWF) as such a system?[71]

FH: When the Fair Wear Foundation was launched, it was still small and only Dutch, while we are established all over Europe and have an international buying department. We have had several talks with them, compared our auditing activities, and concluded that we share goals. But we decided to continue with Socam because that works for us. Nevertheless, I don't rule out future talks. But it has to operate on a European level.

The FWF is in the process of European expansion.

FH: We know. We have told them to call us when they are ready. So far, we have not seen enough added value in cooperative efforts. We think we are doing all right, and we have the leverage of our central buying department.

Another difference between Socam and, for example, the Fair Wear Foundation is transparency: in these cooperative organisations, data are shared.

FH: Our internal transparency is good; our database shows what is produced where, allowing us to control and correct. We've promised our suppliers not to divulge those data. We are open about violations and corrections, but we don't publish names. Of course there are business interests at stake as well. Good production companies represent a value; buying companies will protect them carefully. Working together presupposes trust.

EF: And assuming that corrections are sometimes not only necessary at the supplier but also in the buying company, you can only make corrections in your own, not in other ones.

How many auditors does Socam employ?

FH: About 25, stationed in production countries. Ninety-five per cent of their audits are unannounced. In the future we may invest in extra manpower, because production locations fluctuate greatly. Sometimes audits we did half a year ago are not useful anymore because a supplier has selected other production locations.

C&A's 2008 report shows that, between 1996 and today, the number of audits has decreased.

FH: Auditing has followed an upward learning curve. Initially, the auditing time in factories was insufficient. Our audits are now longer and cover more issues. We have become aware that issues like discrimination and harassment are not easily visible. We still miss them sometimes; we can do better.

Are workers interviewed outside the factory, where management can't hear them?

FH: That is a difficult issue; you have a relationship with your supplier. But when auditors get the feeling that workers can't talk freely, they can leave a card with a telephone number. It is difficult; they will get contrary information. We have relatively many women auditors, about 40 per cent; female workers often find it easier to talk with them. We also have a website and a 'fairness channel' where complaints can be deposited.

But workers are not very likely to use them. If they have a complaint, the auditor's card is all they have?

FH: Plus the unions and NGOs, but they usually contact us, not the auditors. It could be better.

In 2006 it was discovered that illegal Bolivian immigrants were sewing clothes for C&A in São Paulo, Brazil, under very bad conditions. Is there a chance of something like that happening again?

FH: We are regularly confronted with problems – that is why Socam exists. But we are not almighty. When for example a complaint reached us about a factory in Bangladesh, we had stopped ordering there eight months before, which left us powerless.

Which is an argument to cooperate with other companies.

FH: That is what the CCC asked us to do, and what we did. We supported the demands of companies still ordering there.

C&A has changed in 20 years. Its relationship with trade unions is an example.

EF: Absolutely. The windows are wide open. There is no reason at all to fear unions in our consultation-happy Dutch culture.

Production countries often don't have such openness towards unions. It must cause frictions, operating from here in countries like that.

EF: It is a given. We have to be modest about what we can achieve elsewhere; I sometimes feel that we Dutch want to cover the rest of the world with a blanket of our standards and values.

But before we do that, we've interfered in other ways ...

EF: We must also realise that we still have much to do at home.

On that point, we totally agree![72]

2
Destination Elsewhere

In the middle of the 1990s, the pace of relocation of the western garment industry to low-wage countries in the Third World accelerated. Small garment producers were losing ground to large ones. The large ones increasingly disposed of their manufacturing facilities and relocated production overseas, keeping only the most complicated and fashion-sensitive parts of production 'at home' and concentrating on the most profitable pursuits of design, marketing and sales. They turned into 'merchandisers' or 'brands', seemingly freed from the material world of sewing machines and stitching workers.[1] Small retailers formed buying combinations that gradually developed the same structure and activities as large retailers. Mergers and takeovers among brands increased the power of buyers over producers. To keep sales rising, companies began to bring out several collections per year. The secret of the rise of H&M – the Swedish retail chain that in the 1990s conquered the European market – was the combination of an extremely frequent change in collections with a large turnover. Its buying power enabled the company to negotiate low production prices and sell fashionable clothes cheaply.[2]

The primary reasons for relocation are the availability of cheap labour and the absence of workers' organisations in the countries relocated to. An extra advantage is risk avoidance, through shifting the burden of managing and maintaining a labour force in a volatile market – characterised by seasonal and fashion-induced waves – onto the shoulders of producers in developing countries. While these producers and their subcontractors compete for orders and drive each other and their workers to the edge, the brands and large retailers don't have to worry about the needs of the labour force and are free to focus on what they are really good at: selling.

Relocation is facilitated by modern information technology and transportation. Governments in developing countries, eager to attract investment, contribute through favourable tax measures, negation of labour rights and suppression of unions. When the Sri Lankan multinational Tri-Star Apparel showed interest producing in Uganda at the beginning of the millennium, the government welcomed it with a loan of US$5 million. It also converted a warehouse into a garment factory and dormitories, for free. It provided power lines and three standby generators. It recruited 2,000 employees and subsidised worker training. The government paid about 80 per cent of the costs of establishing the factory.[3]

There is yet another, accidental driver of garment industry relocations. When cheap clothes, produced in developing countries, began to flood western markets, they threatened to wipe out the garment industry that had managed to survive there. In order to protect that industry, developed countries began to impose import restrictions on clothes from developing countries with a burgeoning garment industry. This resulted in the 1974 Multi-Fibre Arrangement (MFA), a system of quota restrictions that inadvertently led to relocations from countries with quota restrictions to countries without them. They had been free of restrictions because, until then, they had never had a sizable garment industry. Thus it came about that countries like Cambodia or Laos, where 'making clothes' had until then stood for home spinning and weaving, saw themselves suddenly flooded with garment factories at the end of the 1990s.

The Multi-Fibre Arrangement, intended as a short-term measure to give the industry in developed countries the chance to adapt to the cheap imports from developing countries, governed the world trade in textiles and garments from 1974 to 2004. It was one of the most comprehensive sets of trade restrictions in the world; but so strong was the competitive nature of the industry that the MFA not only failed to prevent the globalisation of the clothes trade, but even helped it along.[4]

The garment industry has always been one of the first to alight on non-industrialised countries, because it has no need for heavy, expensive machinery, for land, or for a educated workforce. For the same reasons, it can be relocated again and again.

Four broad waves of production relocation can be identified in recent decades. The first wave, in the 1960s and 1970s, ran to South Korea, Taiwan, Singapore, Hong Kong and Tunisia. As their economies developed and the Asian countries began to present themselves proudly as the 'Asian Tigers', skill levels and wages rose. Most brands responded by moving into more complex goods in their home countries, and shifting low-skilled, labour-intensive industries overseas to countries with cheaper workforces and weaker or no unions. Korean and Taiwanese investors, in particular, developed design and marketing capacity, while relocating production to other

Asian and even African countries, where they became a powerful economic force.

In the 1980s the second wave of relocation hit the shores of the Philippines, Sri Lanka, Malaysia, Bangladesh, Thailand and Indonesia. By the end of that decade, several new low-cost countries were scouted – the most important being Pakistan, Vietnam and China. Some of them had the added advantage of fewer quota restrictions under the Multi-Fibre Arrangement – though only for a while, since quota restrictions tend to follow export successes.[5] The 1990s also saw the fall of the Iron Curtain, which made the formerly communist economies accessible for western corporations. Industrial and economic collapse in eastern and central Europe provided a new source of cheap labour, with the added advantage of relatively high skills, well-developed infrastructure and proximity to western markets. Finally, Turkey, another one of western Europe's neighbours, began to attract foreign investment to its garment production industry at the beginning of the 1990s, transforming what had until then been a primarily domestic producer into one of the top ten clothing exporters in the world.

The fourth and last wave of this period, gathering strength at the end of the 1990s, has occurred in Cambodia, Laos, Burma and Africa.[6]

In African countries – attractive mainly because of the lack of export restrictions that had restrained Asian production – the lifting of those restrictions in 2004 meant that the industry became extremely footloose. Between 2001 and 2006, the Sri Lankan company Tri-Star Apparel came and went in Botswana, Kenya, Tanzania and Uganda.[7]

While the first-wave relocation countries were able to profit by raising wages and developing skills, most of the countries that came after did not. Competition with lower-cost neighbouring countries undermined their industries before they could upgrade their base of skills and investment to move into higher-value goods in the way their predecessors had.[8] This also undermined workers' lives. The practice of subcontracting orders down through an ever expanding supply chain led to a rampant informal economy where labour rights, social protection, job quality standards and workers' organisation did not exist.[9] By its nature, an informal economy provides maximum flexibility to an industry and maximum insecurity to workers. Union organisation, which can protect and emancipate workers, is not only actively repressed by governments and employers, but also hampered by the vulnerability of workers without contracts or social protection, who are pitted against each other in scrambling for jobs. And even if they succeed in getting off the ground an organisation to voice their demands, they are partly barking up the wrong tree because the local employer is as much a victim of the global dynamic as they are. Thus relocation – promising development to the country of arrival but creating havoc in both the countries of departure and arrival – illustrates the paradox of creative destruction that is so characteristic of globalisation.

Five years after its birth in the early 1990s, the Clean Clothes Campaign was working hard to get a grip on the globalising garment industry. But while every scrap of information was diligently stored, and contacts with workers' organisations in countries of production were cherished, they were at this time still mostly coincidental, rather than systematic. In order for it to be able to effectively monitor the industry's movements and support workers at the grassroots level, there was an urgent need for the CCC to spread its wings. From 1993 on, it set out to map the supply chains of western retailers. Which brands were having their clothes made where, how, and by whom? Ineke Zeldenrust describes their initial research efforts:

> There was no internet yet, so we buried ourselves in the archives of the library of the Ministry of Economic Affairs. We worked like Trojans, looking at thousands of articles, ads and photos, searching for garment labels, cross-referencing names. We went to trade fairs. We asked workers and partner organisations to bring or draw us the labels sewn in the clothes in their factories, and we designed a label index for them to point out the ones they were familiar with. In the production countries we bought trade registers, like for example the Bangladesh Garment Manufacturers Export Handbook, in which factories presented their brand customers. We accessed every morsel of information publicly available.[10]

In 1995 and 1996, Ineke Zeldenrust and her colleague Janneke van Eijk visited Thailand, Bangladesh and Sri Lanka. At the same time Marijke Smit, writer of the C&A epic *The Silent Giant*, went to Indonesia, Hong Kong and the Philippines. Together, using a variety of creative means of gaining entrance, they visited over 50 factories to gather information and forge ties with workers and their organisations. It was the first time the CCC had undertaken this kind of research. Their initial impressions were striking:

What hit me most during these visits were the hours people worked. By the time they were finished and able to talk to us in the local union office, it would sometimes be midnight. Next day, they would be up before sunrise. Another problem that stood out was the difficulty of organising. Any attempts were met with threats of relocation and dismissals. It was very hard for fired workers to find another job, which deterred other workers from organising ever again.[11]

The research disclosed many human and labour rights violations. In a Philippine factory, production targets were raised as soon as workers managed to reach them. Many employers exercised a flat-out non-union policy. It was not uncommon for employers to close their factories and reopen somewhere else as soon as workers organised. Sweatshops employed young migrant women who had no idea about their rights. They worked twelve hours a day for too little money to live on. In a Thai factory, women had to build a dressing room wall themselves to shield them from the eyes of male factory workers. In Sri Lanka, 90 per cent of the women working in the free trade zones suffered from headaches and eye problems and 24 per cent from backaches, while 63 per cent was undernourished, and 20 per cent had undergone abortions in order to keep the job.[12]

The research laid the foundation for the global CCC network. The activists met with union representatives, local researchers, women's groups and other non-governmental organisations. They exchanged addresses and information; they expressed their objectives and needs; they took the first steps on the way to a common strategy for improving labour conditions worldwide. In the following years some contacts evaporated – though most solidified, and many new ones are made. In 2009 the network comprises some 250 organisations working in garment-producing countries in Asia, eastern Europe, and Africa. Contacts with organisations in South and Central America are less frequent. Sweatshops abound there as well, but their markets are mostly in North America and Canada. There is nevertheless a steady exchange of information, and occasionally also joint campaigning with American and Canadian organisations. Simultaneously with the expansion eastward and southward, the CCC network spread within Europe.[13]

Over time, the network has devised a common strategy, though all agree its evolution will be a never-ending process. Some principles are clear and unquestionable: workers have a right to a living wage, to safe and healthy working conditions, to freedom of association, and to collective bargaining. Demands for action have to come from workers and their organisations. There is no single way to reach the common goals.[14]

In November 2007, on a lovely Sunday in spring, the Baan Siri hotel on the outskirts of Bangkok filled up quickly. At the reception desk hugs and handshakes were exchanged between people whose faces still looked sleepy from the flights that had brought them from their corner of the world into this hub of global meeting and greeting.

It was rumoured that this was the largest meeting of international anti-sweatshop activists ever, with over 120 representatives of almost as many organisations. Some came straight from behind their sewing machines, some from behind a stack of law books. Some had shut the doors of small crowded offices behind them, where the telephone had just started ringing again to announce yet another case of mass dismissals. Some had walked away from conference tables where politicians, captains of industry and union representatives were discussing preferential trade agreements. All were part of the global CCC network, and had gathered to attend the International Campaign Forum 2007 of the Clean Clothes Campaign.

There followed four days of heated discussions and world-encompassing strategising; four days of trying to understand each other and reach consensus on essentials. The focus was on two global campaigns. The first one was the 'Play Fair' Campaign, which was going to use the 2008 Olympic Games in Beijing to highlight the labour conditions of sportswear workers. The second was the 'Better Bargain' Campaign, directed against giant retail chains like Wal-Mart, Carrefour and Aldi, who through their unlimited buying power ruled supreme over garment production conditions around the world.

But there was also time for regional consultations between people from southern African or southeast Asian countries, for workshops about factory closures and migrant labour. Time for a visit to striking workers of a transport company, for raising money for an organiser of a Chinese workers' centre in Shenzhen who had come close to being chopped to pieces in an attack on the centre. At night, after the official sessions had finished, small groups could be heard joking and arguing on the grass outside the hotel, in the sultry, polluted Bangkok air.

When the Forum was over, most participants agreed that it had been a good attempt at participatory, unbureaucratic and transparent decision-making. Many old issues had not been resolved, and new ones had surfaced. There were differences of opinion regarding goals, strategies and timelines. The language barrier continued to be a serious obstacle, and the gap between the perspectives of a Malagasy garment worker and a Dutch unionist was wide. The two global campaigns had moved forward. 'But maybe', said Kelly Dent, a long-time Australian CCC participant, 'the most important outcome of meetings like these is the health of the network.'

In the following chapters, representatives of the global network present at the Forum talk about the struggles in their countries and about the role of the CCC, against the backdrop of their national garment industry and its impact on people's lives – similar in many respects, different in others. Each story concentrates on certain issues, leaving out others discussed elsewhere. Each adds a piece to the overall mosaic depicting a network of labour-rights activists fighting the adverse effects of globalisation.

Part 2

A Globalising Network

3
Asia

BANGLADESH: A LETHAL INDUSTRY

Market Darwinism is a term some critics use to describe the mechanisms of the globalising garment industry. But while the 'race to the bottom' resembles the competition of species in more ways than one, there is a fundamental difference: in the garment sector, it is not the fittest that survive, but those exercising the bitterest forms of worker exploitation. That, at least, is how it looks in Bangladesh.

The Bangladeshi garment industry experienced explosive growth in the 1990s. The country had an advantage over competitors whose exports were restricted by Multi-Fibre Arrangement quota. Not surprisingly, it awaited the MFA phase-out in 2004 with some anxiety. Against all predictions, the industry continued to grow. But the way in which it did brings to mind images of the First World War, which saw wave upon wave of soldiers sent to the battlefield – every new platoon more desperate than the one it was to replace. The Bangladeshi garment industry is fed by never-ending waves of slum-dwellers, brought up on a diet of poverty and illiteracy in one of the most densely populated countries on earth. In Bangladesh, 45 per cent of people live below the poverty line; the adult literacy rate stands at 41 per cent.[1]

Even when the 2004 phasing-out of the quota system brought Bangladesh into competition with China, the industry kept growing. But this was not because it was innovative and dynamic – the industry suffered from defective infrastructure and underinvestment – but because, as the German internet magazine *Spiegel Online* pointed out, even China cannot undercut hourly wages of between 5 and 10 US cents.[2]

In 2006, after an outburst of protests in which factories were torched and workers took to the streets, and under pressure from the international brands, the government raised the minimum monthly wage in the garment industry to Taka 1,662.50 or 20 euros. It was the first raise since 1994, and the new wage was still not even close to meeting the basic needs of a worker's family. In the same period, the value of the ready-made garment sector had grown by a factor 4.5. It contributed 75 per cent of the country's export earnings. In September 2006, the powerful president of the employers' association said:

> Last year we had tremendous growth. The quota-free textile regime has proved to be a big boost for our factories. We're confident we can now keep the growth momentum intact and double our exports to more than $15 billion in the next five years.[3]

In 2006 a fire occurred in a Chittagong garment factory, killing more than 50 workers and injuring 100 more. The same year saw the collapse of the Phoenix Building, killing 19 and injuring 50 people, and a deadly stampede of garment workers of the Imam Group factory, who heard the explosion of a nearby transformer and ran into the trap of a too-narrow exit. A chain of factory fires and collapsed buildings punctuates the history of the Bangladeshi clothing industry since the 1980s. In August 2000 the Globe Knitting fire killed twelve and injured one more; in November 2000 the Sagar Chowdhury Garment Factory fire caused 48 deaths, including those of ten children; in August 2001 the Macro Sweater fire and stampede saw 24 dead and more than 100 wounded; in May 2004 the Misco Supermarket Complex fire and stampede killed nine young garment workers, and injured more than 50.[4]

Direct causes included old and haphazard wiring, overcrowded working and sleeping areas, narrow and blocked staircases, locked exits, the absence of emergency exits and fire extinguishing equipment, and a lack of fire drills. In the background there always lingers – in addition to a matter-of-fact nonchalance about the lives of workers – the murderous competition between producers for orders, which prevents expenditure in areas that do not directly benefit production. It leads to an industry that can rightly be called 'lethal', to quote a journalist who described the worst factory carnage to date: the Spectrum collapse.[5]

The Spectrum factory was built on a swampy tract of land outside the capital, Dhaka. Because the city is overcrowded, with skyrocketing land prices, businesses move to the nearest available sites. Even if these are not fit for high-rises, they build them anyway. In 2002 the Spectrum owner added five storeys to his four-storey factory. A couple of days before the collapse, workers had watched a crack gradually widening in one of the walls. They were nevertheless caught by surprise when the floor fell from under their feet, at 1 a.m. of 11 April 2005. To add injustice to injury, they should all have been lying in bed at home, because their shift had officially ended at 6 p.m. the day before. The urgency of meeting orders had prevailed. The accident killed 64 workers and injured more than 70 – some for life. They were found between the red children's pullovers they had been making for the Spanish chain Inditex-Zara, and under the purple-striped women's tops ordered by the German Bluhm fashion group – as the Clean Clothes Campaign was quick to establish. The CCC identified Inditex-Zara, the German KarstadtQuelle, Steilmann, New Yorker, Kirsten Mode and Bluhmod, the Swedish New Wave Group, the Dutch Scapino, the Belgian Cotton Group and the French Solo Invest and Carrefour as buyers, and tried to persuade them to participate in a fund to provide emergency relief and a permanent income to survivors and families of the deceased. Most of the companies had a code of conduct, and an auditing scheme to check whether suppliers were adhering to the code, but none had noticed the safety risks. Some, like KarstadtQuelle, initially denied having ordered at Spectrum. But the German retail giant had to admit to its involvement when someone unearthed the company's own label, 'Le Frog', from the ruins: a French–English label, produced for a German company, retrieved from the rubble of a collapsed Bangladeshi factory.

Inditex-Zara was quick to respond, paying 35,000 euros for immediate relief. After protracted hesitation, several other companies followed. The French company Carrefour distributed 15,000 euros through an NGO, partly in the form of rickshaws and sewing machines. It took eight months before emergency relief measures and medical aid had reached all the affected workers and their families. Nearly every family of the deceased workers received 1,000 euros from the Bangladesh Garment Manufacturers' and Exporters' Association, and most received the additional compensation of 266 euros that the Labour Court entitled them to. Because this was not enough to sustain them in the long run, the CCC and the International Textile Garment and Leather Workers' Federation pushed for the establishment of a fund that would pay survivors and families of the dead a monthly pension, based on their previous salaries. First instalments could finally be paid in April 2007 – the main contributors were Inditex-Zara and KarstadtQuelle, while companies that did not contribute were Carrefour, Cotton Group, New Yorker, Steilmann, Kirsten Mode, and Bluhm.[6]

One of the tools employed by the CCC to break the brands' refusals and evasions was a European tour by two injured Spectrum workers, both former knitting-machine operators. Nur-E-Alam, 29, had lost his arm, and Jahangir Alam, 24, lives with permanent kidney problems and leg pains. In February 2006 they visited Belgium, the Netherlands, France and Germany, where they met representatives of the brands, trade unions, NGOs, consumers, students and the media. In Berlin, CCC activists lit 64 candles in front of a KarstadtQuelle department store and, together with the Spectrum workers, collected consumers' signatures demanding that the company join the compensation fund. Four major German newspapers ran articles about the case.

'A workers' tour is a good way of campaigning', says Khorshed Alam, who accompanied the workers at the time and attended the CCC Bangkok Forum. He is project coordinator and researcher of the Alternative Movement for Resources and Freedom (AMRF), a Bangladeshi NGO.

> It attracts the media and puts pressure on companies. They cannot avoid it; it embarrasses them when workers show up on their doorstep. But we only do it when all other forms of communication have been exhausted. It is quite effective you see, but only if they cannot accuse us of not having tried to talk to them first.[7]

Khorshed Alam was a student of political science in the 1980s, when the garment industry in Bangladesh began to grow. In 2000 he founded AMRF and got involved in workers' rights.

> We research and campaign on labour issues, but also on other subjects like water management. Our aim is to unite and organise people in such a way that they can take care of their own problems, that they are able to bargain with the power and resource brokers. We are part of a diversified network all over the world, and do research for western NGOs. The research can be quite risky; with the labour issue, you are confronting the entire power structure. It is easy to land in jail.[8]

The research is often quite difficult as well. It may cost a tremendous amount of time and energy to find enough workers who will talk:

> They are usually afraid, and have little spare time. Which isn't saying that you shouldn't do it, because when you succeed, the results can be a strong argument in a campaign. We did research for the *Fashion Victims* report of the British NGO War on Want,

that confronted British consumers with the Bangladeshi reality behind the clothes sold by the large retailers Tesco, Primark and Asda.[9] After the report came out, I delivered a speech at a Tesco shareholders' meeting, as a shareholder by proxy. I accused the company of violating the rights of Bangladeshi workers, and proposed a different approach. [Ten] per cent of the shareholders voted in favour, which put enormous pressure on the retailers. They rushed into Bangladesh and started talking to their suppliers.

In 2005 the CCC, keen to highlight the weakness of controls over the implementation of codes of conduct, decided to investigate social auditing practices in the garment industry, and published the report *Looking for a Quick Fix*.[10] Khorshed Alam and his team took part in the global investigation on which the report was based. It is an example of internationally coordinated, locally executed research.

Key researchers of eight countries on different continents met in Amsterdam and developed a general framework, a checklist and questionnaires. We decided on which issues to bring up with workers, factory managers and unions, and agreed that we would try to find out how the audit firms themselves perceive their work. After we had translated the questionnaires into Bangla and explained the objectives to our interviewers, we interviewed 150 workers from six factories, most of them medium-sized, which means they employ 300 to 1000 workers. Most of our factories have that size; only 5 to 10 per cent are larger.

Talking to the workers was challenging, because they start work at 8 a.m. and sometimes work until 10 or 11 p.m., sometimes through the night. Since the managers usually decide on the spur of the moment when to stop the work, it was hard for us to make appointments. Garment workers must be among the busiest people in the world, they have hardly time to cook. They cook only once, at night, and eat that food for dinner, breakfast and lunch. If a worker is willing to receive you in her home at night, answering 60 to 80 questions takes up much of their precious time.

Initially workers seldom want to talk because they are afraid that the owner will learn about it. This fear is always there. But when you get to know them and succeed in building trust, it gradually becomes easier. Some workers are really willing to talk, because they have anger inside them. Others are not very open. As young women with no institutional education, they can be shy. Sometimes they wonder what use the interviews are to them. Interviewing managers or buyers is no picnic either; they are more interested in avoiding you. We use personal channels, people we know who know people. Not one of them wanted to disclose his name. So you see, there is no hard and fast road to do this. But since this type of research always translates into action, it never fails to energise and motivate me.

SRI LANKA: THE FIGHT IN FREE TRADE ZONES

'In 1977, Sri Lanka was the first among south Asian countries to introduce the so-called free economy', says Anton Marcus, one of the two joint secretaries of the free trade zones and General Services Employees' Union of Sri Lanka. He has been in the CCC network ever since Ineke Zeldenrust and Janneke van Eijk met him on their mid-1990s scouting tour of Asia. And he knows how to tell a story.

> The election slogan of the winning political party in 1977 was: 'Sri Lanka, another Singapore!' In 1978, the first free trade zones were opened, with the aim of attracting foreign investment. The president of the country said: 'Let all the robber barons come to Sri Lanka and open up factories.' So they all came.[11]

In 2006, around 275,000 workers were employed in 14 free trade zones, alternatively known as investment processing zones and Industrial Parks. Most of the companies in the zones produce textiles and garments. About 85 per cent of the workers are women. Factories in the zones enjoy fiscal incentives, a guaranteed supply of water and electricity, easy access to telecommunication services, quick administrative procedures, and guarded barriers around them to deter unwanted visitors.[12]

Contributing to the phenomenal growth of the garment industry since the 1970s were the liberalisation of the economy, its focus on exporting, and the educated labour force that distinguished Sri Lanka from many other developing countries. Very helpful was the 1974 Multi-Fibre Arrangement, which held back rival garment-exporting countries that had already fulfilled their export quota. An under-utilised quota in Sri Lanka attracted foreign direct investment, resulting in joint ventures with local investors. In 2005 the garment sector accounted for over 45 per cent of Sri Lankan exports, produced by over 700 factories – up from 2 per cent and five factories in 1977.[13]

Since the 1990s, Sri Lanka has faced stiff competition from other countries in south and southeast Asia, as well as from China. The Sri Lankan industry, suffering from high labour turnover, lengthy labour disputes and a low level of technology, has entered turbulent times. Because it is dependent on imported inputs, the level of value added is low, and the need to import raw materials results in longer delivery times. The pressure on factory owners is passed on to workers, resulting in longer work hours and an increase in production pace.[14] The industry has tried to turn the tide by means of mergers and a shift of focus towards quality production. As a result production has decreased, leading to downsizing and diminishing employment in many firms.[15]

Sri Lanka has ratified the core International Labour Organisation (ILO) conventions on child labour, forced labour, discrimination and freedom of association, and important labour laws are in place. Nevertheless it took until the beginning of this millennium for the first union inside a free trade zone to be recognised. Anton Marcus has worked half his adult life to make that happen. At age 59, he is a sturdy, soft-spoken man who likes to laugh. When he was young, he believed that armed struggle was the way to change the world. When the insurrection he took part in failed, he went underground for some time. He had no experience with unions and did not think much of them. 'I believed in youth, not in workers', he says. Later, as a motor mechanic, he gradually came to see the merits of unions, and became an organiser himself. For more than 20 years he prepared the ground for union recognition in the free trade zones, against employers and authorities who did their best to keep them out.

The government wanted to make sure that labour law wasn't going to be applicable in the free trade zones. When trade unions challenged that before the Constitutional Court, the judge decided that we couldn't have two laws in one country and ordered the zones to accept existing labour law. But in practice the government didn't enforce it, especially not freedom of association. In 1982, we started to unionise workers in garment factories surrounding the Katunayake zone, the largest one. At the same time, we made contact with workers in the zone.

Marcus and his colleagues put much effort into training and educating zone workers. More than 80 per cent of them are single women. They are young, and mostly from remote villages; and they have never heard about unions. They see the work as temporary: most women work five or six years in the zones – sometimes because that is long enough for them to save dowry money, sometimes because they become exhausted. They usually work twelve hours a day, seven days a week. In local boarding houses surrounding the zone they live together in rented rooms – sometimes no more than a few sheets of corrugated iron without sanitary facilities. Some of the landlords force their tenants to buy groceries from them at inflated prices. Sexual harassment is a fact of life; women have to be on their guard at all times, especially when they return home from work in the dark. This tarnishes their name, which is already discredited because they live on their own. Marriage advertisements often state: 'No factory girls'.[16] 'The image of women working in the zones is so bad, people think they can make use of them any time', says Anton Marcus. 'From the beginning, our union has taken up this issue. We have to, if we want to be relevant to these workers.'

Only the day before coming to Bangkok, Marcus was in a picket line in front of a courthouse, to demand justice for a girl who had been raped and killed.

On 20 November we heard on TV that a girl had committed suicide by jumping from the sixth floor of a hospital. Immediately we suspected it might be a worker from the zone and found this to be true. When she was in the hospital for minor surgery, the doctor that was supposed to treat her had raped and strangled her, then thrown her out of a bathroom window. There had been witnesses, who had done nothing to prevent it. We made posters that said: 'Free Trade Zone workers are not play-things', and asked for the doctor to be punished. Of course there were efforts to suppress our protests by accusing the victim of having a loose character. On the day of her funeral, an amazing thing happened. We had asked the factory workers to wear white and in the morning, the zone looked like a giant piece of white lace. Not only our membership, but 99 per cent of the workers wore white. It was an excellent way of demonstrating, very visible, easy to participate in. Nobody can stop you. We are now working to expand the action into a campaign for social dignity of the women workers.

It was not until the beginning of this millennium that the first unions were recognised in the Sri Lankan free trade zones.

Before, we had been organising these workers in every possible non-union way. We cooperated with the women's centres outside the zones, we used the Employees' Councils the government had introduced as an alternative to unions. Sometimes this was successful, as in the case of a garment factory that was not paying salaries on time. For a worker, not getting paid means no money to pay board or food. It is often a sign that the factory will be closed. This one was American- and Hong Kong-owned. We were able to contact Hong Kong trade unions. They organised a campaign and invited the chairman of the Employees' Council of the factory over to negotiate. It was the first time a Sri Lankan woman worker visited another country to negotiate – and won. In the end the Hong Kong management was exposed as fraudulent. The banker of the factory found another buyer and to this day it is in business, with 6,000 workers.

At the time of the 1999 presidential elections, there was considerable pressure, especially from the US – the largest importer of Sri Lankan garments – to allow unions in the free trade zones.[17] The new president enacted a law to the effect that unions in FTZ factories be recognised if they had a membership of 40 per cent or more. Marcus recalls: 'We thought our day had come. In 2000 we established our FTZ Workers' Union. But employers refused to recognise its branches in the factories. Either they dismissed the workforce, or they closed the factory.'[18]

In 2003 the case of the Jaqalanka factory brought a milestone victory. It produced for Nike, which may have contributed to the international exposure and subsequent victory. At stake was union recognition. Marcus's union claimed an 80 per cent membership. A referendum was held to determine the exact figure. 'Management even used death threats to intimidate workers. On referendum day the managers all sat there, registering who would show. Only 17 out of 400 workers came out to vote, and we lost. That's when we started an international campaign.' The international union federations ITGLWF and ICFTU filed complaints before the ILO and the Fair Labor Association.[19] The case was also brought to the attention of the European Union and the US, since Sri Lanka had received preferential tariff concessions in return for ratifying the ILO conventions on the rights to freedom of association and collective bargaining.

The CCC supported the complaints and used the 'urgent appeal' tool, its own global mouthpiece that informs consumers about labour rights violations, which operates through the internet.[20] The urgent appeal asked the public to file protests with the factory management and with western companies sourcing their goods from Jaqalanka. 'More than 4,000 e-mails were sent, Nike got really upset', says Anton Marcus.

> Auditors from Nike visited the factory and finally the company recognised our union. It had an impact on all free trade zones. The Board of Investment governing the zones amended its guidelines to allow for unions and make employers recognise them. We still have many problems, but at least now we have zones with unions. Next month we are going to have two collective bargaining agreements signed inside free trade zones. For the first time.[21]

International support is vital to Marcus's union, he says.

> History tells us that international solidarity is one of our core activities; without it we cannot work. The CCC has supported us in I think eight to ten cases of labour rights violations. Even if not all of them have ended in victory, worldwide publication and support help us to continue our fight. I myself am still alive because of it. Employers and authorities to this day accuse me of damaging the Sri Lankan industry, and I am receiving death threats. In February 2007 my picture on an anonymous poster was all over the place. It said that I was an agent of the Liberation Tigers of Tamil Eelan, and have to be wiped out. It is like a blank cheque, anybody can cash it. The CCC and several unions organised an international protest. This kind of support helps to safeguard our lives.

In the Sri Lankan struggle for union recognition, Marcus thinks that consumer campaigns have strong leverage.

> Even though there are global union federations, I think it is not easy for them to organise international action. Some unions are suppressed themselves, even in developed countries. Some are very traditional and not able to organise the modern workforce. Both unions and consumer pressure could and should play a major

role, but there is often a gap between them. We should close this gap, if workers worldwide are to benefit.

INDONESIA: JOBS AT A DISCOUNT

The Indonesian garment and sport shoe industry offers a panoramic view of the stages a national economy may pass through when a globalising industry descends upon it.

The production of textiles and apparel was important in Indonesia even before foreign investment catapulted the industry on to the global stage. Before 1986 the country had built a wall of import restrictions, favouring local firms selling to the domestic market. In the second half of the 1980s, neoliberal policies opened up the borders for companies from Taiwan, Hong Kong and South Korea, for whom garment and footwear production had been the springboard for economic growth.[22] Hampered by the growing strength of labour organisation and by rising wages in their own countries, these companies had begun looking for greener pastures, and had found some in Indonesia. Indonesia could provide cheap labour, quality products and quick delivery, had an under-utilised export quota to the US and Europe, offered tax exemptions and other extras in export processing zones (as free trade zones are referred to in Indonesia), and could serve as a low-cost export platform to non-quota countries like Australia, New Zealand and Japan.[23]

On the wings of foreign investment, the Indonesian garment and footwear industries grew fast, providing jobs to several hundreds of thousands of people and contributing to average economic growth of 7 per cent per year in the 1990s. In 1998, Indonesia was Nike's biggest production centre, with 17 footwear factories employing 90,000 workers and producing 7 million pairs of shoes each month. C&A, Levi's, Dockers, Ralph Lauren, Marks & Spencer, Umbro, Fila, Puma, Lotto, Reebok, Puma, Adidas and Asics, all enjoyed the favourable economic climate of the Emerald Girdle, as former coloniser the Netherlands used to call the string of islands that constitute Indonesia.[24]

The industry fed on migrant labour – mostly young women from the countryside. There were many cases of labour law violations and abuse of workers, often gender-related. The situation was aggravated by the Asian financial crisis of 1997, which wreaked havoc especially among small and medium-sized enterprises, and caused mass dismissals. In 1998, 25 million Indonesian workers, 26 per cent of the total industrial workforce, were fired.[25] While currency devaluations restored the country's competitive advantage – the daily minimum wage in Jakarta's garment factories decreased to about one-fifth of its original value between July 1997 and August 1998 – the banking crisis choked off credit for the manufacturers, while political and economic instability deterred investors and buyers from attempting to cash in on the cheap wages. In the 1990s, Indonesia was one of Asia's lowest-wage countries.[26]

An often-overlooked consequence of low wages is the effect they have on the family lives of workers. Unable to pay for childcare, and with none provided by their employer, women workers send their children to live with relatives in their home villages, and can only afford to visit them occasionally. Research conducted in the 1990s shows that some employers fail to pay even the minimum wage – which is far short of a living wage – or refuse to pay overtime compensation. Legally allowed time off, maternity leave, menstrual leave and sick leave are denied, or hard to get.[27] Workers in nine Nike contract factories in Indonesia reported in interviews that they had observed supervisors or managers hitting, shoving or throwing objects at workers. Punishments in one factory included sitting in the sun for hours, cleaning the toilets, running around the factory grounds, and being denied use of the toilet.[28]

In 1999 an Indonesian NGO and the German Clean Clothes Campaign investigated companies supplying brands with a high profile in Germany. In two production locations, the researchers found many violations of the ILO conventions, of companies' own codes of conduct, and of Indonesian labour law. Threats and sanctions were used to make workers work overtime with insufficient pay. Wages were partly withheld when workers made mistakes or broke tools. Protesting workers were locked in a room. Newly appointed workers were fired when found to be pregnant. Workers who wanted to take their menstrual leave were subjected to humiliating inspections and threatened with wage deductions.

> Tens of thousands of women go to work knowing they are going to bleed through their clothes for the first two days of their period every single month. For those two days, they will wear dark pants and a long blouse so the stain on their clothes is less noticeable when they walk home from the factory.[29]

Both factories paid less than the legal minimum wage. A working day amounted between 52 and 70 hours in one factory, and between 74 and 80 in the other. Supervisors pulled workers by the ear, pinched them and slapped their behinds. In one of the factories, girls of 14 and 15 worked full days, and nights as well.[30] When asked to comment on the report, the legal department of C&A Germany, one of the retailers involved, responded that C&A had stopped ordering at one of the factories in 1998, and could not find the other one in its books. Nevertheless:

> Your study proves impressively that the reality especially in developing countries is often different from what we would like it to be in spite of all conventions ... These conditions are not acceptable to us, and we take steps against them wherever we can influence them. Unfortunately, due to the complex overall situation, model solutions do not exist. It cannot be in the interest of all parties concerned not to source from these countries at all. Your statement 'Transnational corporations like C&A make use of these conditions in order to obtain maximum profit' is known to be wrong since it accuses us [of being] an accomplice. No, we don't make use of these conditions, but we are confronted with them in the framework of our worldwide sourcing. Besides that I cannot see where you find the big profits that the garment trade is supposed to make due to the furthering of these conditions.[31]

In 1998 came the demise of Suharto, the military dictator who had ruled Indonesia for 31 years. The subsequent democratisation efforts and social turmoil caused problems for employers. Attracted by the more stable political environment and lower wages of what was now known as the third and fourth generation of Asian low-wage countries, buyers like Nike and Reebok began to withdraw orders from Indonesian suppliers. In 1998 Nike spokesperson Jim Small, when confronted with an increase in the Indonesian legal minimum wage to US$2.46 per day, said that there was 'concern about what that does to the market – whether or not Indonesia could be reaching a point where it is pricing itself out of the market'.[32]

Another concern of Nike at the time was the relentless international campaign against the company, exposing the sweatshop conditions in its supply chain. The discovery of child labour in factories producing for Nike in Indonesia and elsewhere did so much damage to the company's image that, even in 2009, people still refuse to buy Nikes despite the fact that the brand has since joined the vanguard in the field of corporate social responsibility.[33] The campaigners used the company's high media profile against it. It was calculated that basketball star Michael Jordan's contract for appearing in Nike commercials, worth 13 million euros, amounted to more than the entire Indonesian workforce made in a year of stitching shoes.[34] In 2002, workers tried in vain to keep Nike and Reebok from taking their business elsewhere. In July more than 1,000 Reebok workers protested for the fifth time that year outside the American embassy in Jakarta, against a cut in orders that they claimed left 5,400 workers without jobs.[35] In August another demonstration was staged to try to keep Nike from cutting its orders to a factory from which Nike was sole buyer. Nike went ahead anyway, leaving 7,000 workers jobless. The factory paid only half the amount of severance pay it owed. When questioned by labour activist groups, Nike and its main competitors Reebok and Adidas stated their commitment to staying in Indonesia. Nike Indonesia's General Manager Jeff DuMont said: 'Any statement indicating that Nike is significantly reducing orders to Indonesia is incorrect ... While business reality and global conditions do impact our business practices, Nike is looking forward to a positive future in Indonesia.'[36] In 2009 Nike is indeed still buying in Indonesia. In 2006 Indonesian garment and textile exports grew by 10.5 per cent, and footwear exports by 13.7 per cent. Decisive in this were trade sanctions that the EU imposed on its competitors like China and Vietnam. They gave the Ministry of Industry reason to expect that the Indonesian footwear industry would have an increasing presence in European markets.

At the end of the first decade of the new millennium, the textile, garment and footwear industries combined still constitute one of Indonesia's largest foreign-exchange earners. But the economic landscape has changed enormously. Many small and medium-sized enterprises have folded. As we have seen, the 1997 financial crisis played its part; the flood of cheap Chinese imports finished the job, taking over the domestic market. The production of sport shoes is now concentrated in the hands of a few Asian companies, themselves multinational corporations that sometimes make more profit than the brands they are supplying. Large Asian companies also dominate garment production.[37] An important characteristic of some of these companies is their vertical integration: in addition to clothes, they manufacture or have easy access to yarn and textiles. For buyers, this offers the advantage of 'one-stop shopping'; industry experts predict that vertically integrated industries will prevail in the long run.

While sport shoe production is concentrated in a relatively small number of large companies, garment manufacturing is still the scene of much subcontracting and informalisation. Its supply chain can be likened to an hourglass: a great many 'western' orders are sent to a shrinking number of Asian multinational production companies, who distribute these orders to a large number of suppliers – suppliers who rely, in turn, on a network of subcontractors.[38] This handing down of production orders promotes an informal economy of unregistered workplaces where people work without contracts, or any other legal or social protection. It also blurs the distinction between the formal and informal economies. There are many forms of subcontracting: from the archetype of sending part of an order to a small workplace or home-worker, to opaque arrangements whereby the factory owner lets an agent hire people to work in his production department, always on a short-term basis and without contracts. Through ingenious schemes like these, informal work extends into regular factories. Informal workers sit side-by-side with permanent workers, under the same roof. According to the ILO, a large and increasing share of the workforce in key export industries in developing countries works under such informal arrangements.[39] For the employer, this allows flexibility in responding to sudden large orders alternating with quiet periods; for workers it means hardship and insecurity. Informal workers are not officially recognised – they can be neither seen nor heard; they can lose their jobs overnight. Precisely because of these factors, it is hard for trade unions to reach and organise informal workers. Nevertheless, there are those who try.

Emelia Yanti is general secretary of GSBI, the Indonesian Federation of Independent Trade Unions. It unites unions in four sectors, including the textile, garment and footwear industries.

> We have recently merged our garment and textile union with the footwear union. We have many issues in common, and our unions have lost many members on account of the factory relocations and closures. The merger makes us stronger in negotiating with employers and the government, which in turn gives our members confidence.[40]

Yanti has come a long way. When she was a teenager her father became unemployed, and she had to drop out of school. Continuously searching for a job with acceptable wages and working hours, she saw the inside of five garment factories in eight years. She remembers the labels that passed before her eyes: Levi's, Dockers, Eddie Bauer, Nike, Ralph Lauren, Marks & Spencer and C&A. Through a friend, she learned about workers' rights and realised that, instead of forever looking for a factory offering better wages and conditions, it might be more effective to make a stand. In 1995, with the help of an Indonesian labour NGO, she began to learn how to organise workers.

> Under Suharto, independent unions were illegal, so we called ourselves an Association. In April 1998, at an international meeting of the Clean Clothes Campaign in Belgium, I met workers from Bulgaria and Haiti, who were suffering like us. I also learned about the code of conduct, as a tool for change. Back home, I told my friends in the Association all that I had heard. It led to a new spirit, a strong spirit to organise an independent union. When Suharto left the stage, we had a chance. We quickly proposed to our groups in the factories to form a union, and began to inform the workers about the code of conduct. After two years, they had a good understanding and began to ask the management for implementation. We found many cases on which to campaign.

Even after Suharto, unions continue to have a hard time. Frequently, when workers try to set up trade unions, companies either fire or demote their leaders and members, making workers afraid to join. Under the 2003 Manpower Act, a union can be dissolved for coming into conflict with the ideology of national unity, and participation in collective bargaining is only granted to unions that win a majority of votes in the workplace. This regulation hinders newly developing, independent trade unions. The right to strike has crippling restrictions, and does not apply to all workers.[41]

Yanti has witnessed the dismissal of many newly elected union leaders. One such case made ripples that reached all the way to Davos, where it was brought before an ILO conference. In 2001, after a strike in which 8,000 workers participated, Ngadinah Binti Abu Mawardi was arrested and jailed. She worked in the PT Panarub factory that produced for Adidas, and was the secretary of an independent footwear workers' union that had merged with Emelia Yanti's union.

> The management said that the strike had inflicted a huge loss on the company, and that Ngadinah had forced and incited workers to join it. She stayed in jail for 29 days, and faced seven years of incarceration. Union members were intimidated, only 10 per cent stayed in the union. The management told the workers that this case gave Panarub such a bad image that buyers might reduce the orders, and Panarub would have to fire many workers. Remaining

members were harassed by security personnel and by supervisors who visited them at home. But by then, we had learned to use the international support. Oxfam, the CCC and the global unions ITGLWF and ICFTU stood behind us. The case was brought before the ILO. Our parliament talked about it, and the Minister of Manpower invited us for a meeting. We became nationally known. It was a good job.

The final court decision set Ngadinah free, and ordered Panarub to rehire her. She got a position in the factory's human resources department. 'The management recognised the union and allowed it to recruit members. But they refused to put it in writing. There is still no office in the factories. We can only approach workers during lunch or after overtime.' Factory closures and relocations cause enormous problems for unions:

Many factories close for just a couple of months, then reopen with workers on short-term or with no contracts. With short-term contracts, all workers can think about is holding on to their job. Sometimes I feel they are afraid when I approach them, because it can endanger their job. At the moment we are trying to organise 100 workers who are embroidering Nike logos, all on a short-term contract. We try, even if we know their jobs won't last long.

Organising workers without any contract is even more difficult. 'We need new strategies. There are so many of them, knitting sweaters for Lacoste or making batiks. It is not easy, but we don't give up. Even if the workers think campaigns have a bad effect, we don't stop. We don't want to see management laughing.'[42]

THAILAND: HOW CATS BECAME TIGERS

On 14 November 2000, the world's best golf player, Tiger Woods, found himself ambushed in the Shangri La hotel in Bangkok by 30 Thais dressed in black. They were former Nike workers and labour-rights activists, and they told Woods that his five-year sponsorship contract with Nike equalled the income of a Thai shoe-stitcher working for 72,000 years on end. 'It was a very successful action,' says Junya Yimprasert, 'we were even on CNN for a couple of minutes.'[43]

Junya's nickname is Lek, 'Little One'. In height, maybe; her personality tilts towards the other end of the scale. When she was a university student of social science and development, she became aware of the fact that very few people got the chance to attend university, and that most of them were rich. 'While universities are highly subsidised, only 5 per cent of the students are from a farmer's background. I decided to work for development.' In 2000 she founded the Thai Labour Campaign, an NGO that is not content with just increasing wages or better code implementation, but wants to 'break the circle of worker exploitation', as Lek puts it.

> In the late 1990s, there were many cases of labour rights violations, and I thought we should send word about that to the world. The Thai Labour Campaign started with just me, my computer and a mailing list of mainly friends. We thought that research and publication of abuses might help Thai workers. We could be a platform for discussion and education, and help to build international solidarity. International organisations gobbled up the information we sent out. There appeared to be a real need for information about the Thai situation.

The motive for the Tiger Woods ambush had been the dismissal of 1,300 workers in a factory that had produced for Nike and other sports brands for nearly 15 years. It was part of the restructuring of the Thai garment sector that had grown in the 1980s and early 1990s, but had since then yielded ground to countries with lower production costs. Factory owners were trying to turn the tide by shifting production to non-unionised subcontractors, to the provinces where wages and benefits were lower, and to border areas where they could make use of migrant labour – in short, to relocate and replace formal workers through informal arrangements. At the same time, buyers scouted for cheaper production in neighbouring countries like Laos, Cambodia, Vietnam and China. While the Asian financial crisis of 1997 was often mentioned as the reason for factory closures and relocations, the structural 'race to the bottom' was always in the background.[44]

Before the Nike action, there had been a labour dispute in Thailand that had given rise to one of the first successful North–South campaigns involving the CCC: the Eden case.

At its peak, the Austrian-owned Eden Group was one of the larger garment exporters in Thailand, employing more than 4,500 workers and producing for brands like Disney and Looney Tunes.

Eden's workforce expanded rapidly during the late 1980s and early 1990s. Wages were low and working hours long, and labour law was violated on many occasions. Workers responded by establishing a factory union. In 1991 the company began subcontracting work to home-based workers and sweatshops, stepping up this practice after the union gained strength and disclosed child labour and extremely low wages paid by subcontractors in Thailand and abroad. An official government warning concerning environmental pollution speeded the process up: the owners began to transfer capital and profits overseas, facilitated by a billing office in Hong Kong. When the company reported huge losses, suppliers and banks began to remove factory equipment. In 1996 Eden suffered a complete breakdown, with mass dismissals, broken promises of compensation, and finally the flight of the Austrian owner. Workers picketed the factory for months on end, taking to the streets and demonstrating in front of the Austrian embassy. When the factory equipment, the capital and the owners had finally vanished, the workers shifted the focus of their actions to the government, asking it to take responsibility. This resulted in the partial payment of compensation to some of the workers. In the long run, the fight contributed to changes in Thai labour law, including measures against child labour and the establishment of a compensation fund to which foreign-owned companies had to contribute. The 1998 Labour Protection Act now guarantees workers' severance pay.

One of the contributions of the CCC to the campaign was a European speaking tour by two Eden workers and a representative of a Thai NGO. During visits to six European countries, the three Thai women met with politicians and representatives of western brands, unions, and solidarity and consumer groups. They participated in actions at brand headquarters and in front of stores selling garments made at Eden. They compared their experiences with those of striking Renault workers in Belgium. Another CCC contribution was an international protest-letter action – in fact its very first 'urgent appeal', although it did not yet make use of the internet. Information was distributed to thousands of consumers, who then wrote protest letters to C&A, Otto and Neckermann. The international exposure generated pressure on the Thai government, and the European tour provided Thai workers with the opportunity of 'seeing' the entire supply chain at first hand. They could confront their foreign employers head-on, and connect to an international labour-rights network. The campaign changed the character of the relation between foreign investors and Thai workers.[45]

But international solidarity campaigns did not always deliver, as the infamous Par Garment case illustrated. Par Garment, producing for brands like Gap, Gymboree, Wal-Mart and Tommy Hilfiger, had a colourful history of union repression and labour rights violations. At the end of 2002, after the company had subcontracted most of its work to non-unionised factories and sweatshops, the owner failed to repay his loan from the Bangkok Bank and fled, leaving the remaining 149 workers without jobs or compensation, and with salaries and overtime unpaid – though this did not prevent him from keeping a financial interest in two garment factories in the provinces. Requests to the brands to take responsibility were fruitless. The Par Garment union[46] called upon the Ministry of Labour to pay the money owed to the workers from the compensation fund, but was told to wait until the company's remaining property was sold. In June 2007, five years after being laid off, the workers received less than half of the compensation owed to them.[47]

Perhaps the saddest story is that of the Gina Form Bra Company workers. In 2003 they sent a triumphant message out into the world saying that, after two-and-a-half years of struggle with the management, they had signed a collective bargaining agreement that included the reinstatement of dismissed union leaders with up to two years' back pay. There were enough new orders from brands like Victoria's Secret and Calvin Klein to provide jobs for the entire workforce. Early in September 2006, Gina workers received word that the owner had decided to consolidate production in fewer facilities. The unionised Thai factory was closed, in favour of production locations in China and Cambodia.[48]

'Bed&Bath, now there is an entirely different story!' said Lek Yimprasert. 'It was a highlight in our campaigns.' Bed&Bath was a Bangkok garment company, owned by a Thai couple, employing 850 workers making garments for brands like Nike, Levi Strauss, Adidas and Reebok.

We had done some research into this company, because workers had reported violations of the law and of Nike's code of conduct – they were well aware of the code, since a short version had been printed on the reverse of their name tags. One of the violations was excessive and forced overtime; the workers said that they were given Cokes laced with amphetamines to keep them going through the night. The worst violation of all happened on 21 October 2002, when they found the factory locked and the owners vanished, owing their employees US$400,000 in back wages and compensation. We found out that the factory and the equipment already belonged to the bank. If the workers were to demand a share of the proceeds of the sale, they would get zero, so they decided to change the strategy. First they would hold the employer responsible; second the government; and finally the brands they had produced for.

The case took three months to settle – three very uplifting months, according to Yimprasert.

It was different from other factory closures. The workers of Bed&Bath were mostly young, high-spirited girls and boys. About 400 of them decided to fight. We saw them transformed from cats to tigers. First they were sitting there humbly, waiting for mercy from the Ministry of Labour. After two weeks, when they realised nothing was going to happen, they blocked the car of the minister when it left the Ministry of Labour. He was visibly worried. At that moment they realised they had power when they acted together. They changed from passive waiting to active intervention. We occupied the ground floor of the Ministry. 'It is our home now,' the workers said, 'we have nowhere else to go.' They walked up every floor and knocked on doors, asking officials what they were doing and telling them about their predicament. They stayed there for three months.

Attempts by the government and the police to remove the rebellious workforce from the building were thwarted by the high visibility of the action, which had not gone unnoticed by international organisations, media and filmmakers. Thai unions brought food and money.

They were camping out there 24 hours per day, cooking meals, playing games, singing songs, taking care of their babies. One of the workers even gave birth there. They went to the offices of the United Nations and the ILO, to the US embassy and the Nike head office in Bangkok. They were very united, and we took care to have maximum participation in decision-making.

After two months the financial situation started to become difficult.

They borrowed sewing machines from one of the unions and began to make T-shirts. We sold them to visitors and labour organisations, and even Ministry of Labour officials asked for special T-shirts. They were earning quite a lot so they borrowed more machines and announced that they were turning the Ministry into a factory.

Since the government could not lay a finger on the runaway employers, negotiations now focused on government compensation.

There was pressure from the brands, which had been informed by international labour rights organisations. The brands refused to pay, but they did threaten to pull out of 900 Thai factories. After three months the government gave in and paid compensation out of the Employee Support Fund. Not 100 per cent, but better than zero. We also managed to raise the level of back-payment of wages and compensation money. The Thai labour movement has benefited from the Bed&Bath struggle.

The story did not end there. While most of the 400 workers went in search of new jobs, about 40 of them, backed by a government guarantee, took out personal loans and pooled the money – a little over 20,000 euros – to open a small garment factory cooperative in Bangkok. They called it 'Solidarity Factory'.

The first two years they took subcontracted orders, to pay back the loan. They worked like crazy; I felt so sorry for them. After that, there was more time for capacity building and for thinking about the future. They divided up the overhead work, and everybody got two tasks: stitching and finance, or stitching and marketing, or stitching and accounting. They decided they should have their own logo, their own brand. They came up with 'Dignity Returns'. In the beginning, nobody thought they'd survive. Worker-owned factories never did. During the first three years, it was very difficult. The number of workers shrank to 14. They didn't earn much; some had to take a cutback of 50 per cent. Many were under pressure from their families. But after they paid back the loan and the factory was theirs, they increased the salary to the living wage, 50 per cent higher than the minimum wage. With direct orders, you generally earn three times more than with subcontracted orders.

Getting direct orders and maintaining long-term relationships with buyers is crucial, and not easy. There are periods of slump, and the local market is barely accessible because sweatshops are too competitive. But international NGOs and unions place occasional big orders, and Thai consumer groups, universities and unions are becoming interested.

I think this is a way to break the circle of exploitation. Thailand is a hierarchical country, a class society. If you are born poor, you will live poor. It is difficult to change this belief into a conviction that everyone is equal, because it is ingrained in the minds of workers themselves. We have introduced many slogans to destroy that mental hierarchy. We made a poster saying: 'The employer is a human being, the politician is a human being, the worker is a human being.' Now unions ask for T-shirts with that slogan, for their members.

While it is not hard to find anti-European and anti-American sentiments in Southern activist circles, Lek Yimprasert does not harbour any. But one issue does concern her:

Ever since we started, the Thai Labour Campaign has had a close partnership with the CCC. For us, they are a resource for campaigning and knowledge about globalisation. Their international work has an impact on our campaigns. But I always have to tell them to slow down. Stop talking to the big companies! We must educate the workers here first; most of them have only primary education. If they don't understand what a code of conduct is, how can we explain the link between an Olympic Games campaign and worker rights? That is why in the strategy planning at the global level, southern representatives are important. A new campaign every year is too much; we need one-and-a-half years to educate and mobilise people, with our limited resources. If you move too fast, you won't have global action because the southern people will just disconnect. We have to recognise this. It will delay the process, but if we really want to move together, we have to.

CAMBODIA: PLASTIC KILLERS AND YELLOW UNIONS

The garment industry in Cambodia is young. At the end of the twentieth century, when Cambodia was struggling to its feet after the devastation of the Vietnam War and the ensuing Khmer Rouge years, the dirt-poor kingdom was suddenly flooded with factories producing garments for international brands. In 1994 there were only 20 garment factories; in 2000 there were at least 200; and, according to the Ministry of Commerce, in 2007 there were 290, employing 330,000 mostly young female workers from rural areas.[49] Most of the factories had owners from mainland China, Taiwan, Singapore, Malaysia and Hong Kong, and produced for western brands.

In 1999 an epidemic of fainting among workers was reported in two factories. Excessive overwork and exposure to chemicals caused them to pass out. The Ministry of Labour investigated, and announced on national television that overtime had to be limited to two hours per day, and paid at a higher rate than the minimum wage. In the same month, in another Phnom Penh garment factory, workers went on strike and staged a demonstration at the Ministry of Commerce. They were up against unrealistic production targets that forced them to do unpaid overtime on a routine, structural basis. Their Chinese employer fired anyone who protested. After the strike and demonstration, the employer caved in to the demands of the workers and their union. Workers would earn the minimum monthly wage of US$40, based on an eight-hour working day, six days per week. Overtime had to be compensated, and all dismissed workers were reinstated.

Did the workers' show of strength impress the employer, or was it the intervention of visiting US State Department officials that had the required effect? Their opinion mattered, because in 1998 a Bilateral Textile Agreement was signed with the US granting Cambodia access to the US market, and thereby attracting investors from China, Taiwan, Malaysia, Singapore and Hong Kong. The agreement tied annual increases in Cambodia's export quota to compliance with the national labour code, as well as to the observance of the ILO's core labour standards.

In 2001 the ILO 'Better Factories Cambodia' project strengthened this agreement. It combined monitoring of working conditions, training of employees, and a search for solutions to abuses. The gender aspect of working conditions was highlighted – over 90 per cent of garment workers were female. A study published in 2006 presented data about issues critical to women workers: health and nutrition, breastfeeding and childcare, personal safety, sexual and other forms of harassment, workplace relations and dispute resolution.[50] The idea behind the programme was that compliance with labour standards is good not only for workers but for business as well, because companies will be able to use socially responsible production as a sales argument. It seemed to work. In 2000, Nike and Gap both cancelled or reduced orders from Cambodia after reports of gross labour violations. According to Cham Prasidh, Minister of Commerce, Gap even sent back a $10 million shipment that was in mid-ocean transit when a particularly damaging report emerged. Labour-rights advocates, including the CCC, pressured the companies not to cut and run, but instead to work with suppliers to make improvements. The companies returned to Cambodia after the ILO agreed to monitor working conditions through the 'Better Factories Cambodia' programme. They have placed large orders since 2001.[51]

Despite the ILO project, cases of abuse and disputes in the Cambodian garment industry continued to surface. They concerned the lack of compensation for injured workers, fugitive factory owners who owed their workers wages, and children making shoes and jeans for Nike and Gap. A name featuring in many of the reports before was that of Chea Vichea, the 36-year-old, outspoken president of the Free Trade Union of Workers of the Kingdom of Cambodia, the country's leading independent union, with over 70,000 members. He was also involved in the political movement criticising the Hun Sen government.

On 22 January 2004, around 9 a.m., he was reading a newspaper at a busy roadside newsstand in Phnom Penh when a man came up to him and shot him in the head and chest, then fled on the back of a waiting motorcycle. Chea Vichea's funeral was attended by 10,000 people. The International Confederation of Free Trade Unions condemned the killing and filed a complaint with the ILO.[52] In the year before the killing, Chea Vichea had received death threats, going into hiding several times, and had been denied police protection despite strong reasons for a thorough investigation. More than one opponent of the Hun Sen regime had been murdered, and Vichea had had several collisions with thugs in the course of his union work. Two men were arrested and later sentenced to 20 years' imprisonment for Vichea's murder.

'But', says Phan Phors, 'they are "plastic killers".' It is the title of a DVD made about Vichea's murder, and argues that the two convicted men became scapegoats while the actual killers – acting on instructions of powerful people – have yet to be caught. Phan Phors is a mechanic in a Malaysian-owned, Phnom Penh-based garment factory – one of the hundreds that operate in Cambodia now.

Every weekend he travels 100 miles on his motorbike to his family plantation where, when he is not rubber-tapping, he studies Chinese in order to negotiate better with the Chinese managers of his factory. He was elected president of his factory's branch of the Free Trade Union of Workers of the Kingdom of Cambodia. 'The court hearings in the Chea Vichea case have been denounced by a special representative of the United Nations', he says. 'The International Trade Union Confederation and Amnesty International have asked for a new investigation. After Chea Vichea two more union leaders have been killed. They were my friends.'[53] Seven unions are registered in the factory Phan Phors works for. 'But mine is the only one independent of the government', he says. 'The other unions often make trouble for us. They threaten the workers with factory closure if they demand better pay or a holiday.'

'That is how "yellow unions" operate', says Ath Thorn, president of the Cambodian Labour Confederation, which unites four union federations. He used to be a worker in the garment industry, and is now completing a law degree at Phnom Penh University. Like Phan Pors, he is in his thirties, and like Phan Pors he was present at the beginning of independent union organising in Cambodia.

> Employers create 'yellow unions' when we begin to organise ourselves. They cooperate with factory management and interfere with the work of the free trade unions. Employers and government don't like the independent unions. Officially we have freedom to strike; the government has ratified the core conventions of the ILO. But corrupt officials, in cooperation with factory owners, hire gangsters to threaten us. Union leaders are dismissed and dragged into court. When we demonstrate, the police will use violence. In the past year we conducted three strikes, and every time the police arrested the activists and fired their guns at the sky.[54] From 1996 to 1999, working conditions were very bad. In 1998 a Cambodian labour NGO began to train workers. We learned how to organise and negotiate with the employers, we studied the ILO conventions and labour law – which didn't exist in Cambodia until 1997. Then we started local unions in factories, and in 2000 the federation of independent unions was established. Before the unions, the employers could exploit the workers without any restraint.

In 2000, workers from 69 garment factories went on strike to demand an increase in the minimum wage. At the end of 2007 it stood at US$50 per month – up from US$40 in 1997, but still not enough to fulfil the daily needs of a Cambodian family. In 2006 Oxfam estimated that the average living wage in Cambodia should have been US$85.[55] People worked overtime whenever they could get it.

The industry is permanently on the lookout for new ways of reducing the cost of labour and preventing the formation of workers' organisation, says Ath Thorn. He mentions two.

The owners use short-term contracts, that exclude workers from benefits like annual or pregnancy leave, and if they join a union, the contract is ended. Even people who have worked in a factory for three years cannot get a permanent contract. Sometimes an employer fires all workers and rehires them on a short-contract basis. Another problem is that since 2007, factories will use home-based workers if they get large orders that have to be filled quickly. It robs the regular workers of their overtime hours, which they need badly because the minimum wage is not enough to live on. It is difficult to organise the home-based workers. They are usually entire families, including children, working day and night; they have no choice. They are not interested in unionising. If they did organise, the factory would not send them orders anymore.

Being part of the CCC network is important:

We met the CCC in 2004, at a meeting it had organised to design a strategy for the Olympic Campaign. We believe that consumer pressure on brands in Europe and the United States can be effective. The brands can force factories over here to respect labour rights. We score most of our successes in this way.[56] I feel much stronger, now that we are in contact with labour activists from all over the world. We can achieve more by cooperating globally. If we demand an increase of the minimum wage in Cambodia, the CCCs in Europe can demonstrate in front of the brand offices and the big stores. If they can be satisfied with a little less profit, we can raise the minimum wage. If we stand by our demands, and western customers threaten to stop buying in their stores, the corporations must negotiate with us. I believe in the power of the CCC in Europe, in the democratic countries where they respect the labour movement. We have joined the CCC family.

Phan Phors agrees.

> Three of our union leaders are dead already. I myself am afraid
> sometimes. I work from half-past five in the morning till half-past
> five in the evening. Always two hours overtime. At night I go to
> university to study English, until half-past eight. When I return
> home late I am alone on my motorbike. Once, five men tried to
> stop me, and I was lucky to escape. But I have to continue my
> studies, because I need to speak English and get more knowledge.
> If we give in to fear, we cannot improve the working conditions,
> we cannot develop our country.

CHINA: WHERE THE SUN NEVER SETS

Over the past 20 years, the poetic description of China as 'the land
where the sun never sets' has acquired a more prosaic meaning for
the millions of internal migrants working in the Chinese 'twenty-
four/seven' economy. A still from the documentary *China Blue*,
which shocked western audiences with its images of exhausted
factory girls sleeping between heaps of blue jeans, features two of
these teenagers trying to stay awake by using clothes pins on their
eyelids.[57] When the documentary was shown to a packed Amsterdam
cinema at the end of 2006, the public was clearly moved. A member
of the audience said that he wanted to pay five euros extra for every
pair of jeans he bought in future, provided the money went to
the girls that made them. The screening was followed by a debate
organised by the CCC. One of the panel members was Yuk Yuk
Choi, a Chinese activist based in Hong Kong. When somebody
asked what 'we in the west' could do, she replied: 'You may call
the transnational companies to account.'

Choi is a small, soft-spoken woman who was born in mainland
China and grew up in Hong Kong. After studying sociology,
she started working in an NGO that conducted poverty relief
programmes in rural China. It educated her about the hard life
of rural communities. The Chinese – approximately one-fifth of
humanity – live on 7 per cent of the world's arable land. It is one
of the reasons why so many, mainly young people begin looking
elsewhere for a living. Most of them are young girls.[58] They pack
some clothes and a toothbrush in a bag, and take a bus to the city.
Not only are they going to earn the family some cash income – they
are also going to have fun! You can buy almost anything in the city:

there are movies, music and cars, and if you work hard you may get to enjoy it all.

It is estimated that China now has 200 million internal migrants – partly those from rural areas, and partly workers who became unemployed when state-owned enterprises shut down after the introduction of the market economy. Most migrants work in the industries of the coastal provinces, especially in the south. These days Yuk Yuk Choi works there as well, in the Pearl River Delta, which is referred to sometimes as 'the workshop of the world', sometimes as 'the most polluted area on earth'. Her organisation is the Hong Kong-based NGO Worker Empowerment (WE), which supports self-organisation by migrants.

> Our work is necessary because the only trade union allowed by the government is distant from the workers. But I have to say: it is difficult. WE is small; we don't even have ten staff members. Most of them used to be migrants who started work at 14 and have little education or skills. But they all suffered under the injustices of their work and want to make a change, together with their fellow workers. In our centre on the mainland we train workers in labour law and labour rights; we try to help them get compensation when their fingers are smashed in a machine, to show them where to look for support when they have a conflict with the boss. In the long run, we aim to build capacity, confidence and trust between workers, as a basis for organisation. The companies and the Chinese government are keeping a close watch on our work, but even if there are restrictions, there are also successes. Compared to other countries, labour law in China is not all that bad. It is not implemented, but we can refer to it.[59]

In November 2007 a worker centre associated with WE was attacked, and one of its organisers stabbed by two unidentified men. In July 2008 the centre reopened in another location, with its permanently handicapped organiser back in the saddle.

After the devastation of the Cultural Revolution, the Open Door policy engineered by Deng Xiaoping in 1979 ended China's economic isolation by attracting foreign capital, technology and management skills. The first special economic zones were set up in Guangdong province, next to Hong Kong, and in Fuijian province, on the strait between China and Taiwan. Tax exemptions, free foreign exchange transactions, concessions on land use, and minimal regulation of labour management were effective in luring foreign direct investment to these zones, and soon much larger coastal areas were opened up for foreign capital and trade, finding a huge labour force willing to work for little money.[60]

The Chinese textile and apparel industry was quick to absorb modern technology and procedures, partly because of the financial and marketing expertise of the Taiwanese, Korean and Hong Kong investors who came in and began to act as intermediaries between China and western brands and retailers. China soon gained an advantage over other garment-producing countries.[61] In 2002, even when still restrained by the quota rule of the Multi-Fibre Arrangement, China produced over 20 billion pieces of clothing – almost four for each human being on earth.[62] In 2005, in the first month after the end of the quota regime, Chinese exports to the US achieved a 75 per cent jump, while its exports to the EU increased by 46 per cent.[63]

It is hard to avoid superlatives when describing the growth of the Chinese economy. Until the western financial and economic crisis of 2008, China's economy showed double-digit growth; in 2007, China produced 40 per cent of the world's shoes; Dutch households save 300 euros every year because of cheap Chinese imports; the number of Chinese millionaires and an affluent middle class are growing fast; the large cities have branches of Starbucks, MacDonald's, Häagen Dazs, Gucci and Louis Vuitton.[64] This economic transformation has reduced the numbers living in absolute poverty, but the gap between rich and poor is widening; China ranks among the most unequal of nations. While city centres surpass western cities in the number and size of their high-rise buildings, shopping malls and cars, about 200 million out of 700 million rural inhabitants have an income of less than one dollar a day. When they move to the cities in search of jobs and income, many find 16-hour working days, starvation wages and unhealthy working conditions instead. In 2005, according to official estimates, industrial deaths amounted to 127,000, and the number of workers suffering from occupational diseases was 200 million (out of 758 million workers across China). In the Pearl River Delta, some 40,000 fingers are severed each year in work-related accidents.[65]

China has had a minimum wage since 1994. It is set by local or provincial governments, who are required to take into account the cost of living in their area. The Labour Law also sets the standard working week at 40 hours, with overtime not exceeding 36 hours per month, and paid accordingly.[66] The reality is different. Although average wages have increased every year in China since the late 1980s

– the average wage in urban areas in 2006 was 170 euros (US$224) a month, four times higher than the figure for 1995 – the incomes of low-skilled workers in primary industries have not kept up. Those most adversely affected are migrant workers in areas such as the Pearl River Delta, where the cost of living has increased rapidly over the last few years. A National Bureau of Statistics survey in 2006 reported the average monthly wage of migrant workers in the Pearl River Delta to be 600–700 yuan (58–67 euros, or US$76–89), only enough to buy four bowls of noodles a day.[67] In 2007, three people died and 31 were injured when a crowd stormed a Carrefour store that had announced a sale of cheap cooking oil. This signalled the increasing difficulty people have had with the steadily rising prices of food and energy.[68]

Average wages are higher than the minimum wage, but some employers fail even to pay that. When Jasmin in *China Blue* starts work in the jeans factory, she earns US$0.08 an hour; the minimum wage at that time was between US$0.45 and US$0.48 cents. In 2006, the minimum monthly wage in the Guangdong province was between 43 euros (US$57) and 75 euros (US$100). In order to earn a living, many people worked between 12 and 14 hours a day, seven days a week, with one day off each month. Workers paid on a piece-rate basis were confronted with unrealistic quotas, and had to work long into the night to earn wages that might still be lower than the minimum wage. Western people experience 'burnout'; the Chinese suffer from 'overwork death': *guolaosi*. In 2002, a 19-year-old girl died after having worked for 21 hours without a break.[69] Conditions are worse for temporary workers and for those who have no contracts, and women generally earn 20–30 per cent less than men for the same work.[70] Payment of wages is often delayed, and earnings are reduced by fines charged for misdemeanours such as 'looking around' or 'sitting cross-legged'.

Migrant workers are considered 'temporary guests' in the cities, and are barred from all kinds of social provision. Place of residence largely determines benefits and opportunities, and rural people have fewer entitlements than city dwellers. The *hukou* system of resident registration that tied people down to a particular place has been gradually dismantled to meet the demand for a flexible labour force. But, while people are now allowed to migrate, it is still difficult to obtain an urban *hukou*. This makes it hard, for example, for children of migrants to attend public schools. Workers and their families are denied healthcare by employers who fail to pay for the legally required medical insurance.[71]

In the autumn of 2006, the European parliament passed a resolution that highlighted the difficult situation of migrant workers and asked China 'to combat all forms of modern slavery, child labour and exploitation, particularly of female workers, so as to ensure respect for the fundamental rights of workers and discourage social dumping'.[72]

In September 2007, the Hong Kong-based NGO *China Labour Bulletin* published a report indicating that child labour had become an increasingly serious problem. This was confirmed in 2008, when more than 1,000 children were discovered in a situation of forced labour in Guangdong province. A criminal organisation had lured them to factories, where they earned between 22 and 34 euro cents per hour.[73] A more 'normal' form of child labour were the 'work–study programmes' using children to work in factories or on fields on the understanding that employers contributed to educational costs. At the time of writing, some 400,000 children are estimated to be involved in these programmes. One example cited by Human Rights Watch concerns 500 children from a middle school in Sichuan working 14-hour shifts in a factory during the summer. They sleep in overcrowded dormitories, are fed insufficiently, suffer work-induced health problems, and are fined for production mistakes. Employers often use children when trying to evade government regulations on seasonal work.[74]

Although the level of organisation among migrant workers is low and in many places non-existent, their sheer despair has led increasingly to 'wildcat' strikes and other forms of protest. Efforts at organising outside of ACFTU – the only legal trade union federation, since China has not ratified the ILO conventions on freedom of association and collective bargaining – are usually met with repression by the government, which considers social instability a great threat. The lists of imprisoned labour-rights activists compiled by the International Trade Union Confederation and by *China Labour Bulletin* are eloquent: people continue to be 'reformed through labour' or incarcerated in psychiatric wards.[75]

But repression is not the only governmental tool for shaping labour relations. In recent years, the Chinese government has introduced a series of laws and regulations to protect the rights and interests of workers, and 'from a strictly legal standpoint, it would be fair to say that the protection of workers' rights in China is systematically improving', says Han Dongfang, the renowned labour activist who, since his release from a Chinese prison, supports workers on the mainland through *China Labour Bulletin*.[76] The Contract Labour

Law of 2008, for example, is designed to regulate the explosion of short- and no-contract labour. The Law also sets limits on working hours and overtime, and implies a curbing of employers' influence. It prompted the American–Chinese and the European–Chinese Chambers of Commerce to protest strongly and threaten a withdrawal of orders. This corporate interference in the country's legislation elicited a storm of indignation, at which point the European–Chinese Chamber of Commerce retracted its objections. But the Law continues to be undermined by the excessively low piece-rate wages that force workers to seek overtime.[77]

Under these circumstances, corporate social responsibility (CSR) is at most a flawed and inadequate tool to improve working conditions. Even brands that are serious about their code of conduct and audit their suppliers regularly cannot prevent the boundless violations of basic labour rights in their supply chains. When the CCC and global trade unions, as part of the 2008 Play Fair campaign on the occasion of the Beijing Olympics, investigated four Chinese companies awarded licences to produce official Olympic goods for firms such as Nike, Wal-Mart and Disney, they found many abuses that had not been discovered by the auditors assigned by brands and retailers to investigate the factories. The Play Fair coalition concluded that, without freedom of association and collective bargaining, no sustainable change could be effected.[78]

In a *Business Week* article titled 'Secrets, Lies and Sweatshops', a CSR manager for a major multinational company commented that the percentage of Chinese suppliers cheating on payroll records stood at 75 per cent in 2006. A study commissioned by Nike in 2005, investigating 569 of its suppliers in China and elsewhere, found code violations in every single one, as well as many tricks for hiding them. Factory managers complained that they could not afford better labour standards as long as western buyers were unwilling to pay more for what they ordered. Like the Play Fair research, the article raised the question of whether it is possible to improve working conditions in a country without 'real unions and a meaningful rule of law'.[79]

According to *China Labour Bulletin*, there is a growing network of labour rights NGOs across the country, with 40 in Guangdong province focusing on migrant labour alone. They provide information and training on labour rights, and assist in legal proceedings. They operate in a grey area, since registering as an NGO is difficult. Some register as businesses, while some present themselves just as private salons or clubs. Still, pressure for change is growing. *China Labour Bulletin* reports:

> China's citizens are increasingly campaigning openly, at the community level, on a wide range of local rights violation issues – ranging from unauthorized and uncompensated land seizures in the countryside, urban evictions to make room for city development projects, serious pollution from local factories, police violence against protestors, and of course [there are] collective protests by workers.[80]

In support of these actions, labour-rights groups doggedly continue to explore routes between the rocks and hard places within Chinese society. To get an idea of their modus operandi, it is useful to take a closer look at the work of one of these groups, which for reasons of safety will remain unnamed. It is a Hong Kong-based group, and over the years its activities have changed from being research-based and organised from the top down to having direct involvement with mainland workers. They provide training to workers in factories on employment relationships and health and safety issues. At first, access to factories was gained through cooperation with brands ordering from those factories, and needed to adhere to their codes of conduct prescribing training programmes. Later, the group also forged direct relationships with workers and grassroots organisations, since it appeared that brands could be unreliable: sometimes they simply packed up and left. The training has in some places resulted in the establishment of worker committees, or in trade unions affiliated to the state union federation. The impact on working conditions has been limited, but the emerging organisations are a way of identifying active workers who dare to stick their necks out. This is important, since one of the major obstacles for workers in standing up for their rights is their lack of confidence: they do not have the experience of their voices being heard. The many labour protests that occur are usually one-off events without long-term planning, or even much hope of success. The organisers often leave the factory immediately afterwards – either because the authorities have detained them or because management will discriminate against them if they stay. Building solidarity and sustaining an organisation is difficult. Since the lack of organising experience is another major obstacle, the group arranges contacts between mainland workers and workers from other Asian countries, and stimulates the exchange of information.[81]

It is groups like these that provide the clean clothes movement with anchorage in China. They supply information from the ground and try to express the needs and demands of Chinese workers. Western groups in turn pressure brands to develop decent labour standards in their Chinese supply chains, and give direct support through the urgent appeals system, through worker exchanges, and in other ways. When the CCC organised the showing of *China Blue* throughout Europe, it not only conveyed an inconvenient truth to the western public, but also facilitated contacts with the European labour movement for the Chinese activists who accompanied the film.

A major anti-sweatshop campaign on China involving the Hong Kong partners was the 2008 Play Fair campaign. The Olympic Games in Beijing presented a challenge: while China wanted to use the global profile conferred by the games to demonstrate its progress and achievements, labour and human rights activists saw a chance to shine a light on the people at the losing end of China's success stories. The campaign had to move carefully to avoid endangering individuals and groups working in mainland China. The coalition – consisting of the CCC, its partner organisations, and the global ITUC and ITGLWF unions – published two research reports. One investigated four companies licensed to use the Olympic logo, which was hugely profitable: the official Beijing Olympic mascots alone were estimated to have brought in more than US$300 million. All four companies violated one or more standards for wages, overtime, child labour, or health and safety. Employees of a headwear company worked more than 13 hours a day, seven days a week, while they received less than half the minimum wage. Workers reported that management instructed them to lie to the auditors of western brands investigating their factories. There was no form of worker representation.[82]

The second report was built on interviews with over 320 sportswear workers in China, India, Thailand and Indonesia, and on reviews of company and industry profiles, reports, newspaper articles, websites and factory advertisements. It concluded that, despite more than 15 years of corporate social responsibility, violations of workers' rights were still the order of the day. It identified low wages, precarious employment, violations of freedom of association, and factory closures as the four main hurdles to overcome.[83] Street actions of the European CCCs and their global partners, a virtual Olympic torch relay using mobile phones and the internet, and the media attention generated by the reports culminated in a day of action in Hong Kong, five days before the Games began. The International

Olympic Committee, itself a major brand asked to undertake action, did not give an inch; but some of the sportswear industry's major players agreed to take part in a working group that discussed sector-wide solutions to the hardships of garment workers.

Staphany Wong used to be staff member of the International Hong Kong Liaison Office (IHLO) of the international trade union movement, one of the CCC's partner organisations active in the Play Fair campaign.[84] The IHLO supports this movement in Hong Kong, and monitors trade union rights and labour developments in China. 'In Play Fair we had a good working relationship with the CCC', says Wong. 'We like each other instinctively. Their approach is direct, there is little bureaucracy. For us it is good to be involved in bigger international campaigns and learn the technique of working with different groups. It has been good media training too.'[85]

The IHLO itself has no staff working in China, but is in close contact with other Hong Kong groups that meet workers on the mainland in 'service centres' or elsewhere.

> Most younger workers are familiar with the internet; they enter discussion forums on which we are also active. The majority move from city to city to look for better employment, and uses the internet to keep updated on the minimum wage level and the best positions in a city. The core problem is the absence of freedom of association, but they will not mention this. They have never had it. It is one of the difficulties of organising in China. The official trade union ACFTU does not represent the workers. Foreign trade unions often think that they have to collaborate with the ACFTU because it is big and powerful, but we think they could explore other roads as well. We try to brief them about the key labour-related issues in the regions they visit, about the labour activists in prison there. But sometimes they are afraid to upset the ACFTU. It is a hot issue to touch, but they should at least try because after all, freedom of association is the foundation unions are built on.

Wong has worked on labour rights for several years now, and has recorded much repression. But she sees positive changes as well. 'Despite local obstacles, labour legislation is improving, and people are more aware of their rights.'

May Wong works with Globalization Monitor, a Hong Kong NGO that supports workers in industrial zones in China, focusing on labour, the environment, women's rights, and globalisation. She agrees with Staphany Wong: Chinese workers have become more aware of their rights, and are using them.

They file court cases against employers, and there are more possibilities for grassroots organisation now. When I started to work in the industrial zones in the mid-1990s, it was much more difficult to do research and interview workers. These days, workers even provide information to journalists. Few can afford a computer, but in chat rooms you see some fierce criticism on the direction of the economy. You can get away with it as long as you don't organise any long-term actions. That's where government draws the line. It is the reason we see so many cases of 'wildcat' strikes and blocking of highways without any apparent leadership.[86]

The worker service centres on the mainland are a growing influence, she says.

The government knows we are there and what we do. They just monitor it. Worker Empowerment[87] uses a special strategy: it supports a worker centre near an industrial zone, and the centre encourages active workers to gather signatures under a petition to raise the minimum wage, because food prices are going through the roof. The workers ask the local labour bureau and government representatives to adopt it. Campaigns like these are a new development in industrial zones. The future is difficult to predict, but the seeds are sown. The ACFTU is trying to connect to this movement. They are trying to monitor labour disputes and migrant workers by recruiting them into the union, and actively encourage local chapters to recruit migrant workers.

Past experiences have made Wong wary of working with brands on corporate social responsibility.

If workers had their own unions, we wouldn't need these CSR interventions. Since 2001, the Hong Kong groups [have worked] with Nike, Reebok and Adidas on health and safety in their supplier factories in China. Unfortunately, we have not gotten best practices yet. There are problems: no full commitment of the brands, incapable CSR personnel, much resistance from the supplier factories, and no full participation of workers throughout the project. We were very frustrated and disappointed. We have to be careful when companies invite us to do a project. When they only use us to show their willingness to work with local stakeholders, we lose credibility. But working with international partners is important. We face many obstacles and risks, and international support is crucial.

Because of sharp controls on capital movements, Chinese banks were believed to have escaped the current western credit crisis and recession; but, in the course of 2008, they arrived in China anyway. While the years of expansion and labour shortage have not brought workers' emancipation, the crisis is not likely to turn that tide. The export sector in general is suffering from shrinking orders from western brands and retailers; since the end of 2008, double-digit growth has ceased.[88] For about a year before the crisis hit, the Pearl River Delta had already seen an increase in closures and relocations of low-end, low-profit and highly polluting enterprises – including the clothing sector – as the central government sought to move away from them towards higher-end production.[89] The crisis, extending into 2009, has stepped up the momentum of this trend, and millions of workers have been fired. Businesses seek government support in the form of tax breaks, special loans and suspension of the Labour Contract Law. Social stability is at risk. Provinces like Sichuan and Chongqing are bracing themselves for the return of millions of migrant workers. Poorly educated workers, especially, are having difficulty finding jobs. In November 2008, fierce protests erupted in the southern Guangdong and Jiangxi provinces: workers destroyed the windows and computers of a toy factory when they were dismissed without compensation. In Guangdong alone, 67,000 of over 700,000 factories were shut down in just a few months. In many cases, social security payments that would have ensured compensation to dismissed workers has not been made by employers.[90] At the beginning of 2009, millions of workers in the textile, toy and furniture industries lost their jobs. In February, immediately after celebrating the Chinese New Year in their home villages, many of them returned to the Pearl River Delta, hoping to find new work and prepared to accept lower wages and worse conditions than before. The Chinese government announced provisions for modest compensation and training for migrants who had been fired. Now it is preparing for social instability. The People's Army has been called upon to be 'steadfast and loyal' to the Communist Party.[91]

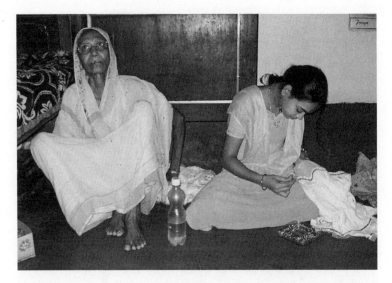

1.   Grandmother and child home-worker, India 2008. © Clean Clothes Campaign

2.   Sweatshop, India 2008. © Clean Clothes Campaign

3.   Participants in the European tour push the broken-down bus, Brussels 1996. © Clean Clothes Campaign

4.   Made with Love, label in a C&A brand sweater, Utrecht 2007. © Liesbeth Sluiter

5.   Emelia Yanti, general secretary of GSBI, an Indonesian federation of independent trade unions, Bangkok 2007. © Liesbeth Sluiter

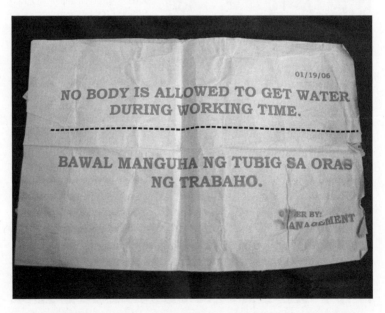

6.   Sign in a Philippine factory supplying Wal-Mart, 2006. © Clean Clothes Campaign

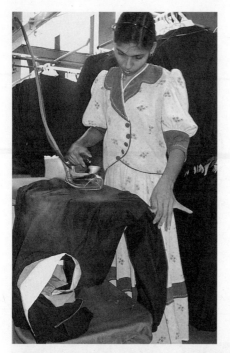

7. (left) Worker in economic processing zone, Sri Lanka 2002. © Clean Clothes Campaign

8. (below) Worker tour of Sri Lankan and Indonesian workers and unionists. Indrani Wijebandara of North Sails Lanka visits the sportswear shop of a former Dutch surf champion, 2003. © Clean Clothes Campaign

9.   Solidarity Group, a cooperative garment factory established in the wake of a strike in a regular factory, Bangkok 2007. © Liesbeth Sluiter

10.   Knitwear factory in Madagascar, 2004. © Clean Clothes Campaign

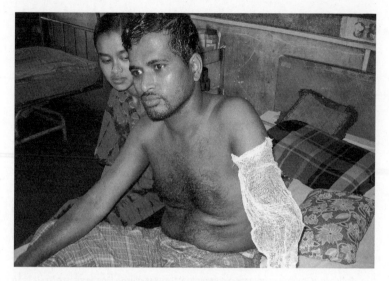

11.   Nur-E-Alam lost his left arm after waiting 17 hours to be rescued from the collapsed Spectrum factory, Dacca 2005. © Clean Clothes Campaign

12.   Spectrum workers demanding the arrest of Spectrum owners after the factory collapsed, killing 64 and injuring 70 workers, Dacca 2005. © Clean Clothes Campaign

4
Africa

While labour rights may be putting down roots in African soil, it is not easy to find them flowering. *Un jour, ça va arriver*, says Françoise Rabary Harivelo, employee of a Madagascar textiles factory: one day, it will happen. She is a representative of the STM, the Syndicat Textile Malagasy.

'This is the first time for me to participate in an international meeting', she said towards the end of the 2007 Bangkok CCC Forum.

> I think that the projects discussed here are a little big for my union and co-workers. But we have to try to connect with other countries. It has become clear to me that everybody has the same problems. Capitalism dominates. The multinationals are the same in America, Europe, Africa and Asia. I believe we need an international solidarity to fight them. We have been too isolated, we don't know what happens elsewhere. This morning we have decided to form a regional group with South Africa. We need to know about each other's problems, and try to solve things that we cannot solve alone.[1]

In her factory, Françoise is supervisor of a production line cutting textiles. She works between 10 and 14 hours a day, six to seven days a week.

> Apart from wages, our main problem in Madagascar is contract work. Workers will get a six-month contract; after that they are fired and hired again for six months. This repeats itself, there is hardly a steady job anymore. I think the brands that buy our products should pay attention to this. There is one that can be an example to the others: Gap. Before they place an order, they ask us about wages, food, transport, hygiene and safety.

Organising is difficult.

When we hope to organise a public meeting, we are afraid the government might repress it, like it did some political demonstrations. When the unions try to improve the living conditions of workers, the factories move. They go to Kenya or the Seychelles. We always fear for our jobs. There is a saying in Madagascar: it is better to work for little money than go to bed without food.

Accompanying Françoise Harivelo in Bangkok was Hanta Andrianasy, a quiet woman whose modest appearance hides a strong will and determination. She is a medical doctor, and also in charge of the gender and union promotion programmes of a German political foundation, the Friedrich-Ebert-Stiftung (FES). In this capacity, she facilitates the organisation of garment workers in Madagascar.[2]

During the first years of the 1990s, I began to notice that many of my patients were tired women. They had abortions, they missed their periods for months, and they were all very tired. When I asked after their profession, they were all seamstresses, and all of them worked in the same knitwear factory in an economic processing zone. I wondered, what is happening in this factory? In 1996, FES agreed that we should try to do something about these tired women. I felt their diagnosis was not physical but social, and wanted to go straight to the cause of their fatigue. We began to organise meetings with unions, labour inspectors and worker delegates, in which labour laws and rights were explained. We identified needs and topics that interested the workers, and made radio programmes.[3]

The unions were reluctant from the start.

There are many unions in Madagascar, sometimes six in one factory. Some are politically oriented, and focus not so much on the work floor as on supporting or opposing political regimes. They found it difficult to work with NGOs on labour rights issues, because they were afraid we would break up the union movement. But we didn't mean to replace unions; we thought the meetings might be a place for dialogue between union members, non-unionised workers and the inspectors. A place to discover what is really happening.

In 1997 Hanta Andrianasy met Esther de Haan, then international campaign coordinator of the CCC, for the first time.

We talked about these issues. In 2003 we met again, this time in the company of Jabu Ngcobo and June Hartley from South Africa, who represented the global union ITGLWF that had opened an African office in 2000. It led to an association of about 20 elected worker delegates from garment and textile factories, close to the workers. When the unions protested, the delegates promised to discontinue the association if the unions would begin working together. They thought the profusion of unions weakened the workers' struggle. The unions refused, so the delegates went ahead.

Of the original 20 delegates, only two or three are now still working. Some lost their jobs because of factory closures; many were fired.

Some of the dismissals could be justified by labour law, on the grounds of unauthorised absence. To understand why workers would risk such punishment, you have to understand the importance of cultural events in our country. Certain rituals identify you as a member of the family. If you don't attend them, you cannot be buried in your family tomb. For Malagasy people, this is no option. The family tomb and the ancestors are part of daily life. So sometimes people will leave work even if management doesn't allow them. Some dismissals were due to causes like these, some were just punishment. We concluded that the delegates needed more tools, to prevent further misery. Our cultural way is to have a dialogue – Malagasy people are known to be peaceful. So together with the Friedrich-Ebert-Stiftung we have produced a handbook for the delegates, a practical tool for social dialogue in the private sector. We have also tried to get delegates reinstated by asking for international support through the CCC urgent appeal system. In one case we were successful, but then the factory closed. Another delegate accepted a settlement that at least provided some compensation, after a two-year process. Even after the Labour Department had judged the dismissals to be unlawful, management refused to comply.

New delegates joined, and the association continued. In 2005, delegates and workers decided to create the Syndicat Textile Malagasy (STM), a union specialising in textiles.[4] 'It was necessary in order to focus on textile sector issues. The founders were also looking for ways to improve the union movement in terms of efficiency and internal democracy', says Hanta Andrianasy.

Now STM is still in a learning phase. Although the union members are women, the leaders are men; Françoise is the only woman on the executive board. Because we are a French-speaking country, it always costs extra energy to communicate with the English-speaking regional and international world outside. In the beginning almost nobody could use a computer; now we ask the experienced worker delegates to take the new ones to a cyber café and teach them. Also, communicating within the country is not always easy because travelling takes a great deal of time and many workers cannot afford a cell phone. Still, in 2006 the STM mobilised more than 1,000 workers. But this year only 100 paid the fee, even though it is only one euro per year. Some earn no more than 25 euros per month and are never sure about their job. But I think that, with support, the STM has potential. Even if the government isn't used to seeing the union as a partner in the socio-economic field, even if the unions have to face up to leadership problems ... sometimes you just want the workers to win.

SOUTHERN AFRICA: RESEARCH IN ACTION

'In southern Africa, so much energy has gone into unionising!' says June Hartley, mother of four and proud grandmother. As a blanket-weaver, she stood at the crib of the South African union movement and was one of the first black women to defend workers' rights against white factory managers and government officials. 'Formation of unions was the beginning of life', she says. 'We realised we were not alone.' She survived eight months of solitary confinement during the Soweto uprising. She has held different positions in the trade union movement, has a Masters in the sociology of labour and a Master of Business Administration; she set up workers' colleges in South Africa and was a literacy teacher. She tells stories that should fill another book some day.

'The research of the Clean Clothes Campaign in southern Africa has been critical', she said at the breakfast table on the third day of the Bangkok Forum.[5]

The international perspective brought depth of understanding about the processes at work in the industry. The research data were shared and immediately used for campaigns against abuses, as in the case of the dismissed worker delegates in Madagascar. These campaigns not only benefit individual workers, they can also fortify unions because you can talk about flowers all you like: until people see them they are not real. Workers need to experience that management cannot get away with unlawful dismissal. We have seen all these newly industrialising places in southern Africa. New factories, new trouble. Unions try hard to recruit members, but of course factory owners don't need them! The CCC has been instrumental in getting union recognition in several places – Lesotho, for example.

In Lesotho, a garment worker was stabbed in the neck with her scissors by a factory guard. CCC research quickly revealed which were the buying brands, one of which was Gap.

The CCC contacted Gap and the American garment union Unite, and the campaign was focused. The general secretary of the Lesotho union visited America to negotiate with Gap and talk to consumer groups. Finally the injured woman took a settlement and the union got recognition. Organisations like the CCC can never replace unions. But it works like a machine, with all the parts delivering a concerted effort. The CCC fills a gap at the international level.

In 2008 Esther de Haan was a researcher for CCC partner SOMO, as well as a member of the CCC International Secretariat.[6] Since the mid-1990s she has visited countries in sub-Saharan Africa several times to research the textile and garment industry. In these research projects she cooperated with the South African Trade Union Research Project and with the Civil Society Research and Support Collective, based in South Africa.

The researchers were at the heels of the footloose garment industry itself. Since the beginning of the 1990s, textile and garment factories had proliferated in countries like Swaziland, Botswana, Lesotho, Mauritius, Madagascar and Kenya. The quota restrictions of the Multi-Fibre Arrangement on Asian exports had turned low-wage African countries into an interesting alternative for garment production companies. Preferential trade agreements like Lomé/Cotonou and AGOA, which allowed duty- and quota-free African exports to Europe and North America respectively, added to the bright prospects, even if African infrastructure and workforce education were generally less developed than in Asia.[7] African governments oiled the wheels by promising investors tax incentives and infrastructural facilities, often in export processing zones. According to de Haan,

We wanted to document investment patterns and working conditions in the industry. From the beginning, we understood the research to be campaign-oriented action research. We worked together as much as possible with local and regional worker organisations, and fed the findings into educational processes and campaign strategies. Ideally, workers' organisations set the research agenda, and would decide to what end the results would be used. In the meantime, we also tried to build up research capacity in local organisations. One important finding of our research was that, in the wake of international brands, large garment producers had now also begun to shop around globally for favourable production and trade conditions. Multinational production companies from Asia such as Tuntex and Nien Hsing, the largest jeans-maker in the world, had set up shop in African countries like Lesotho and Swaziland. These companies, empires themselves, operate without the worries of brand imaging and consumer pressure. They are therefore difficult to influence on issues such as labour conditions.[8]

According to *Made in Southern Africa*, the report that presented the research results until 2002, trade agreements and the absence of a quota system were more effective in attracting investment than government incentives like a cap on wages, tax holidays and repression of unions. Where these were on offer anyway, they made workers suffer.[9]

The garment industry did bring employment opportunities; in Swaziland for example thousands of people found factory jobs. But these factories can tear the social structure of a community apart. When they are dropped into a village, there is often no infrastructure to receive new, migrant families of workers with their children. Sometimes a factory claims water that farmers need to irrigate their fields. Waste water from factories causes pollution. In cities, new factories tend to induce migration from the countryside, which also uproots and destabilises communities. More questions arise when you take the durability into account of an industry that depends on trade agreements that are bound to expire one day; these companies deserve their epithets 'footloose' and 'quota-hopping'. And even if foreign investors stick to one location, much of the profit leaves the country anyway.

It is also difficult to appreciate employment opportunities if working conditions and wages are as appalling as we found them to be. In 1997 I visited a factory in Kenya where, six months earlier, a fire had reduced half of the building to ashes. Employees were making socks in the middle of the sooty debris. Very dirty socks indeed. It looked like hell in that factory.

Unions are usually repressed. A worker in Swaziland told us that, when union representatives tried to contact the homeward-bound workforce outside the gates, they ran past them as quickly as they could. They were afraid to be seen talking with them.[10]

AGOA and foreign investment have created employment, and have increased garment exports from sub-Saharan Africa, although they decreased again after the 2004 MFA phase-out. But in countries like Lesotho, Swaziland, Tanzania and Uganda hardly any locally owned garment companies have been set up, and most of the fabrics for the foreign-owned companies came from Asia. Foreign companies have been the main beneficiaries of exports. Some local entrepreneurs have benefited as well, like transporters and food vendors that sell meals at the factory, but there are very few links to the local economy.[11]

Michael Koen, a South African researcher with a background in the union movement, has worked closely with Esther de Haan.[12] He has seen the consequences of the macro-economic changes in Africa close-up:

Southern and eastern Africa used to have a clothing industry of their own. As countries moved into the global economy they had to drop the import tariffs that had protected their domestic production. That opened the gates for imports of second-hand clothes. They flooded Africa in huge quantities; there is even smuggling to countries that still refuse to let second-hand clothes in. This was the first major blow to the domestic industry, which had been developed as part of the import-substitution strategies that preceded neoliberal economic policies. Once the used clothes hit the streets, the domestic industry died overnight. Hundreds of thousands of jobs were lost. The factories that survived became dependent on foreign markets, and were finally taken over or replaced by foreign, mainly Asian companies. Twenty years ago, most garment factories in Africa were African-owned. Now fewer people are employed in them, almost none are locally owned, and most are ready to move at the drop of a hat. They are supplying to retailers that are often vicious in their demands and expectations. And this is supposed to be development? The idea of domestic manufacture for domestic consumption has been obliterated. Governments have bought into the idea that economies will become healthy through export-led growth with foreign direct investment and cuts in state expenditure on social benefits. But while there has been growth in gross domestic product, the social indicators in Africa have been falling through the floor. Some of that is HIV-related, but there is also a statistical convergence with the neoliberal policies.

We must find a way to pressure national governments into taking their responsibilities. I don't buy the argument that neoliberalism makes nation-states weak. I think they just give the power away. But a prerequisite for African countries to take that power is integration among themselves. They should stand together as a bloc, but they don't. Internal trade is insufficient; the colonial focus outward has never disappeared. There are about 25 blocs in Africa, in the form of common currencies, local preferential deals and trade blocs, which isn't good integration. An integrated African region might develop the sort of gutsy moves that are needed to stand up to the structural adjustment programmes that even the World Bank itself is now having doubts about.[13]

Koen echoes Esther de Haan's criticism of the type of employment the garment industry has created:

The jumping around of the industry creates continuous disruption. The employment gains of new factories are offset by closures elsewhere. Nobody can plan a way out of poverty, because there is no notion of a job beyond next week. This process of disruption is debilitating people and affecting the unions. They have suddenly been confronted with foreign employers who are completely intransigent and nasty. By the time they had gained some ground, bang!, the Multi-Fibre Arrangement ended, taking away the African advantage. Lesotho lost a number of factories almost instantly. Swaziland lost some – Malawi too. Many unions are quite small and dependent on membership fees; when factories close, union fees dry up.

The research in southern and eastern Africa was intended to contribute to changes for the better, and in some cases it did – notably in Lesotho. After publication of the findings in 2001, the Lesotho government and the clothing union Lecawu launched their own investigation into the garment industry. It supported the previous

research, listing 29 serious violations of the Lesotho Labour Code
and leading to the recommendation that the labour commissioner
instruct companies to comply with the Labour Code in short
order.[14] The Lecawu union became stronger by linking up with
the international network of unions and NGOs. The international
garment union federation ITGLWF organised regional workshops
on codes of conduct and campaigning, in which the Lesotho findings
were used as a benchmark. Because the research had identified
retailers sourcing in Lesotho, unions and NGOs were able to stage
campaigns focusing on these retailers' western headquarters.

The report findings also served as ammunition for local and global
campaigns targeting the Taiwanese-owned Nien Hsing factory.
Buyers like K-Mart, Sears, Gap and Cherokee were confronted
with the conditions in Nien Hsing's Lesotho workplaces. Taking
advantage of the country's high unemployment rate, Nien Hsing
employed workers on a 'casual' basis, allowing them to pay less
than the minimum wage. Some workers had been employed as
casuals for ten years or more. They were reminded not to raise their
voice against the physical abuse and locked emergency exits in the
factory by the hungry unemployed sitting outside the gates every
day, hoping to be hired. Supported by regional and international
campaigns, Lecawu negotiated a historic agreement that committed
management to recognising the union and agreeing to collective
bargaining, on condition that the union enjoyed majority in the
factory. Several other factories followed. Lecawu membership
increased from 3,000 in early 2001 to 16,000 in 2003.

Although international support and research were instrumental
in reaching this agreement, they are never a substitute for effective
grassroots unionism, according to de Haan and Koen.[15] 'But research
can fast-track processes of organising', says Koen.

When we went to a factory in Malawi to get information from
workers about pay-slips and working hours, many came out to
talk to us. They wanted to form a union, and we could have
signed on several hundred members on the spot that afternoon.
The existing union was maybe 350 members strong. So the
research showed up organisational weaknesses and indicated
targets for recruitment that the union and the ITGLWF-Africa
then could build on. The Malawi union grew to 6,000 members in
one year. In Swaziland and Lesotho, Asian manufacturers formed
an association that began to negotiate with the unions.

In local negotiations, external power sources like an international network can be helpful.

> Once your foot is in the door, the game changes. Now it's about perceived power. The employer is thinking: How much can they hurt me? If the company next door has been the target of an international action, he is aware of that. Confronting him with violations of ILO conventions in his factory may corner him. That kind of thing is a club in your toolkit. But it is imperative that it doesn't replace the basic union power, which consists of the ability to withdraw labour. Without that, a union doesn't have power at all. Using it in a globalised context is more difficult than before, because the factory owner can always pack up and go. Therefore you have to use it very carefully, and it helps to have international pressure, preferably urging the employer not to pull out, but to stay and correct the problem.

But the principal effect of international support, Michael Koen says, is giving a voice to marginalised people. 'By opening up space for them at strategic junctures, it can increase their power.'

5
Europe's Neighbours

Asian and African countries were not the only ports of destination for the flight of the European clothing industry at the end of the twentieth century. Close by, there were other countries with attractive production regimes, and they had the added advantage of short delivery times, well-developed infrastructure and an educated labour force.

The fall of communism in 1989 had caused unprecendented economic earthquakes in central and eastern Europe. Bettina Musiolek, living in the former East Germany and a member of the German CCC, describes what happened to the textiles and garment industry in her country:

> The markets in Russia and other eastern European countries disappeared overnight. Partly because poverty was on the rise; partly because everybody with a little money now bought the western clothes they had longed for, which were dirt cheap to boot. Everybody started ordering from the catalogue of Otto, the West German mail-order company. To be able to compete, the East German factories had to adapt to a higher and more intensive pace of work, and produce many different collections per year. They needed a whole new marketing system and network, and had to use the West German currency, of which they possessed very little. They also had to adopt the cheapskate strategies of western companies: informalisation of work, the use of short-term contracts and home-work, and outsourcing to low-wage countries. Of course they didn't succeed. Between 1989 and 1991, employment in [the textiles and garment industry] was reduced by half; 140,000 workers lost their job. In 2008, production has vanished altogether. I think that, in East Germany between 1989 and 1992, we saw the biggest industrial collapse in history.[1]

In the midst of industrial collapse, the export-oriented textiles and garment sector in other eastern European countries gained in importance. As in developing countries, low-technology industry and an economy oriented towards foreign markets provided a survival option. In 1997, 1998 and 1999, representatives of the International Secretariat and the German CCC visited factories, trade unions and NGOs in Poland, Romania and Bulgaria. They found that, in some places, the industry had risen from the ashes since the shockwaves of the early 1990s, and had been integrated into European and even global trade – albeit in a very different form than before.[2]

Instrumental in this development was a new trade and investment mechanism established by the European Union. It is called 'outward processing trade', or OPT, and it entails exporting fabrics and materials like zips and buttons from the EU to eastern European countries, where they are assembled into clothes and then sent back to EU buyers. It enables the buyers to protect and promote western European textiles and to profit from cheap production costs, as well as saving extra because they only pay tariffs on the value added abroad, and not on the fabric and materials. For the eastern industries, OPT is a short-term answer to shortages in capital. It allows for a relatively fast cash-flow without taking too much risks; and it brings new clients, new money, and in some cases technological upgrading. On the other hand, factory managers complain about the low profit margin. They see this, in addition to the inflation in their countries and the high interest rate on credit, as an obstacle to much-needed investment. OPT is a survival strategy, rather than a form of development. Added 'bonuses' are the decay of domestic textile industries, the loss of expertise in design and marketing, and dependency on western buyers who exert adverse pressure on wages and delivery times.

As a result, soon after the transition from a state-led to a market-led economy, the eastern European garment industry was largely transformed into sweatshop production. When, in 2007, eastern European countries were admitted to the EU, and OPT ceased to be an option, the loss of skills and investment reserves diminished their competitive capacities and their ability to upgrade the industry. Ironically, upgrading had been the strategy advised by EU and World Bank.

EASTERN EUROPE: INDUSTRY-TURNED-SWEATSHOP

European buyers turned to eastern European countries not so much because of their low wages – although in countries like Romania and Bulgaria, they hardly surpass Asian levels – but primarily because of fast delivery, the level of skills and education, and production quality.

In Poland, CCC researchers, including Bettina Musiolek, visited 19 factories at the end of the 1990s and found working conditions a little better than in other eastern European countries, and wages a little higher – though below the needs of a family aspiring to a decent standard of living. European buyers such as Adidas, Nike and Wal-Mart considered the country an attractive production location because of the advantages of rapid privatisation and relative political stability. The industrial landscape offered a mixed view. There were formerly state-owned factories where labour law and remnants of social benefits were still upheld for a shrinking number of workers; there were small private companies that often downplayed their workforce, because firms with fewer than 40 employees were exempt from certain labour laws; there were subsidiaries of multinationals interested in penetrating the market. A large 'grey economy' made use of short-term contract work, and home-work was on the rise.

In Bulgaria, changes seemed to occur slowly after the transition, because western business interest was minimal. The economic situation deteriorated when the Bulgarian garment industry lost the Soviet and east European markets. Privatisation disclosed existing unemployment and the Bulgarian currency devalued rapidly, which had a negative impact on domestic purchasing power. Political turmoil followed. The CCC investigators found that, between 1989 and 1996, the output of the garment industry had shrunk by a third – by two-thirds if the informal economy was not considered. Nonetheless, this sector was one of the few still functioning. Ruen, a previously state-owned trust appointed to privatise the knitwear and sportswear industries, now controlled the entire sector. It acted as an intermediary, collecting orders from multinationals like C&A, Puma and Reebok, and selecting the cheapest contractors. Women made up 80 per cent of Bulgarian garment workers. Wages were the lowest in the country's labour market, covering about 12 per cent of basic needs. Working conditions were pitiful. Overtime was often not paid until targets were reached. There were reports of seamstresses being locked up so that they were unable to have a break, or forced to strip naked to prove that they had not stolen anything. Greek garment manufacturers employed seamstresses in sweatshops across the border in Bulgaria. The completed pieces were transported back to Greece, often illegally, and then exported to western Europe.

In Romania, the CCC researchers visited 23 production locations at the end of the 1990s, ten of them former state-owned companies that either had been fully privatised or were still partly owned by the state – privatisation had made slow progress. Because they were often large and unproductive – with surplus capacity and old machinery, and usually not fully functioning – they were not popular with investors. Many of them were vertically integrated; they produced textiles as well as garments, making them less appropriate for the 'outward processing trade' that prescribed imported textiles. Since client contacts used to be centrally organised, managers often had no experience in that field and lost their clients to new, privately owned businesses.

Before 1989, Romania had been a major clothes producer, and exported to western countries. The textile and garment industry used to be the country's second-largest employer – Bucharest had boasted a factory with 16,000 employees. The collapse that occurred after the transformation of a communist to a market economy was partly reversed after 1990, when the country became a favoured production location for western companies. It combined the advantages of skilled labour, low production costs, experience in producing for western European countries, and proximity to the EU market. But the 'outward processing trade' left the industry with low profit margins, leading to the demise of domestic textile production. Between 1993 and 1997, Romanian textile and garment exports increased by 220 per cent. The main share of production was exported to western Europe, especially to nearby Italy and Germany. Earnings were very low: in western shops a Basler shirt cost 25 times more than the amount for which it was produced. In the private companies, labour laws were at best partly upheld. In economic terms, some of them were doing rather well; they had built up a customer network, and their workforce grew in line with production. Labour law dated back to communist times, and everybody agreed that it was relatively good: the problem was implementation, especially in small factories. A joke from the old days went: 'We pretend to work, while the state pretends to pay.' In 1998 the wages were still a joke, but the pace of work no longer was. Workers – 85 per cent women, with husbands often unemployed – complained that a 40-hour working week was not enough to reach production targets. They sometimes worked 16-hour shifts, and overtime was not paid accordingly. When there was no work, they earned nothing.

In none of the three countries visited had the 'code of conduct' taken root at the time. If managers knew that the western companies ordering at their factories had a code, they were in the dark as to its meaning, and understood it to be a set of recommendations instead of requirements. More often, their only experience with buyers' standards concerned quality and delivery times. These buyers included H&M, Gap and Benetton.

Another common trait of these three countries was the ineffectiveness of trade unions in improving working conditions. In the former, state-owned factories, the old unions were still present; their members were often strongly aware of their rights as laid down in labour law. In the new, privately owned and usually small companies, unions had no hold whatsoever, and the existing trade union federations had no policy to organise workers actively. Some union leaders even felt a tension between the economic development of their country and worker organisation. As a Polish union leader put it: 'Solidarnosc has a difficult position because it should work in the interests of the workers, but I myself also feel responsible for the economic well-being of the firm. Frequently these interests are contradictory.'[3] Even if unions succeeded in negotiating collective bargaining agreements, the road to implementation was paved with obstacles. In Bulgaria, unionists were harassed and laid off. In Romania, factory owners established 'yellow' (fake) unions.

Between 2003 and 2005, the CCC carried out new investigations in eastern Europe, this time including Serbia, Macedonia, Moldova and Turkey – countries that had also developed a considerable garment industry. It appeared that, eight years after the first research, working conditions remained essentially the same. Although in some cases the involvement of multinational retailers and efforts at corporate social responsibility had effected improvements, basic labour standards continued to be violated, and seamstresses were still languishing at the low end of the labour market everywhere.[4]

Non-governmental organisations are a relatively new phenomenon in central and eastern Europe. Most NGOs have limited experience with international work, and at the time of the research the CCC found no NGOs working specifically on labour issues and women's work – although some unions and NGOs expressed an interest in collaboration. They attended CCC seminars, and some took part in international campaigns. German CCC member Bettina Musiolek says:

Campaigning is a real problem in this region. Many unions are still more state- than worker-oriented, and there is no NGO tradition. Existing NGOs don't like labour issues, because they are still associated with the communist regimes. Voluntary work is always a problem; when there is no money for a project, it will not happen. People have a hard time maintaining themselves.[5]

Several strategies were formulated to develop organisational capacity and build a network. In Romania, Poland, Bulgaria, Serbia, Macedonia and Turkey, a series of 'Train the Trainers' workshops took place between 2002 and 2004, in which women learned how to interview workers and managers, how to interpret documents and write reports. An exhibition was staged about conditions in the garment industry in Macedonia, Serbia and Montenegro.

POLAND: CAUGHT IN THE MIDDLE

After 2000, a cooperative relationship developed between the CCC and Karat, an NGO network focusing on gender issues, and extending over central and eastern Europe and the Commonwealth of Independent States, with a secretariat in Poland. The seeds of this network were sown on a train.

'In 1995, women left from Warsaw for Beijing, to attend the fourth UN World Conference on Women', says Joanna Szabuńko, programme manager of Karat. 'While they crossed many eastern European countries and picked up conference participants on the way, they held workshops on the train. After seven days, they arrived in Beijing with a common regional vision.'[6] From there on, the road has been bumpy. The NGOs were inexperienced and had little confidence. Political frictions made work on common issues difficult; the dynamic changed all the time – and still does. Karat conducts several gender programmes, one of which focuses on economic and social justice, involving labour market issues and working conditions in sectors with many women workers, such as the garment industry.

'In many of our member countries the garment industry has either been important for a long time, or became important after the change to a market economy', says Joanna Szabuńko.

In Poland the industry goes back to the nineteenth century. The city of Łódź was famous for it – they called it the City of Women. There was communist propaganda depicting the garment workers as heroines building our socialist country. There were absurd pictures of garment workers partying after work, or getting a massage.

The change to capitalism hit the sector hard.

Large factories with thousands of workers [were] bankrupted, workers were left without severance pay. There was huge unemployment and little retraining. Surviving companies were drawn into the supply chains of foreign brands. Straight from the socialist dependencies, they jumped into new, capitalism-driven ones. The younger, mostly smaller factories followed suit. Soon 80 per cent of production was done under the 'outward processing trade' system. That contributed to the problems of today, because when the brands left for lower-wage countries, the factories did not have a strategy of their own: no special products, no managerial skills, no marketing or acquisition departments. There is just a boss and a lot of workers. The flooding of our domestic market by European products after 1999 didn't help. Of every four zlotys spent on sportswear and athletic footwear in Poland, three go to Adidas, Nike, Puma, and Reebok, in that order. In Polish, the word 'adidasy' is synonymous with sports shoes.

It is hard, because of the 'grey economy', to acquire reliable data about the amount of factories and workers. Factories falsify data to evade payment of taxes and social benefits. Unions have no presence in the smaller factories. It is estimated that there are about 100 sportswear and 2,000 garment factories, usually employing between five and 30 workers. Opinions about the future of the industry are divided. According to Szabuńko:

University specialists tell us the situation will decline if the industry doesn't change its strategy and develops innovative materials, designs and technologies, like they do in Europe, maybe even adopt an 'ethical' image to differentiate ourselves from Asian production. Some Polish brands, notably in outdoor products, are successful because they follow the EU strategy for development, from labour-intensive to research-intensive, but they outsource in Asia as well!

Trade unions and producer organisations claim to see a revival in mass production.

> They say that more orders are coming in and big companies are coming back. I don't think so, we'll see. We are concerned with the present-day problems of women workers. Because factories are going through hard times, there is much precarious employment. We've heard about women making a deal with the boss for unpaid overwork, and of women reporting sick in the white economy while working in grey-economy factories. Seamstresses usually get a piece-wage, which drives them into overwork. The minimum amount they get for the assigned workload is about 290 euros, while they would need at least 450 euros to survive.

The Polish garment industry has become contingent on global developments.

> Karat is presently working on a sportswear project, together with the German and Austrian CCCs. When we wrote the application, Adidas and Puma were still producing in Poland; when the funding came, they had left.[7] Precarious employment, low wages, the disappearance of social benefits – it is all related to our being drawn into the global economy. It is hard to find a strategy for improvement; industrial innovation is not our job. Cooperation with trade unions doesn't come easy. The ones that formerly were affiliated to the Communist Party didn't really reform. When we tried to contact one, the representative said he would only talk to us if the factory owner agreed. The unions that were rebellious at the time, like Solidarnosc, are now involved in politics.

> But Poland is not only a production country anymore. Its 'ascension' to the status of consumer country was metaphorically marked in 2006 by the opening of a giant shopping complex called 'Manufactura' in a former garment factory in Łódź. Its pointed slogan is 'Manufactura drives the economy since 1852', and the mall features the world's brands and retailers, from C&A to Zara. 'Because our economy has grown, we have an increasing number of consumers with a "western" lifestyle', says Szabuńko.

> Poland is now somewhere in the middle between being a production and a consumption country. Recently this has opened the doors for consumer campaigns, but when we started this line

of campaigning in 2005, we bumped into several problems. For ages, people couldn't buy anything; the shops were empty. When they filled up in the 1990s, there was no money. Now that people are earning money, they can finally go to the giant supermarket and buy what they have craved for so long. When somebody then turns up to tell them that their clothes are made by exploited workers, they tell them to get lost!

In addition, the international perspective doesn't come easy.

It has been hard to inspire solidarity with workers in, for example, China. 'Bad working conditions in China? My mother is working just as hard in Łódź!' We try to link with Polish reality by explaining that bad working conditions in China will lose Polish women their jobs, because the orders will go wherever conditions are worst.

After a few years in which no response seemed to be forthcoming, the tide may now be turning, according to Szabuńko.

In 2007 and 2008, the media and the public have grown increasingly interested. We are cooperating with a consumer group and a youth organisation that have formed an association on fair trade issues. We organise events with an environmental organisation that campaigns on fair trade. Apparently these new approaches take time.[8]

TURKEY: LABOUR RIGHTS ARE CONSTITUTIONAL RIGHTS

Three years after the first eastern European investigations, CCC researchers focused on Turkey, another EU neighbour with a large clothing industry. Export-oriented garment production had been on the rise here since the 1980s, when government support and low labour costs had attracted foreign buyers. In 1980, garments constituted less than 10 per cent of total exports; by 1995 this had grown to 28 per cent, and in 2000 to 36 per cent. In 2004, textiles and clothing had become a major industry.[9] In 2007, Turkey came fourth on the World Trade Organisation's list of leading clothes exporters.[10]

The overwhelming majority of enterprises are unregistered. Because of this, data about production locations and the workforce are generally unreliable. While the Ministry of Labour and Social

Security set the number of garment workers in 2002 at half a million, both employer and employee associations estimated it to be at least 3 million when workers in the informal economy were included. This implies that the Ministry failed to register about 80 per cent of the garment workforce. In 2004, the Under-Secretariat of Foreign Trade estimated the total number of companies in the sector at about 44,000. More than 80 per cent of them were small to medium-sized, and manufactured ready-made clothing for export.[11]

Since 2000 the growth of the industry has slowed down – partly because of a series of financial and economic crises, partly because of growing competition from Romania, Bulgaria and North African countries. Companies exporting to the markets for cheaper bulk goods in Asian countries and Russia have suffered in particular, many going bankrupt; companies supplying the high-quality markets of the EU and the US have tended to survive, because they have more stable and long-term relations with buyers.

Turkey's aspirations to be a secular, modern, industrialised republic with good international trade relations have led to labour legislation offering workers protection, including social security. Although this leaves much to be desired, and despite continuous pressure to adapt labour law to the demands of the volatile market, registered workers in the textile and apparel sectors have generally stood to gain from this regime. Most problems have arisen in the large informal economy. It seems that the good old-fashioned sweatshop has found a footing here once more, with working days of between 14 and 16 hours, and women and children required to work at night. This is prohibited by law – children under 16 are not allowed to work, for example – but the law is toothless as long as the Labour Ministry is understaffed and enforcement is lacking.

Women make up the larger part of the garment and textiles workforce. Many of them have migrated from their villages to Istanbul, the hub of the industry, but they also come from the Balkan states, Russia and the Middle East. Many are home-workers, either because they are too old to go out or because they have small children. Cultural factors also play a part in this – first-generation migrant women are generally reluctant to work out of their homes; neither they nor their husbands are ready for the change in gender roles it implies. When their daughters familiarise themselves with urban ways of life, they gradually gain more independence and get jobs in workshops. Nevertheless, home-work is there to stay. After the economic crises that befell Turkey before and after the new millennium, many women who had been employed in workshops were fired and took up home-work once again.

In 2004, the ILO launched a programme to address unregistered employment in Turkey, and published a stock-taking report. Formalisation of all enterprises, the report stated, was not expected to come about soon; the informal economy took the form of a vicious cycle: for a worker, turning down an unregistered job often meant no job at all. Employers save up to 50 per cent on labour costs, but miss out on the benefits of the formal system, such as access to credit, management development, investment in human resources, technology and new markets. The employers therefore remain unable to escape the low-cost, low-value-added sectors, and cannot move up the value chain. Most small and medium-sized enterprises, which are often family-owned, operate within such narrow margins that forcing them into the formal economy overnight would result in insolvency. The government, dependent upon the formal sector for financing social security, has difficulty keeping these systems afloat; and because they are thus expensive and weak, they remain unattractive for unregistered companies.[12]

Unions are a familiar part of the Turkish industrial landscape, and Turkey has ratified the ILO conventions on freedom of association and collective bargaining – but this has not resulted in the adaptation of national legislation. Efforts to organise workers meet with obstruction on several levels. The level of union membership is extremely low. Even the most optimistic experts estimate that only between 3 and 4 per cent of garment sector workers are members, with only 1 per cent actually benefiting from collective bargaining rights.[13] There are legal restraints on unions, such as the restriction of collective bargaining agreements to unions representing at least 10 per cent of the workers employed by a sector, and which have registered more than 50 per cent of the workers employed by a workshop;[14] or the law stating that a worker must be registered as such if he or she wants to join or establish a union, leaving the multitude of unregistered workers out in the cold. Another inhibiting factor is the requirement that workers formally register their membership of a union with a notary public – for which a fee is charged. But the biggest obstacle may be the anti-union tactics of employers. In particular, smaller enterprises engaged in export-oriented subcontracting, and facing the pressure of global competition, are fiercely opposed to unionisation. The cases of Paxar and Desa serve to illustrate this.

The US-based Paxar factory in Istanbul supplies labels and logos for an illustrious clientele, which in 2006 included Marks & Spencer, Next, Adidas, Wal-Mart, Levi Strauss, Puma, Disney, Gap, C&A, Otto, Esprit, Nike and Tommy Hilfiger. In 2006 it became clear that Paxar had violated not only Turkish law, but also the codes of conduct of the brands by attempting to destroy trade union organising. All the brands took action in this case, forcing Paxar management to negotiate with the Teksif union. This set an example of what corporate social responsibility could accomplish. In the agreement, reached in 2007, wages were pegged to inflation, while the union was officially recognised and accepted as the legitimate representative of its members at Paxar.[15]

Six organisations in Turkey participate in the CCC network.[16] One of them is the Women's Rights at Work Association, founded in 2004 and focused on gender and labour issues. At the end of 2008 it was actively involved in the Desa case. Bilge Seckin, who studied political science and theatre history – disciplines that complement each other surprisingly well, she jokes – is its founder-president.

> The global crisis is speeding up the process of informalisation of workplaces. Registered workplaces are closing, and new unregistered ones open up. This affects all workers, women even more than men. We want to support women workers, especially in the textiles and garment sector. They are the most vulnerable part of the workforce. When a family has the opportunity to give some of its children an education beyond the mandatory eight years, they choose the sons, not the daughters. So most women are unqualified when they enter the labour market, and end up with the low-paid jobs. They even get paid less than men for the same jobs. These women struggle with all kinds of difficulties. Some of them have been child workers. Most of them have a job until they have babies, then later take it up again because the family needs the money. Many women have to fight husbands and family for a little bit of freedom, and for some a sewing job is an opportunity. But there is no social support, no day care for the children in the factory, even if the law prescribes it. Husbands may also object if their wives want to join a union. It is a pity so few people are unionised. We have good relations with the unions, but gender is not an easy issue for them. If the women succeed in overcoming all these hurdles, they can become great union members, because they have grown stubborn. Like we see now in the Desa case, with Emine Aslan.[17]

Desa makes leather bags, jackets, gloves and other accessories for luxury brands like Prada, Louis Vuitton, Mulberry, Samsonite and Marks & Spencer, as well as for British designers Nicole Fahri and Luella. The company also sells its own Desa brand of products in about 60 stores in Turkey and abroad. Two Desa factories and one tannery in and around Istanbul employ 1,800 workers, 500 of whom are women. They regularly work 36-hour shifts; some workers record 220 hours of overtime each month, but are not paid accordingly. Wages are low; a number of workers are not covered by health insurance; maternity leave is not granted; and there are no facilities for nursing mothers or day care. Many have to quit work to look after their children. One of the factories has no ventilation – particularly dangerous given the chemicals used in leather processing. The few available toilets are dirty, and in one of the factories workers have to drink water from a hose on the floor of the toilet.[18]

Emine Aslan – 44-year-old mother of four and a textile worker since her early twenties – had for eight years been an employee of the Desa factory in Sefaköy, a working-class district of Istanbul. Unhappy with some of the working conditions – in particular the excessive and mandatory overtime – she decided to meet with the leather workers' union Deri-İş, which had started organising in Desa factories at the beginning of 2008. The union's efforts had already provoked the intimidation and dismissal of 42 workers in one of the factories. When Emine invited colleagues to her house to talk about unionising, she became the next victim. She was fired in July 2008, without compensation. Since then she has arrived at the factory gates every morning at 8.30 a.m. wearing an apron displaying the text: 'Unions are a constitutional right'. She plants a few banners, pours tea from her thermos and sits through the day, ready to tell her story to whoever wants to listen. It is the first strike she has ever been involved in. She has been subjected to threats and efforts at bribery, and fined by the police for occupying the pavement, but she will not budge.[19] And while she perseveres in front of the Sefaköy factory, the 42 workers who were dismissed have taken up picketing at Desa's factory in Düzce.

'We try to give a voice to women like Emine', says Seckin.

If they only stand in front of the factory, few people can hear them. We try to get journalist acquaintances to publicise labour issues. Apart from the small leftist newspapers, the media don't like to tackle those issues because the companies spend a fortune on advertising. But the Desa case is attracting publicity. Emine was on the front page of a national newspaper, and a reporter from the Italian newspaper *Unita* visited and wrote a long story. Leather workers from İzmir sent her postcards, teachers from the Black Sea province of Tokat offered support, and her name is heard as far away as Germany.

The Women's Rights at Work Association uses the consumer angle to put extra pressure on companies.

Every Saturday, we go to the Desa stores to demonstrate and ask the public to boycott Desa products. We don't think it will destroy the factory, because 75 per cent of Desa production is for export. We also asked international organisations for support. LabourStart, an international union website, hosted our campaign on the internet.[20] The International Textile, Garment and Leather Workers Federation (ITGLWF), their Spanish and Italian affiliate unions, and the CCC contacted the brands that order at Desa, and when that did not move things forward, their people began to write letters to the brands and to Desa. Almost 5000 have already been sent. We have learned from the CCC to use the consumer angle. Up until this case, our contacts with the CCC were limited to eastern European and southeast Asian organisations in the network. In March 2009, Emine Arslan will tour Italy, France and Spain to talk to government officials, trade unions and NGOs. It is good to know that we have friends all over Europe. We don't feel lonely anymore. It is a source of power for us.[21]

Part 3

The Campaign in Action

6
Strategic Developments

Mouraria is an old quarter of Lisbon, nestled against one of its hills. The name goes back to the Muslim Moors that lived on the Iberian peninsula between the eighth and fifteenth centuries AD. Today the buildings along its steep alleys house people from all over the globe, along with the far descendants of those Moors. This hill is the birthplace of fado, the bittersweet Portuguese soul music.

At the end of April 2008, a group of about 20 people climb the streets of Mouraria, talking all the way in a mix of Portuguese, Spanish, Italian and English. Their destination is a building almost at the top of the hill – a mansion formerly belonging to a family of nobles. Their ghosts still move through the blue-tiled rooms, under painted ceilings and copper chandeliers. Now the mansion is home to the neighbourhood community that keeps the fado tradition alive, and whose members are fervent football aficionados, as demonstrated by a room full of glittering cups and medals. The top floor, with posters celebrating solar energy and denouncing genetic modification, looks more like a campaign centre. It is the office of Gaia, the environmental organisation that hosts the Mediterranean meeting of the Clean Clothes Campaign, for which the group has assembled. Gaia's members are young and spirited, and they enjoy their footing in this neighbourhood with its age-old traditions.

In one of the larger rooms of the mansion, surrounded by portraits of Portuguese kings and a single lone queen, European CCC coordinator Marieke Eyskoot explains the general principles and practices of the Campaign to newcomers. 'We're an informal and international partner network that aims to improve working conditions in the global garment industry', she says. 'We have a common goal, while working methods may differ. This meeting is intended to help Gaia establish a Portuguese CCC, to strengthen the ties between the CCCs in Mediterranean countries and devise regional strategies.'

Over the next two days, subjects range from a campaign on home-workers stitching footwear in northern Portugal to the global 'Better Bargain' campaign on giant retailers like Wal-Mart and Carrefour. There is a discussion about the dangers of working with companies on corporate social responsibility while fighting them at the same time. In small groups, people share experiences of handling urgent appeals and the media. They identify companies active in the Mediterranean area as targets for common action, like the Spanish firm Induyco, which supplies uniforms for the Spanish Guardia Civil and the Italian Carabinieri. The Spanish and Italian governments, they say, should be asked to buy only decently produced uniforms. One of the Italians jokes that she would have preferred the Carabinieri to go naked; she participated in the 2001 G8 protests in Genoa, where the police shot an activist.

At the end, the general feeling is one of growth and achievement – but for one sad fact: almost none of the Portuguese NGOs that Gaia invited to the meeting in the hope of launching a CCC coalition have turned up. That might be connected to derogatory portrayal of Gaia in the press, because of its opposition to genetically modified crops. Gaia volunteer Sara Leão offers another explanation. 'Portuguese organisations prefer to go alone. When there was a boom of fair trade initiatives in our country in 2000, we tried to unite them in a platform but didn't succeed. The collective process doesn't come naturally to Portuguese people.'[1]

Leão, a psychology student and photographer, joined Gaia for its horizontal organisation model and its focus on environmental issues.

I like campaigns on basic needs, like food and clothes, issues that affect us all. They are about our way of life. I became interested in the garment industry through a campaign on responsible consuming. You have to focus on something near to you. Most important to me about this meeting was learning about the home-workers in northern Portugal. That is an issue we can tackle, something near and relatively small. The 'Better Bargain' campaign demands a bigger structure than we have at the moment.

A Portuguese CCC would be the 14th offspring on the European campaign-tree. At the time of writing, the organisation consists of 13 CCCs in 12 European countries: Norway, Sweden, Denmark, Germany, Netherlands, the UK, Belgium (one in the Flemish part, one in the French-speaking part), France, Switzerland, Austria, Italy and Spain. The process of European expansion, the adopted strategies and the various forms and focuses that national CCCs have developed, can be seen as an answer to globalisation on the one hand, and to the need for concentrated, local action on the other. Think globally, act locally, as the saying goes.

NGOs WITHOUT BORDERS

In the middle of the 1990s the Dutch CCC took up a structured approach to international network-building. Partners in eastern and southern production countries were sought out through scouting trips and action research, and by engaging with congenial groups in the international labour movement. Expansion of the European network began at about the same time and more or less in the same way, although the playing field was radically different.

The European garment industry had been outsourcing production since the 1970s. While, at the end of the 1980s, 70 per cent of garments sold by European retailers were still European-made, in 1993 this figure had dropped to 35 per cent. Employment in the garment industry had declined in northern Europe more extensively and faster than in Mediterranean countries. In the EU, more than half of the garment industry jobs disappeared between 1990 and 2000, and the trend continues in the twenty-first century.[2] In September 2008, the European Globalisation Fund paid 35 million euros to 6,000 Italian textile workers who had been dismissed because several companies had relocated production to low-wage countries.[3] The only production remaining in western Europe is that which, for reasons of craftsmanship or fast delivery, can only be carried out here – often in backyard sweatshops and by home-workers.

For the CCC, the exportation of jobs and abusive working conditions made its own expansion an obvious priority. In April 1993 the first English-language Clean Clothes newsletter was published. It described how, since the official launch of the campaign in 1990, the focus had shifted from actions against one specific company to the development of a 'Charter of Fair Trade' – the forerunner of the CCC 'model code of conduct', and a tool to improve working conditions sector-wide. It placed responsibility with the brands and retailers at the top of the supply chain, and its implementation would address the forces underlying specific abuses.

It was a multiple shift of focus: from street to office, from one company to the entire garment industry, and from 'opposing to proposing' – a strategy that persists until today. In order to achieve this – to take on the entire industry and gain access to the sweatshops of the world – the CCC needed to grow. While at home in the Netherlands the CCC was spreading the message among rural women and city youth, gathering support at provincial fairs and muddy pop festivals, links were being forged internationally with groups in the US, Canada and Europe. The newsletters published reports from the International Textiles Garment and Leather Workers' Federation, the UK's 'national group on home-working', and the Asia Monitor Resource Center in Hong Kong. CCC activists attended an international seminar in Paris about industrial codes of conduct and social clauses in trade agreements, with a focus on Nike and Levi Strauss. In 1994, a group of Canadians launched the Maquila Solidarity Network that, with goals and strategies similar to the CCC's, became an overseas twin organisation. While the CCC focused mostly on Asia, because the bulk of Europe's clothing was made there, the Maquila Solidarity Network reached out to Central and South America. The two campaigns complemented and reinforced each other. Step by step, the bases of knowledge and partnership grew.

In different parts of the world, organisations similar to the CCC were gaining momentum, fuelled by the scandals surfacing in what has been called the 'Year of the Sweatshop'. In 1995, the sportswear line of famous US talk-show host Kathy Lee Gifford was found to be 'stitched by a ghastly combination of child laborers in Honduras and illegal sweatshop workers in New York', and 'Mickey Mouse was letting his sweatshops show after a Disney contractor in Haiti was caught making Pocahontas pajamas under such impoverished conditions that workers had to nourish their babies with sugar water.'[4] The activists of the American National Labor Committee cleverly juggled statistics into statements that galvanised the public: 'Wal-Mart's annual sales are worth 120 times more than Haiti's entire annual budget ... it would take a Haitian worker 16.8 years to earn Disney CEO Eisner's hourly income.'[5] A *Life* magazine story on Pakistani children sewing footballs for Nike sent consumers on to the streets to protest in front of sporting goods stores across the US and Canada.[6] US Labor Department officials discovered slave labour in a garment sweatshop in El Monte, California.[7] In December 1995, following a campaign against Salvadorian sweatshops producing for Gap, an unprecedented agreement between Gap and the National Labor Committee provided for human rights monitoring of Gap production sites – not by Gap itself, but by an independent institution.

Nike 'watchdog groups', which already existed before the 'Year of the Sweatshop' and had followed the company's global flight patterns, became stronger and more extensive – the CCC became a part of this movement when it launched a Dutch Nike campaign in 1995.

In 1998 a Fair Wear Campaign got going in Australia, focusing on the more than 300,000 home-workers on the continent, and trying to get companies to sign a code of practice that would grant home-workers some protection.[8] The NGO Homenet facilitated the exchange of information and contacts between home-workers and their organisations in countries such as India, the Portuguese island of Madeira, Indonesia and the UK.

It seemed the time was ripe for NGOs without borders. In March 1995, the CCC and SOMO, the Dutch centre for research into multinationals, launched a 'European Campaign project', with the aim of raising awareness of the 'struggle of women workers in the garment industry in developing countries and Europe'.[9] They set out to strengthen existing ties with Belgian, French, British and German groups, and to broaden the movement by establishing autonomous Clean Clothes Campaigns in these countries. The EU gave financial support to the project, which included local training workshops, followed by a European tour in 1996 by CCC activists, garment workers and unionists from six Asian countries.

'It was a wonderfully colourful party', recalls CCC's Ineke Zeldenrust. 'Almost the entire garment labour movement was represented. We had two unionists, two labour researchers, a home-worker and a factory worker on board. Five women and one man. Most of them are network-members to this day.'[10] The journey through Europe in a flaming-red, former public transport bus is still fondly remembered by everybody who took part. In one month, the passengers met with unions and workers, and with women's and consumer organisations. They visited garment company headquarters, participated in Labour Day festivities and youth festivals, attended a 'tribunal' on the relative merits of different codes of conduct, and carried out street actions. 'It was incredibly inspirational', says Frieda de Koninck – then the newly appointed coordinator of one of the two Belgian CCCs.

These feisty women – and one man – that told us stories we had never heard before and appealed for joint action ... they were so different from the academic lectures on global problems we were used to. It was like a living visiting card: this is who we are and this is what we work for.[11]

The photograph of the passengers pushing the broken-down bus with all their might provides a fine metaphor for the spirit of the undertaking, as well as of the tasks ahead.

The public response was beyond expectation. In the Netherlands, 18 newspaper articles, nine radio interviews and six television appearances dealt with the tour and its message.[12] Cha Mi Kyung of the Asia Monitor Resource Center in Hong Kong – one of the participants – described the burgeoning factories in China to an audience of British, Mexican and South African women workers in the UK, and was in turn surprised to find the wages of Manchester garment workers lower than those in Hong Kong. The visit to Paris sweatshops made the Asians more aware of the intricacies of the global supply chain. British teenagers were shocked to hear that Indian women worked twice the hours of European workers and earned only £28 a month. In the Flemish town of Schellebelle, a Filipina and an Indonesian woman, both working in factories producing underwear, exchanged views with the owner of a Belgian underwear factory that outsourced most of its production. Organisers of the German leg of the tour wrote that 'we can already say today that there is now a much more sound political and personal base for the development of a longer-term CCC in Germany'.[13] The German Clothing and Textile Workers Union, which had been dragging its feet for months, joined the German CCC. It was part of the increasing rapprochement of trade unions and NGOs.

At the concluding meeting of the bus tour, Chanda Korgaokar – a researcher for an Indian trade union and organiser of Mumbai home-workers – emphasised the need for coordination between the European CCCs, and between North and South, commenting that 'differences in goals and strategies can be used by the retailers to "divide and conquer" and in that way offset the effects of the campaigns'.[14] This was generally acknowledged, and led to the establishment of a European Coordination Committee, the forerunner of the CCC International Secretariat. Tasks perceived to be necessary included coordination of actions on European retailers, the establishment of a clearing house for information and international contacts, the drafting of a model code of conduct, and the design of a system to monitor code implementation involving grassroots participation.

The European workshops in 1995 were attended by many organisations that remain part of the CCC European network at the time of writing. From Germany, for example, there were Südwind and the Evangelische Frauenarbeit Deutschland, both groups with religious backgrounds focused on women and development, which were already working on garment issues before joining the CCC. The French NGO Artisans du Monde had also been running a garment project, called Libère tes Fringues or 'Liberate your outfit'. In the French-speaking part of Belgium, the fair trade and development NGO Magasins du Monde had been conducting a clothing campaign called 'Made in Dignity', together with the Swiss NGO Erklärung von Bern. In Flemish Belgium, the starting point was Wereldsolidariteit, the Third World organisation of the Christian labour movement. In the UK a coalition called Labour Behind the Label had been formed as a platform for several NGOs that had taken up garment and labour-rights issues – including the recently launched Homenet, which focused on home-workers, Women Working Worldwide, and the NGO Nead.[15]

Reading and campaign materials – among them the model code of conduct – were translated and sent to the organisations in Europe that were about to launch a CCC, and to other global partners. In 1996 and 1997, the new CCCs distributed hundreds of thousands of postcards to consumers in Belgium, France, Germany and the UK, who were asked to send them to retailers. The cards requested details about working conditions in the retailers' supply chains. Somewhat to everybody's surprise, several companies responded. Apparently, consumer power was not imaginary. In France, 50 cities were introduced to the Clean Clothes Campaign on an action day, with fair trade fashion shows to the rhythms of African and Latin American music. The Germans' first step was research into leading German companies like Adidas and Puma. All the CCCs scouted for organisations to strengthen their coalitions, especially trade unions.

A small item in a 1995 CCC newsletter announced the launch of a website dealing with campaigns on the garment industry. It presented information on the industry, as well as on the campaign and its expansion, and it published 'urgent appeals, cases of workers struggling for their rights who need international solidarity and help'.[16] The EU provided money for six modems, which facilitated fast communications in the budding European network. A little later, an interactive mailing list was set up.

The internet arrived just in time. By connecting people all over the world in milliseconds and providing access to libraries, archives and the latest news across borders, it proved an immensely powerful resource for a globalising movement. As Naomi Klein wrote in *No Logo*:

> Each day, information about Nike flows freely via e-mail between the US National Labor Committee and Campaign for Labor Rights; the Dutch-based Clean Clothes Campaign; the Australian Fair Wear Campaign; the Hong Kong-based Asian Monitoring and Resource Centre; the British Labour behind the Label Coalition and Christian Aid; the French Agir Ici and Artisans du Monde; the German Werkstatt Ökonomie; the Belgian Les Magasins du Monde; and the Canadian Maquila Solidarity Network – to name but a few of the players.[17]

But the internet did more. It had a direct influence on organisational structures:

> Indeed, the beauty of the Net for activists is that it allows coordinated international actions with minimal resources and bureaucracy ... the Net is more than an organizing tool – it has become an organizing model, a blueprint for decentralized but cooperative decision-making. It facilitates the process of information sharing to such a degree that many groups can work in concert with one another without the need to achieve monolithic consensus.[18]

This description fits the CCC like a glove. The campaign views itself as 'performing a coordinating function between already existing organisations who share the same concerns, and bringing these concerns together in action and campaigns'.[19]

THE NETWORK IN ACTION

After the bus tour, the European network began to grow more spontaneously. A Swedish campaign, Kampanjen Rena Kläder, took off with a running start in 1997, when retail and industrial unions on the one hand, and four large garment retail companies on the other, appeared interested in working with the CCC Code of Conduct, and started a pilot project called 'Dress Code'.[20]

In 1998 the newly established Spanish CCC, Campaña Ropa Limpia, organised an international forum called 'New proposals for Dignity in the garment industry', in which trade unionists and labour activists from Europe, Bangladesh, Zimbabwe and Nicaragua participated. That same year, Spanish consumers sent more than 50,000 campaign cards to players in the Spanish national football team asking them to express their concern about working conditions in the sportswear industry to the large brands. (None of the players responded.) The Swiss NGO Erklärung von Bern had been working on garment labour issues since the 1980s. In 1999 it used the name Clean Clothes Campaign for the first time, when it staged a month of public mobilisation together with several Christian organisations in the month of Lent (the 40-day liturgical season of fasting and prayer before Easter). This Lenten campaign was so successful that, after one year, three large Swiss companies adopted the CCC code of conduct.

The 'older' CCCs, while contributing to joint campaigns, continued on their paths, conditioned by national circumstances and resources. A short, by no means complete description of their activities illustrates the scope and focus of the movement.

The French CCC set out on an ambitious programme, running from early 1996 to 1998, when the football World Cup was held in the country. The ubiquitous presence of the large sports brands made it into an obvious occasion for campaigning. After the initial awareness-raising festivities in 50 French cities, the campaign on companies began at the end of 1996 under the name l'Ethique sur l'Etiquette or 'Ethics on the Label', which was subsequently adopted as the French CCC's name. It targeted retail clothing chains and large clothes-selling supermarkets, and aimed to collect 100,000 signatures under a petition to the National Council of Commerce, asking companies to adopt the Fair Trade Charter. In 1997 this target was reached, and apparently the number of concerned customers impressed at least a few companies: in June 1997, a federation of large retailers with members including C&A, Le Printemps, Monoprix, Prisunic and Les Galeries Lafayette expressed the intention of adopting a set of ethical standards forbidding slave labour, child labour and illegal labour. Hypermarché's Auchan and Carrefour, and the women's leisurewear chain Camaieu, entered into negotiations with campaign representatives about adopting a code of conduct, which Auchan went on to do. A pilot for independent monitoring was in the pipeline, and the CCC participated in the training of company buyers.[21]

In 2003, the French CCC published a 'company barometer', ranking 26 supermarkets and large retailers of sportswear according to their performance on corporate social responsibility. All were found to be seriously lacking compared to Nike, Reebok and Adidas. The barometer was a tool for the 2004 campaign Jouez le Jeu, or 'Play the Game', targeting the 26 companies. Over 300 events were organised all over France, and a huge demonstration took place in front of the Eiffel tower. In 2005 the campaign's focus narrowed to six big retailers: Carrefour, Auchan, Decathlon, Leclerc, Go Sport and Intersport. The CCC wrote a guidance manual for activists, and 40 local groups requested meetings with managers of 144 supermarket and retailer branches across the country, of which 26 agreed. Soon after, l'Ethique sur l'Etiquette found itself in troubled waters. In retrospect, the organisation seemed to have stretched itself too thinly, with a great many local organisations that were nominally affiliated but in practice not rooted in CCC's philosophy and working methods. In 2007 a process of rebuilding began, and in 2008 l'Ethique sur l'Etiquette was back in business, under the control of a new board and with local groups slimmed down from 140 to 30.

In Flemish Belgium, the CCC has a good working relationship with trade unions. It succeeded in getting consumers to send 230,000 campaign cards to H&M, Levi Strauss Belgium and C&A. The companies responded to each individual sender personally, and asked for a meeting to discuss the content and implementation of codes of conduct. Workshops were held by 600 youth groups and schools, and a youth delegation convinced the Royal Belgian Football League to sign the code of conduct of the International Football Federation. The CCC of French-speaking Belgium, Vêtements Propres, organised a youth campaign in 1996 called Défaut de Fabrication or 'Faulty Fabrication', involving 30 student groups stoking the fire among other students and high school pupils. More than 40,000 campaign cards were sent to Nike, Adidas and Reebok, and 12,000 old trainers were gathered and delivered at Adidas's Belgian headquarters. 'Quite a smelly event', as a campaign organiser remembers. The Belgians are good at creating visually attractive events. For the campaign that convinced the Swiss lingerie company Triumph to withdraw from Burma, they strung a 1.2 km line of bras in the garden of the company's office.

In 2002 Vêtements Propres joined an international campaign targeting the toy industry, which has much in common with the garment sector. Toys, like clothes, are near to people's lives and pose direct questions about consumption patterns; they are also often made under sweatshop conditions. The toy campaign provided a new opportunity to reach consumers. In opening up the clean clothes movement to other consumer goods, Vêtements Propres also initiated a debate about this within the CCC network.[22]

The Dutch CCC was very successful in its campaign on ethical public procurement. It convinced most Dutch work-wear companies to join the code-monitoring initiative Fair Wear Foundation, and persuaded local and national public authorities to favour these companies when buying their civil servants' work-wear.[23] In 2007 the Dutch came up with another remarkable campaign idea. When its owner put the popular low-end department store Hema up for sale, the CCC immediately called upon the Dutch people to buy it collectively, in order to maintain availability of its cherished products while also improving working conditions in the supply chain. The media liked the campaign, and financial pledges flooded the CCC's newly created Hema website. When a British investor outbid the 340,000 euros that the CCC had to offer, the campaign transformed into 'Friends of the Hema' – the first critical fan club of a department store. The Friends were invited to Hema headquarters, where the company agreed to explore the possibilities of investigating its garment supply chains.[24]

The UK clean clothes organisation Labour Behind the Label (LBL) hacked a new path into the jungle with its 2005 Fashion Colleges project. Through workshops, training events and an attractive, state-of-the-art website, it introduced 'clean clothes' to fashion teachers and students, with the aim of fertilising some of fashion's roots: the designers, buyers, merchandisers and technologists – the people at the top end of the garment commodity chain. Fashion students and teachers appeared interested in all areas of sustainable fashion, from fair trade to recycling. The project was so successful that Karat in Poland and the CCCs in Austria and the Netherlands adopted it in 2007.[25]

In 2006, responding to consumers' need for guidance in ethical shopping, LBL launched a report and a website with profiles of the main UK supermarkets and 'fast fashion' retailers. 'Fast fashion' was the new buzz word referring to clothes that reach the rack just five or six weeks after they are first seen on the catwalk. They cost very little, so people can afford to wear them twice and then replace them. The website contains information about where and how collections are made, and the impact they have on the lives of garment workers. And since we are now in the twenty-first century, the website is interactive: visitors can blog, share information, and sign on to urgent appeals.[26]

The German CCC, Kampagne für Saubere Kleidung, had gathered 40 organisations under its banner in its first year. Two books were published immediately – one a compilation of essays on the national and international garment industry, written and assembled after the European bus tour; the other reporting on research into the Chinese and Philippine garment industries supplying German companies.[27] While, after its first year, the Kampagne decided to intensify its efforts at mobilising the public, it put strong emphasis on getting companies to accept and implement the CCC code of conduct. On the one hand, it targeted large retailers like Tchibo, Aldi, Lidl and Otto Versand; on the other, it increased pressure on the national sportswear brands Adidas and Puma with a variety of actions and media projects including documentaries, street protests, and speeches at shareholders' meetings. When, towards the end of the first decade of the twenty-first century, structural changes were not forthcoming, disappointment surfaced in the Kampagne für Saubere Kleidung, leading to its reorientation. While work on companies continues, its sights are set on legally binding rather than voluntary regulation.[28]

CODES AND COMPANIES

Welcome to the twelfth edition of the international newsletter. Find in this newsletter reports on the campaigns in Europe; some of the actions, debates and educational activities that are being developed [and] the ongoing pilot projects on independent monitoring ... The concept of Clean Clothes Communities, in the US, the Netherlands and France might provide some new food for local campaigning ... Europe is preparing for the European Football Championship and so is the Clean Clothes Campaign.[29]

This editorial in the international CCC newsletter sketched the plans of attack for the new millennium: a primary focus on companies, codes and independent monitoring; the new approach of clean clothes communities and ethical procurement of clothes for public servants; and joint European campaigns centred on large sporting events.

The work on codes and implementation was arduous, but the need for it was felt to be pressing because it would enable everybody concerned to speak with one voice, and prevent companies from playing one stakeholder against another, or stalling decisions by bickering about definitions. In 1998, after lengthy deliberations throughout the network, after draughts and re-draughts, the CCC presented its Code of Labour Practices for the Apparel Industry including Sportswear. The code includes the core ILO conventions and sets standards for freedom of association and the right to collective bargaining, maximum hours of work, health and safety, a living wage, and security of employment; it forbids forced labour, child labour and discrimination.[30] It was signed by three international trade union federations,[31] several Asian labour organisations and networks, and by the approximately 250 NGOs and trade unions in the CCC network.

But a code provides no guarantee of its own implementation. In the second half of the 1990s, the Dutch CCC worked hard on the preparatory work for a foundation consisting of retailers, trade unions and NGOs, that could develop a monitoring policy and guarantee its implementation. Regular, random audits in supplier factories by an independent agency were considered indispensable, as was meaningful input from local groups and garment workers. Any company signing up to the Code should, upon detecting abuses, supply funds and allow time to find a remedy, rather than relocating its production. Companies complying with the standards could carry a trademark.[32] In 1999, after five years of negotiations, the Fair Wear Foundation (FWF) was established in the Netherlands as a multi-stakeholder initiative (MSI). Undersigning it were the Dutch CCC, the development organisation Novib (later to merge with Oxfam), the two major Dutch trade union federations, and two industry organisations – one representing small and medium-sized retailers, one representing producers.[33] They agreed to a code of conduct very similar to the CCC Code and including independent monitoring. The participants stated explicitly that the Code should not replace collective bargaining agreements or undercut national labour law. An organisational structure was provided, chaired by a former environment minister. Most important among its guiding principles were independent verification of self-monitoring by companies; links to other European monitoring developments; proper complaints procedures for workers; an end to 'cutting and running' if abuses were found, in favour of the implementation of a developmental approach; and recognition of the limited influence of the small and medium-sized companies that were members of the Foundation.[34] At the end of 2007, the Fair Wear Foundation was evolving from a Dutch into a European organisation. Member companies now included German, Swiss, Swedish, UK and Belgian companies.

The FWF was neither the first nor the last multi-stakeholder initiative in the clothes business. In 1996, American president Bill Clinton gathered representatives from the garment industry, trade unions and NGOs to establish the White House Apparel Industry Partnership, with the Fair Labor Association (FLA) as its governing body. The SA8000 programme, launched in 1997 by the New York-based NGO Social Accountability International (SAI), was designed to bring about global consistency in code of conduct standards and third-party verification procedures. In the UK, the Ethical Trading Initiative (ETI), founded as a multi-stakeholder initiative in 1998, was intended to produce a learning process of affiliated organisations and companies through pilot projects and the exchange of best practices. In 2000, the anti-sweatshop movement of American and Canadian students established the Worker Rights Consortium (WRC), which assists universities with the enforcement of their codes of conduct when they buy apparel and other goods bearing university logos.

In 2003, a first step was made towards cooperation between the FWF and other multi-stakeholder organisations. The CCC, FWF, ETI, FLA, SAI and WRC formed the Joint Initiative on Corporate Accountability and Workers' Rights – Jo-In for short – and embarked on a lengthy pilot project in Turkey to work out best practices in code implementation. Turkey was chosen because it was a large exporter to global markets, and because the MSIs did not yet have a meaningful presence there. Turkey, moreover, had a strong incentive to cooperate, because it wanted to join the EU. Eight multinational brands joined the initiative, each taking part in one of the MSIs: Adidas, Gap, Gsus, Otto Versand, Marks & Spencer, Nike, Patagonia and Puma.[35]

The corporate world, feeling the various multi-stakeholder initiatives breathing down its neck, and trying to keep control, responded by setting up its own global monitoring programmes. Some companies acted on their own – like C&A, when it created Socam in 1996 – while some created a larger base. In 2002 the American Apparel and Footwear Association launched Worldwide Responsible Accredited Production (WRAP). In 2003, the Brussels-based Foreign Trade Association founded the Business Social Compliance Initiative (BSCI), which extends to all countries and all products.[36] In 2006 the supermarkets Carrefour, Metro, Migros, Tesco and Wal-Mart launched their own Global Social

Compliance Programme (GSCP). Representing enterprises with combined annual sales of over $500 billion, this initiative is likely to overshadow all others.[37]

After 2000, the auditing of factories became a booming business in the new context of corporate social responsibility. Tens of thousands of audits were now conducted each year, with a proliferation of profitable commercial auditing firms. Wal-Mart alone claimed to have commissioned over 16,000 audits at 8,873 factories in 2006.[38] Since this burgeoning world of auditing did little to improve working conditions, the CCC International Secretariat set up audit research projects in Kenya, Romania, Bangladesh, Pakistan, India, Morocco, Indonesia and China. The resulting 2005 report, 'Looking for a quick fix', became a valuable resource for everybody involved in improving working conditions in the garment industry.[39]

Codes and their implementation were not the only issues on the company front, and the International Secretariat was by no means the only CCC player in this field. In the UK, Labour Behind the Label took the lead in a 'living wage' campaign with the report 'Wearing Thin: The State of Pay in the Fashion Industry', outlining the idea of a living wage as opposed to the minimum wage, and illustrating its necessity with examples from across the world.[40]

The Swedish CCC made headway with its Dress Code pilot project, designed to develop a reliable verification procedure. In 1999 and 2000, local researchers conducted worker interviews, followed by unannounced audits of the factories they worked in, in Bangladesh, China and India. It uncovered labour rights violations that had not been noticed during regular monitoring, and established the need for worker education on labour rights and for reliable complaint procedures – especially in sectors without any real worker representation. In 2001 the Dress Code project collapsed when trade unions and companies disagreed about the process of monitoring and verification.

In 2000 the Swiss CCC, supported by 50,000 consumer campaign cards, convinced its major national retailer, Migros, along with two others, to accept the CCC Code of Conduct, and undertook a pilot project on independent monitoring and verification at four production locations in Asia.[41] The pilot resulted in a Swiss verification body that later merged with the Fair Wear Foundation. A helpful tool in pressuring companies was the regular publication of a company score list that detailed companies' performances on social standards.

In France, l'Ethique sur l'Etiquette participated in an informal verification committee with the supermarket chain Auchan, which focused on a pilot project in Madagascar. After a year, a working group involving the federation of large retailers was established to exchange information and experiences on codes, monitoring and verification.[42]

The German Kampagne für Saubere Kleidung continued to batter at the gates of German companies. Supported by thousands of consumer signatures, campaigners discussed the CCC code of conduct with retailers C&A, Otto Versand and Adidas, and with garment producer Steilmann Gruppe. They were disappointed by the results. The companies stuck to their own codes and refused to accept independent monitoring.[43] Disillusion grew when, in 2000, Adidas reneged at the last minute on its commitment to allow an independent monitoring project into six of its supplier factories in El Salvador, where gross malpractices had been found.[44] In 2001, Puma rejected cooperation with Kampagne, maintaining that its own code of conduct and auditing procedures were satisfactory.[45] The same year saw the targeting of KarstadtQuelle, a huge department store chain and mail-order business. While it supported fair trade initiatives like the Rugmark certificate for tapestry, and sold environmentally sound products through its subsidiary Hess Natur, KarstadtQuelle retained its own auditors and its own code, which specified no living wage requirement and only a vague standard on working hours.[46] In 2003 a pilot project began with Hess Natur to develop a verification system for medium-sized and small companies. Hess Natur joined the Dutch Fair Wear Foundation.

The Austrian CCC sent out questionnaires to 200 garment companies. Seven were returned, of which four were from eco-clothes companies. Their codes of conduct appeared to be worse than C&A's. CCC Austria had to abandon its plan for a brochure that would have informed the public on where to buy 'fair wear'.[47]

The Ethical Trading Initiative, a British multi-stakeholder initiative, carried out a range of pilot studies to test monitoring and verification systems. It continued to grow, with corporate members including Levi Strauss Europe and Marks & Spencer. In 2006 it published the results of an impact assessment conducted over the previous three years. In general, it appeared, there had been improvements in the area of health and safety, but little in those of precarious employment, the living wage, or freedom of association. Positive changes were found most strongly in situations where workers and managers received training on codes, and where buyers, agents and suppliers had stable relationships. Suppliers complained that complying with the buyers' code of conduct cost them money and time, while the prices paid for their products did not increase and deadlines remained inflexible.[48]

Women Working Worldwide, one of the constituents of Labour Behind the Label, launched a worldwide project on international subcontracting chains in 2000. The project combined academic investigations and educational programmes in production countries into an innovative form of action research. One of its offshoots was the book *Threads of Labour*, a study of the theory and practice of globalisation.[49] The organisation and education of workers were identified throughout the network as prerequisites of code implementation, because without workers' input codes are considered merely a public relations tool on the part of companies, which may even facilitate anti-union policies: what is the point of a union if the company code already offers labour-rights protection?

With so many initiatives in the field of codes, monitoring and verification, it was felt that experiences should be pooled to develop generally accepted procedures and standards. From 2001 onwards, the CCC and SOMO compiled information and organised several conferences on the subject, in order to identify best practices and recurring pitfalls. In the garment industry, with its long and sweeping supply chains, monitoring and verification were obviously not simple tasks. At the same time, it was considered a priority to present an alternative to the flawed procedures of the industry itself.[50]

THE LEGAL ANGLE

In the spring of 1998, the International Forum on Clean Clothes in Brussels brought together for the first time CCC partner organisations from western and eastern Europe, Asia, Africa and Central America. The event was staged as a judiciary tribunal, with indictments against seven brands: Adidas, C&A, Disney, H&M, Levi Strauss, Nike, and Otto Versand – though only H&M turned up. The jury consisted of experts from the Permanent Peoples' Tribunal; 15 witnesses brought testimonies from the sweatshops of the world.[51]

While human and labour rights had been central to the CCC from the beginning, the legal angle was new. The objective was to arrive at a legal approach, on the one hand, to consumers' right to information, and, on the other, to the liability of contractors and subcontractors in the supply chain. As Naomi Klein has said, drawing lessons from the worldwide campaigns against Nike, Shell and McDonald's: 'The courtroom is the only place where private corporations are forced to open shuttered windows and let the public look in.'[52]

Several companies had already been taken to court. Shortly before the Forum, consumer groups filed a lawsuit against Nike at San Francisco Superior Court. They claimed that Nike had misrepresented working conditions in the factories of its Asian suppliers – an allegation substantiated by a Bangladeshi witness at the Tribunal. In June 1998, a Chinese dissident who had been imprisoned sued Adidas for his having been forced to stitch Adidas footballs in a prison camp.[53] Also in 1998, the famous Saipan sweatshop lawsuit took off. It involved 26 retailers and 23 garment factories on the Pacific island of Saipan, the largest island of the US Commonwealth of the Northern Mariana Islands. It was home to a garment industry that produced US$1 billion worth of clothing sold annually to the US, and employed 10,000 workers – almost all young women from Asia – in slave-like conditions. With the help of the US Department of Labor and anti-sweatshop activists, the women won a four-year legal battle, bringing them the promise of a landmark $20 million settlement in back payments, and of a programme of independent monitoring of Saipan garment factories – the first of its kind to be legally mandated.[54]

Not surprisingly, the jury of the Brussels Forum voted for consumers' right to information not only about clothes' materials and quality of manufacture, but also about their production conditions. It also stated that codes developed by companies themselves should be 'transformed into agreements with unions, consumer organisations and other popular bodies'. The judges gave some suggestions as to how legal tools might be used, such as pressure on legislators to make the provision of information about production conditions mandatory, and legal actions against companies that have adopted a code of conduct but failed to make themselves accountable, thereby exposing themselves to the charge of misleading the public.[55] In the closing meeting, participants cheered the Forum, seeing it as a chance to grow stronger as a network. But there was also criticism: representatives of the Haitian workers' organisation Batay Ouvriye regretted the Tribunal's lack of real judicial power; they also rejected codes of conduct as a 'bourgeois tool' that only masked class struggle, without fighting capitalism as the cause of workers' exploitation. In less Marxist language, but with the same suspicion of an industry whitewash, the codes debate would continue to haunt strategy discussions in the clean clothes movement.

After the Forum the legal angle would continue to be pursued, though less vigorously than campaigns targeting companies and raising public awareness. The French and Belgian CCCs would be involved in efforts to sharpen the law on corporate social responsibility, in amending a law on the disclosure of company information to consumers, and in getting a law approved that would hold companies responsible for acts that violated Belgian law but had been committed abroad – equivalent to the law enabling the prosecution of child molesters who can be convicted in Belgium for sexually abusing children in Thailand. Carole Crabbé of the Belgian CCC Vêtement Propres says:

> We worked on that from 1998 to March 2008, when the judge decided to not decide anything at all. It was a defeat. The work on the corporate social responsibility law was very interesting. It built upon a case in the USA in which Nike was indicted for lying to customers by misrepresenting working conditions in its supply chain. We pursued that line of thought by asking: Is it possible to consider the code of conduct as a tool to attract the consumer, and consequently the non-appliance as a lie? We worked on it up to 2002, then we couldn't find any new roads, or the time to go forward. Now the European Coalition for Corporate Justice has taken it up. I am not optimistic, because there is no political will to go there. It is interesting, but sometimes it's more effective to push companies than to push elected politicians.[56]

In 1999, the European parliament voted for a resolution of the British member Richard Howitt to promote the accountability of European-based multinationals by supporting code of conduct initiatives. The parliament asked the European Commission to instate a 'European Monitoring Platform', proposed hearings, and asked for legal measures to monitor multinationals. Since the resolution was not binding, and companies and governments offered resistance, the Platform never materialised. In 2009, despite two new parliamentary resolutions, there is still no European legal framework to hold multinational corporations to account.

In 2001, a legal working group of the CCC with 20 participants from eleven countries discussed the possibilities and risks of suing companies. Also on the agenda were the guidelines for multinational enterprises established by the Organisation for Economic Cooperation and Development (OECD), which unites 30 of the world's most industrialised countries. A few years later, the CCC contributed to the United Nations' 'Ruggie process' – consultations aimed at building an international legal framework for business and human rights.[57]

CLEAN CLOTHES COMMUNITIES

In 1999, 'clean clothes communities' were on the CCC agenda for the first time, and they were there to stay. This strategy involves local organisations and communities, public authorities – and indirectly companies as well – by organising communities to ask their authorities to buy work-wear for government employees from socially responsible companies only.

The seeds of this initiative were sown by American and Canadian students, who discovered in 1998 that the US$19.95 university caps they wore were made by workers earning 8 cents apiece. The students questioned the contracts between their institutions of learning and the big brands acting as licensees of the university and college logos. They unleashed a forceful anti-sweatshop movement on campuses nationwide. After several universities had adopted a code of conduct, the students – organised as United Students Against Sweatshops and Students against Sweatshops Canada – proceeded to tackle the question of code compliance. To this end, they developed the Worker Rights Consortium, an organisation that verifies code compliance, strengthens local organisations in production countries, builds a network to inform workers of their rights, and allows them to report abuses confidentially. By 2000, 56 colleges and universities had joined the Consortium; by 2008, that had risen to 170.

The idea of a campaign demanding the ethical spending of public money soon spilled over into local communities. The city of Bangor, in Maine, declared that ordinary people should have something to say about the behaviour of businesses, large or small, operating in their community. 'We would never permit local vendors to sell us rotten meat, or stolen property, or illicit drugs because such behavior offends our community values. Likewise we do not condone international corporations supplying our retailers with items made under conditions that equally offend our sense of decency.'[58] In 1999 there were more than 20 'anti-sweat' cities, including San Francisco. In 2003, local 'sweat-free' campaigns across the country coalesced into the SweatFree Communities network. In 2007, more than 170 school districts, cities, counties, and states in the US had adopted 'sweat-free' procurement policies.[59]

In the Netherlands, university and high school students do not wear uniforms, but public servants do. The CCC targeted local authorities and politicians. Public authorities are the biggest single consumers of work clothes, employing a considerable part of the working population, many of whom wear work clothes: police, the army, public transport workers, rubbish collectors, city gardeners, hospital staff, fire-fighters. With this much buying power, public authorities can exert considerable pressure on companies. The CCC hoped that the 'clean communities' campaign would lead to an involvement of local communities and individuals in the global agenda for a sustainable world. The idea was that local campaigns could have the effect of a double-edged sword, addressing international issues of solidarity and environmental protection while also affecting citizens and politicians at a local level. To get things going, the CCC developed a handbook and organised a series of workshops for local groups. In 2000, Amsterdam City Council adopted a resolution to the effect that all purchases paid for with public money should take labour and environmental standards into consideration. When the CCC investigated existing policies, it appeared that city employees in charge of buying work-wear had no idea about the origin of the clothes, let alone about their production conditions. Most thought that, since as a rule delivery times for work-wear were short, the clothes were made in the Netherlands. But they hardly ever are: most are made in North Africa and eastern Europe, in factories with no code of conduct whatsoever. Because such orders are usually very specific – for reasons of personnel visibility and safety – supply chains are short, and relations between buyers and producers have a long history. This produces conditions favourable to code implementation, and it was not long before most work-wear retailers joined the Fair Wear Foundation – which in turn made it easier for cities to become clean clothes communities. In 2003, the Dutch government passed a resolution stating that the government's purchasing policy regarding clothes should refer to internationally accepted environmental and ILO standards.[60] In 2007 the government committed to buying only sustainable goods by the end of 2010 – though this obligation was not enforceable by law.[61]

In 2004 and 2005 the public procurement campaign was taken up all over Europe. In mid-2005, 250 French communities adopted a 'clean clothes' resolution. In 2008, 80 out of 306 communities in Flemish Belgium, plus several public institutions, passed a resolution calling for ethical procurement, and a Clean Clothes at Work project was launched with trade unions. French-speaking Belgium counted 30 clean clothes communities in 2008. The Spanish CCC embarked on an ethical procurement project in three Catalan cities; the UK saw a broad campaign on public procurement for various products; and Sweden took the same road, organising a seminar for local authority buyers.

Nevertheless, actual progress left much to be desired. When SOMO was commissioned in 2005 to carry out a study on seven major European work-wear companies (two of them members of the Fair Wear Foundation), it concluded that most companies, including the FWF members, were lacking in transparency, and lagging behind in terms of corporate social responsibility policies compared to major sportswear and clothing brands.[62] On the progress of the project in Flemish-speaking Belgium, CCC coordinator Frieda de Koninck comments:

> Now that we have created a demand for clean clothes, you'd think companies would organise the 'ethical' supply, but they don't. Disappointed communities or institutions come back to us, and since it is asking a bit much for them to organise supply chain control, we still have to step in. European expansion of the Fair Wear Foundation would help.[63]

Carole Crabbé, of Vêtements Propres, says:

> Together with the Fair Trade movement, we have been lobbying hard for the new European directive on public procurement, but that law turns out to be rather flexible. When governments translate it into national law, they use that flexibility to create space for non-compliance. Compulsion is for example dependent upon market share, and especially work-wear companies as a rule don't have large market shares. The CCC, together with an organisation of European cities, is now going to lobby local authorities about implementing the law. It's a new turn for the campaign, because we have to show expertise and become operational. We must make the connection between demand and supply, and help community officials to handle social criteria and evaluate companies.[64]

SPORTSWEAR CAMPAIGNS

The European Football Championship of 2000, held in the Netherlands and Belgium, was the occasion for the first concerted European campaign. As an event with enormous visibility, it was used by sports brands to advertise their shorts, sweatshirts and shoes. The CCC saw it as a stage from which to proclaim its message to a large public, to the brands, and to the national and European football leagues that were owners of powerful brands. It used a range of tactics including football tournaments; 300 runners in the Vienna marathon (not exactly football, involving lots of sportswear); a tour of Thai workers to the cities hosting the matches; street theatre; a meeting in front of Adidas headquarters in Germany; distribution of educational materials in schools; the returning of heaps of old sports shoes to Nike and Adidas; ad-busting (twisting brand images in such a way that they criticise or parody the brand); an exhibition; and a documentary. The development organisation Novib, the major Dutch union federation FNV, and Amnesty International all took part in the campaign. The director of Euro 2000 promised that a code of conduct would be included in contracts with sponsors, suppliers and licensees of the Euro 2000 logo. It was the very modest code of the World Federation of Sporting Goods Industry, which included no provisions for monitoring or verification.[65] Campaigners had won the hearts of the public, but lost the game.

But there would be other opportunities. After Euro 2000, sportswear campaigns accompanied every European and world football championship and every Olympic Games – winter and summer. As well as reaching an audience of billions, these international campaigns served to expand and solidify the network. The 2004 Play Fair campaign targeting the Olympic Games in Athens was the biggest international mobilisation of workers' rights of its kind that had then been undertaken. It achieved unprecedented levels of collaboration between international and national trade unions, Oxfam, the CCC, and Southern partners. For the smaller NGOs, the ability to use the huge resources and distribution channels of Oxfam and the trade unions was a gift from heaven. The trade unions profited from the direct approach and creative action methods of the smaller organisations. Worker exchanges organised between and within production countries were considered particularly successful, because shop-floor wisdom could often be put to immediate use. For this type of campaign, the new media proved to be ideal communication channels. The 'fairolympics' website served its purpose as an incredibly fast information highway and focal point. Over 500 actions were held worldwide. On 1 May, 50,000 people took part in the biggest-ever Thai labour march. A week before the Games, more than 1,000 garment workers and activists from seven Asian countries gathered in a Bangkok stadium for the 'Asian Worker Olympics'. A cycling trip from Leuven in Belgium to Athens was participated in by 30 activists. In Dublin, women ran a Fair Play mini-marathon. The Greek god Zeus presented the Play Fair research report to the Dutch Olympic Committee in the Amsterdam Olympic Stadium, while an open-air sweatshop 'sew-in' on an Athens rooftop attracted worldwide media attention. From Vancouver to the Swiss Alps, from Taiwan to Australia, the rights of garment workers were bathed in the glare of the spotlight turned on by the Play Fair campaign.

The International Olympic Committee (IOC) was presented with a petition carrying 500,000 signatures, which it refused to accept. The sports world is a tough opponent. Although some were able to look beyond the swimming pools and running tracks, most athletes and sports VIPs rejected the 'mixing of sports and social problems'. The IOC appeared to be the champion of this mindset and moved very slowly, if at all. Various national Olympic committees were just a little more sympathetic to the cause – the Dutch one added a clause on labour standards to the contracts with its sponsor Asics.[66] The European parliament passed an emergency resolution in support of the campaign, calling for a sector-wide solution to violations of workers' rights.

Some contacts with individual sportswear companies proved productive – for example, when they led to meetings with trade unions in production countries, or to the training of workers on codes of conduct. Some companies reviewed their codes of conduct practices. Member companies of the Fair Labor Association, including Nike, Reebok, Adidas and Puma, took steps to give more credibility to their monitoring programmes – notably the promotion of freedom of association.

More discouragingly, the internal network evaluation of the 2004 Olympics campaign revealed that the focus had been too 'western', with too few results for the garment workers in production countries. While taking into account that real change takes time, it is recognised that

> while the campaign provided plenty of scope for participation
> in consumer countries, campaigns in producer countries often

felt they had fewer ways to get involved. Moreover, not enough thought had been given to how the outcomes of the campaign (in particular the advances made in dialogue with sportswear sourcing firms) could be used by workers themselves to bring about change ... organisations in the producing countries must be placed at the centre of any future work ... With this in mind, the International Textile, Garment and Leather Workers' Federation (ITGLWF) embarks on a program with its affiliated unions in Asia to develop their knowledge of the supply chains of the major multinational sportswear companies sourcing from their countries.[67]

Massive sports events create an opportunity for addressing the sportswear industry as a sector – the whole fleet at once instead of just one ship at a time. These campaigns can move beyond damage control and aim for structural change. They have the added advantage that companies cannot hide behind arguments of competitiveness and the need for a 'level playing field', because that is exactly what a sector-wide campaign is about.

The 2004 Play Fair campaign hammered home the fact that current models of code implementation had not been able to stop exploitation and abuse, and that freedom of association was a key area for improvement. Also, for the first time in a large international campaign, the CCC introduced multinationals' purchasing practices as a potential lever for change. It urged companies to 'change their purchasing practices so that they do not lead to workers' exploitation, with prices being made fair, deadlines realistic, and labour standards given the same status as price, time and quality'.[68]

Four years later, the 2008 Play Fair Campaign, organised at the occasion of the Beijing Olympics by the International Trade Unions ITUC and ITGLWF and the Clean Clothes Campaign, did not beat about the bush: 'For years key sportswear brands have argued that they can't raise wages single-handedly. Play Fair 2008 believes that collectively they can – these companies control the sportswear and sports shoe markets.'[69] Despite huge profit increases over the past four years – not only for western brands, but for giant Hong Kong-based shoe manufacturer Yue Yuen as well – a Chinese Adidas-stitcher would still have had to fork out a month's salary for a pair of those shoes, and the income of Vietnamese workers failed to cover daily expenses.

Play Fair recognises that more than a decade after sportswear industry companies began to address problems in the sector, some progress has been made on some issues, however there is no disputing that workers' wages in real terms have not improved. [T]he prices set by sportswear company buyers shape that market.[70]

The 2008 Play Fair campaign was launched with the publication of a report titled *No Medal for the Olympics on Labour Rights*, which disclosed cases of violations of labour rights in four Chinese factories manufacturing Olympic merchandising products licensed by the IOC.[71] In some factories the nineteenth century appeared not yet to have ended, with 13-hour working days and seven-day working weeks, failure to pay even half the minimum wage, unprotected work with hazardous materials, and child labour.

Though forbidden by law, child labour is still widespread in China. Enforcement is lagging behind because insufficient resources are allocated to it, and because of the failure of government to address its underlying causes – such as a lack of access to free education, and unemployment among the rural poor and migrant communities. In order to supplement school budgets, some schools force children to work. In 2001 a fireworks workshop attached to the Fanglin village school in Jiangxi province exploded, killing more than 60 children and three teachers. Many children work in the footwear industry and in smaller workshops producing textiles, shoes and related products. In 2004 a primary school headmaster in Huizhou city was found to be employing his pupils in the toy factory he owned. In 2006 a shoe factory in Guangdong province was discovered to be exploiting a large number of schoolchildren in the guise of an 'internship' system. They worked twelve hours a day.[72]

When confronted with the evidence of abuses in factories licensed to make Olympic merchandise, the Chinese organising committee did exactly what the campaign asked it not to do: it ended the contracts.

For some brands, however, years of Play Fair campaigning seemed to have hit home. A month before the start of the 2008 Olympics, a press release reported the launch of a 'ground-breaking' new working group in Hong Kong, after a conference about the Play Fair research report titled 'Clearing the Hurdles'. The report highlighted the failure of more than 15 years of CSR in the sportswear sector. The four hurdles to overcome were identified as low wages, precarious employment, violations of the right to freedom of association, and factory closures.[73] In addition to the Play Fair campaigners, the new working group encompasses representatives of Nike, Adidas, New

Balance, Umbro and Speedo. They will explore incentives for trade unionism and collective bargaining, and for improving wages across the sector. The brands recognised that the training of management and workers in supplier factories was indispensable, and it is one of the issues the working group will examine. Eight international sportswear campaigns in as many years have consumed enormous financial and human resources – but, little by little, labour rights are gaining ground.

URGENT APPEALS

International solidarity actions are an important part of the CCC's activities, as illustrated by the many 'urgent appeals' mentioned throughout this book. About 50 per cent of total CCC resources is spent annually on urgent appeal work. It is one of the tools the CCC uses to inform western consumers about production conditions, while at the same time supporting workers and their organisations.

Urgent appeals begin with requests for action – from workers in a production country or from their organisations – on a specific case of labour rights violation. When the International Secretariat or a national CCC receives such a request, it decides whether to take it up based on criteria such as the amount and quality of the information 'from the ground', and the link with garment companies in the CCC's own country. When the information is verified, the CCC approaches brands and retailers buying from the factory in question, in an attempt to resolve the problem. If that fails to work, an appeal for action is distributed throughout the relevant part of the network.

An example of a successful urgent appeal is the one that ran in 2000 and 2001 concerning a Nicaraguan factory owned by the giant Taiwanese production company Nien Hsing. When union leaders were fired for going on strike for a wage increase of 8 cents a day, support came from all sides. A union in a Nien Hsing factory in Lesotho declared its solidarity; Taiwanese activists campaigned in their own country for the right of the Nicaraguan workers to organise; American anti-sweatshop activists protested in front of 400 stores selling jeans from Nicaragua produced by the company; and the CCC set its army of letter-writers to work. In the spring of 2001, following a court ruling in favour of the unionists, the management caved in, reinstating the unionists.[74]

Another successful urgent appeal forced the Swiss lingerie company Triumph to withdraw from Burma in 2001, using the unforgettable image of a woman wearing a bra made of barbed wire. Usually the CCC tries to ensure that companies do not 'cut and run'; in this case, the opposition in Burma asked for an economic boycott to isolate the country's dictatorship.

Some actions have been less successful, such as that against the Austrian brand North Sails. In the Sri Lankan factory that produced North Sails' high-quality surfing sails and gear, 270 workers were fired or suspended because they had mounted a strike when their quality bonus was cancelled. The contrast could not have been more pronounced between the carefree surfing crowd on the world's beaches and the girls sewing their outfits in sweatshops. Campaigners made use of this contrast by staging actions on beaches in Australia and the Netherlands; the Austrian CCC demonstrated in the centre of Vienna; in Sri Lanka, the Free Trade Zone Workers Union picketed in front of the Zone, and brought the case before the Sri Lankan Labour Tribunal; the global union ITGLWF filed a complaint with the OECD, using the guidelines for multinational enterprises – all to no avail. Then Sri Lankan workers toured Europe and, together with the CCC, tried to find North Sails' headquarters. It appeared that, in the meantime, the brand had been licensed to a company named Boards & More, which could not be found at its official address in Zürich, Switzerland. The international campaign was re-launched twice, in 2004 and 2005; but neither the licensed company, nor the distributor, nor the buyer, nor the factory responded. In 2005, 37 out of 270 workers started legal proceedings. In 2008, the court ruled in 27 of these cases, ordering North Sails to pay the dismissed workers compensation of 2.5 months' salary for every year worked. In 2007 a complaint was filed at the Austrian national contact point (NCP) of the OECD. The ensuing mediation efforts failed, and at the end of 2008 the NCP's concluding statement remained unpublished.[75]

GENDER

'For me the garment industry provided a thematic crossroads of issues like women's labour, globalisation of production, the power of transnationals and international solidarity', said Ineke Zelderust in the 2005 publication *Made by Women*.[76]

From the start, the core of the clean clothes movement has been female: the campaigners are predominantly women, and their cause is women's labour. Precisely because jobs in the garment industry are low-paid, low-skilled and insecure, it is the female part of the workforce that does them: 85 per cent of the workers in the clothing and sport shoes industry is female, amounting to around 30 or 40 million women worldwide. These women are mostly young, without schooling, and poor. Many have migrated to industrial centres from their villages, or from countries with no employment opportunities. Some are just looking for a way to keep themselves and their families alive. Others are dreaming of a better future in which they can buy Nike shoes and go to the cinema, be independent and have fun with friends. Because they are powerless and vulnerable, they have no other choice than to enter a factory and begin gluing the first pair of what will become an endless mountain of shoes; or to take in home-work and stitch the first of a thousand miles of seams.

The stories in this book illustrate what this means: women whose children sleep beneath the sewing machine and begin to help out as soon as their fingers can manage to thread a needle; women who wear nothing but black clothes to work when menstruating, because toilet visits are restricted and stains on their clothes will shame them; pregnant women who stand all day; women who are sexually harassed and psychologically intimidated; women who get paid less than men for the same job; women who have to leave their babies with parents far away. These are problems specific to women, and they add to the problems that male garment workers experience as well: the low pay, the long hours, the lack of rights, the worries about the future of one's job.

The CCC has always strived to take into account this gender dimension of the labour-rights struggle; it has been a part of the analyses, campaigns and demands, and of the network itself. In CCC meetings, nationally as well as internationally, women are over-represented – articulate, outspoken and well-versed women, at that.

Although it has been a matter of principle not to treat gender as a separate issue, but instead to let it pervade the day-to-day work of the campaign as it pervades the day-to-day garment business, the participants in a 2001 international CCC network meeting in Barcelona concluded that the issue needed extra attention. One of the outcomes has been the publication of *Made by Women*, a cooperative undertaking by women in the network.[77] It relates how a major area of gender-related stress for garment workers is the work awaiting them when they come home after a long day in the factory. All over the world, women are the primary caretakers of household and community life. Hungry children, neighbours who have fallen ill, aged relatives who need groceries, religious feasts prescribing elaborate cooking and decorations – it is usually women who take up these tasks. For most western women, protected from exploitative working conditions by labour law and the results of union negotiations, the combination of a job and work at home can be taxing; for women who are underpaid and overworked, this challenge is of a different order.

A second area that warrants special attention in relation to women's needs is that of health and safety. You might think it would be hard to overlook the fact that women can and do have babies, but the lack of menstrual, pregnancy and maternal provisions seems to prove otherwise. Wilful neglect also occurs, as in the case of a Chinese factory that hired only very young women, because pregnancy and children are just too troublesome.

Women, being the weaker sex biologically, always run the risk of sexual harassment and violence in a workplace characterised by insecurity and male supervision. There is almost no situation more conducive to sexual abuse than one in which a woman is in urgent need of a job and men are in charge of hiring and firing. Women are also up against violence outside the factory – especially when they return home late after working overtime. In some societies, girls are considered to have loose morals just because they are living alone, without their families. A slogan of the demonstration in Sri Lanka that mourned the rape and murder of a garment factory girl was significant: 'Free Trade Zone workers are not play-things'. Referring to the plight of women in the free trade zones, Sri Lankan union leader Anton Marcus commented: 'Our union has taken up this issue. We have to, if we want to be relevant to these workers.'[78]

A development that hits women particularly hard is the increasing informalisation of economies and employment relationships. All garment workers suffer under precarious employment, but it hurts women more because they are by far the most numerous among its victims. They often have only short-term contracts, or none at all, because they are not considered the main breadwinner in the family – not 'real' workers; and that is even truer if they are migrants, with no legal status.

Organisation of women workers has its own, gender-related obstacles. Most trade unions have a tradition of male leadership and a male-oriented culture. In 2007, of all ITGLWF affiliated unions, a little over 17 per cent were led by female general secretaries or presidents. That was not representative of female membership, which accounted for about 50 per cent of all workers represented – and it was even less representative of female workers in the sector as a whole, of which they were estimated to make up 85 per cent.[79]

Irene Xavier, Malaysian labour rights activist and coordinator of the union-associated NGO Transnational Information Exchange Asia, says:

> All initial organising of women in the garment industry was led by men. They have done good work, but sometimes they are an obstacle for women to become effective trade union leaders. We have just set up an alternative network for women leaders, a space for them to talk about their problems, which they wouldn't do otherwise. They all blame themselves for not taking leadership responsibilities. They say they don't know enough and don't understand economics, that globalisation is too complicated for them. From a practical point of view, it is really difficult for women to lead a trade union, because it doesn't fit in with their reproductive roles. The fact that they are mothers and housewives is not taken into account; it's up to them to sort out the difficulties of combining these tasks with work for the union. They have conflicts in their families – some must even choose between the union and their family.
>
> The other challenge we are facing is the traditional trade union structure with one leader who directs everyone, without a clear second line of leadership, and without transparent governance systems. We raise those issues, but people are not comfortable with them. In trainings, I have asked women whom they would approach when they have a problem. They would name the male leader, even if there was a female secretary appointed for the task. It is always a shock for them to realise this – they have never thought about it.[80]

Not all unions are addressing this problem, or are even aware of it. But, according to Doug Miller, former Head of Research of the global union ITGLWF, many initiatives are underway that try to empower women. 'The trade union movement is working on this constantly', he says. 'There are gender projects and women's leadership workshops in several Asian countries.'[81]

Unions are, of course, not the only organisations facing the urgency of the gender issue. Companies must take it to heart when they adopt a code of conduct and investigate factories, governments when they make labour laws, and the anti-sweatshop movement when it plays its watchdog role and proclaims itself an advocate of labour rights.

THE ELASTIC NETWORK

Before 2000 the CCC had grown fast to a total of ten coalitions of NGOs and trade unions in nine European countries. After 2000, new coalitions were established. In Italy the campaign was called Campagna Abiti Puliti (2005); in Norway, Kampanjen Rene Klær (2007), and in Denmark, Clean Clothes Campaign (2007). Portugal and Ireland may both see CCCs established in 2009. The national CCCs operate autonomously and find their own financing, but work together whenever possible. Outside Europe, the CCC network is not organised into CCC coalitions, but consists of trade unions, labour and women's organisations, related campaigns like those on bananas and coffee, research groups, and individuals involved in the work at hand. There are some regional CCC networks or taskforces. No formal organisation has ever been established – cooperation is structured around projects and campaigns. Individual partners maintain communications with each other directly or through the International Secretariat, which receives its guidance from the network and is accountable to it.

J. John, director of the Centre for Education and Communication – an Indian NGO and partner in the CCC network – characterises the working model as follows:

> We see the emergence of new organisations in the socio-political world. Workers' rights used to be the exclusive area of trade unions; now, on the global scene, networks are also becoming significant agents. The CCC is taking that shape: amorphous, without much structure, trying to be very democratic, and at the same time having an influence on the economic and political centres. It is a new realm of dynamics in global politics, where we can only be effective if we manage to establish a cross-linkage across nations. Only an organisation assuming that character can be significant. The CCC has acquired that kind of character, but the democratic and interactive character of its relationship with producing countries determines its effectiveness.[82]

Khorshed Alam, a project coordinator and researcher for CCC partner Alternative Movement for Resources and Freedom in Bangladesh, develops this point:

A loose partnership like ours allows for an open and critical relationship. The CCC network tries to accommodate different strategies and opinions, while at the same time sticking to its principles. I think that flexibility makes it strong and quite attractive. People feel comfortable to be involved. What helps is the lack of hierarchy and the fact that processes don't depend on a few persons only. Sometimes you need this feeling that many people are doing the same thing. The feeling of friendship, of sharing information. Is this way of working inevitable in a global network? I'm not sure. I think the CCC never meant to form a huge organisation, which enabled them to focus on work. I've seen other organisations losing the focus of their constituents when they expanded. The CCC is expanding; it should be on guard.[83]

Autonomy is an empowering democratic principle, but without consultation it may affect the work of others in a network in unacceptable ways: think of Southern organisations besieged by various NGOs trying to help in different ways, tripping over each other and depleting available human resources; or of a national CCC on the verge of opening up talks with a multinational corporation when another CCC happens to be launching a campaign against it. Communication is vital in working relationships like these. As the 'CCC partnership framework' puts it:

> Organisations active in the CCC network, within the context of CCC principles, respect political and organisational variety and welcome different approaches and methods. The CCC network aspires to be dynamic, flexible, pro-active, open to change, unpredictable and to avoid bureaucracy. At the same time, it also aspires to internal transparency, accountability, joint strategy development, shared responsibility and democratic decision-making processes. These goals are often at odds with each other. We challenge all those active in the CCC network to actively cooperate in realising both sets of aims, and to welcome the inevitable debates and compromises. We make the road by walking.[84]

In large part, the walking takes place on the high and low roads of the internet, but face-to-face communication is much appreciated throughout the network. The national CCC coordinators meet at least three times a year in so-called Euromeetings, where they report on their activities and strive for agreement on the parameters for national and joint campaigns. To ensure that the input of partners in production countries forms the basis of strategising, regional and global meetings are organised on both specific and general issues.

While there is a marked hesitancy about formalisation and a strong preference for 'natural' growth, one of the tasks of the International Secretariat is the strengthening and expansion of the network. That is exactly what Marieke Eyskoot, coordinator of the European network from 2003 to 2008, has been doing.

> It is quite a network already, and still growing. Not only the amount of people has increased, but also the number of issues and their complexity. Some actions are on a grander scale than before, and the knowledge and database are expanding all the time. Communication is crucial, especially since we are talking about people with very different levels of knowledge and experience. We have to be flexible, while also closely following each other's development, nationally and internationally.[85]

Aspiring CCCs are initially briefed and guided by the European coordinator.

> They can develop their own priorities, within the parameters of the four aims and areas of work of the CCC: pressure on companies, support [for] workers, awareness-raising among citizens, and development of binding regulations for companies. When people want to start a CCC, I visit them and explain what our guiding principles are, what a CCC is and what is expected of them. I ask them a thousand questions. Who will be their coalition partners? Are they experienced in awareness-raising, in global issues? Is there anybody to take on the secretariat and coordinate the coalition, to communicate with the International Secretariat and attend the Euromeetings? Do they see a way to get funding? Of course they have a thousand questions as well. After my first visit, the Swedish coordinator e-mailed me ten questions per day.

Eyskoot also does a round of 'internships' with the national CCCs. 'I visit two of them each year and take part in their day-to-day work. I familiarise myself with the national issues and we talk about the support I can offer. It works well.' An effective CCC, she says, is one that does not take on every passing issue or approach, but works with a focused plan.

It should have a core group of motivated organisations and preferably some more on the sidelines, to offer support when needed. Participation of trade unions is valuable since they represent workers, have access to companies and are experienced in negotiations. A secretariat is a must, as is money. These people are very motivated and tend to invest enormous amounts of time and energy until they run into a lack of money, and when it isn't there anymore the whole train comes to a screeching halt. Finally, a little luck is helpful. Some event in your country, a football championship, an urgent appeal concerning a company with a high national profile.

It is useful to have campaigning experience, but not indispensable.

A hard-core activist profile can even work against you when you deal with companies and the public. We welcome people who are experienced in working with companies, who know the industry and corporate culture inside-out. Buyers, CSR staff, people who are in the know about companies' sensibilities. The Dutch CCC is going to convene a panel of experts in this field, and the Fashion Colleges project has this angle as well.

The focus of national CCCs can be diverse.

We think it is the only way it can be done. A CCC's focus depends on the constituent groups of a coalition, on the public debate in a country, on its economy and history. The Swiss have a strong focus on companies, the Swedes are good at youth campaigns. Sometimes CCCs have serious differences of opinion about strategies. It may confuse issues, and when a joint campaign has to encompass the demands of every CCC the scope may become too wide. But when the various approaches complement each other, they can make for a colourful, well-rounded campaign.

Organisational models differ widely. In some countries one single NGO has a strong ownership of the campaign, in content as well as financially; in others, several organisations have equal stakes, with an independently funded secretariat and coordinator. Some CCCs have a little of each model. Ideally, the relationship between coordinator and affiliated organisations is one of mutual support; in practice coordinators tend to do a lot of pushing and pulling. But even if they all mention the heavy workload, all are unboundedly enthusiastic about the democratic values governing the network model, and the opportunities it offers for empowerment and creative action.

For joint decisions, European CCCs try to reach consensus through mutual adjustment – a little like the procedure followed by tribal elders in Africa: sit down and talk until everybody agrees. Unfortunately time is always scarce, so an additional process has been adopted, called 'explicit consensus'. It implies that each representative must express his or her appreciation of a decision, and it provides three options: you can agree; you can stand aside but allow the decision to be taken; or you can block it. In the latter case, an alternative proposal is obligatory. 'It works', says Eyskoot.

And proceedings have improved since we have used an outside facilitator to lead Euromeetings. A facilitator can reduce the influence of language problems, and also of dominant people. The International Secretariat [IS] of course has a 'natural' advantage, sitting in the centre of the web and also peopled with CCC pioneers. Member organisations resent dominance, but also want the IS to give analysis and guidance. The IS appreciates the national focus of CCCs: without the 'nationals' the network is nothing. But their input on international issues is needed. There are still major steps ahead here. We could cooperate better in common-language regions, sharing educational and campaign materials. We could improve on coordinating the work on companies.

'Can I mention some more things on the up-side?' she asks.

Several national CCCs have been malfunctioning for a period of time. Sometimes the work is not rooted enough in the affiliated organisations, which comes to light when a country coordinator moves on. Sometimes the coalition partners are not getting along and don't agree on division of labour and resources. But every CCC that landed in a rough spot has been able to pull through. They show resilience and tenacity. Debates are lively, and there is a general sense of urgency. The mutual respect in the network is remarkable; I like to think it expresses the spirit of equal rights that is the basis of our work.

Our campaigns confront companies and authorities with a consistent package of ideas and demands, and we are partly responsible for the general acceptance of the notion of corporate social responsibility. We have seen a shift from outright denial of responsibility to taking it seriously. Now we are at a new turning point. We're no longer only talking about cases of labour rights violations, but about preventing them altogether. The reach of voluntary corporate initiatives is obviously limited. Therefore, we are expanding our strategic repertoire. We develop a sectoral approach, and do more work on legislation and regulation, on lobbying governments and international bodies – the same trend you see in similar campaigns like the ones on coffee, bananas and ethical investing. Crucial are expansion and strengthening of the Fair Wear Foundation and similar multi-stakeholder initiatives. We think they can help workers and corporations to find a way out of the chaos created by global trade.

Interlude:
The European Network Up-Close

The profiles presented here have been distilled from face-to-face interviews, held in the course of 2008 with the coordinators of all European CCCs and a few long-time campaigners. Their thoughts and views add flavour to the more abstract processes of organisation described in this book. To facilitate reading, the profiles have all been cast in the same mould, to the effect that each one is focused on five themes: the network; successes; distinctive approach; room for improvement; and personal motivation.

MALIN ERIKSSON (24), KAMPANJEN RENA KLÄDER, CCC SWEDEN

The Network

'One of the great things about a network is that you can have planning and anarchism side by side. We want to attract young people. They want to do practical stuff without paperwork or planning a year ahead, actions that are easy to take part in even for newcomers. At the office we do of course make plans, but we present them as a framework, not as a limitation, so they can use their imagination and just go ahead and do it.

'In 2006 we had a first meeting of NGOs and trade unions in neighbouring countries engaged in activities similar to ours. Now there is a Norwegian and a Danish CCC, and we have regular Nordic consultations that are very useful, because we partly deal with the same companies and the same culture.

'I support the idea that we should act locally while thinking globally, and an international network fits this strategy. It is also difficult. As a coordinator I sometimes feel vulnerable, because my colleague coordinators work abroad.'

Successes

'Our campaign on ethical public procurement began in 2006. It started out with research into supply chains in India and Pakistan that found child labour and labour rights violations that surprised even us. We launched the campaign "My tax money" – we Swedes pay a lot of taxes! It has three statements: I want human rights for my tax money; follow the companies (that are actually ahead of public authorities); and an ethical profile benefits your community. From a grey zone that politicians and civil servants were afraid to enter, it is now something everybody wants to be a part of. Ten cities already have "fair trade city" certification, and recently the three biggest county councils have adopted a code of conduct for buying practices. We are involved in the implementation process. Generally, the demand for ethical consumption and buying practices is on the rise. Our office phone never stops ringing and e-mails come in every minute. Consumers ask what they should buy, companies what to do.'

Distinctive Approach

'We have many awareness-raising activities targeting young people. The internet network Facebook now has a Rena Kläder profile on it, plus those of 600 CCC activists who share information, visuals, poems and action tools. Trade unionists visited over 50 high schools throughout Sweden, to bring clean clothes to classrooms. We have good cooperation with unions, and the cooperation between them and the youth organisations in our platform is very productive.'

Room for Improvement

'Now that we shook up the fashion world – which is quite big in Sweden – we cannot offer it a platform to improve its practices. We don't have the Fair Wear Foundation, only the industry's low-standard BSCI initiative, which companies are increasingly joining.'

Personal Motivation

'When I was twelve, I already wanted to go to Tanzania and save poor people. Later on I understood that it's not about helping people, it's about working together to defend our human rights. A course on global issues after high school set me on my course. I was very happy to find the CCC, because it wasn't only about reading and discussing but also practical. I have to do something to feel that I make a difference. These moments that things actually move forward ... it is an irreplaceable feeling. It beats drugs.

'Still, I may not be doing it forever. I think I will end up having children, and I'm so personally involved and work such irregular hours, I don't see how to combine it with a family. Also, I'm not sure how long you can really engage your soul in campaigning. I sometimes feel that I'm turning the wheel around again – how long can you keep that up without losing the spirit?'[1]

CAROLE CRABBÉ (47), VÊTEMENTS PROPRES, CCC FRENCH-SPEAKING BELGIUM

The Network

'We are now 31 organisations, from trade unions to green consumers, from rural women to socialist teenagers. I'm happy to be in this large network where people respect each other and don't take leadership positions. As a network we are strong because we don't have to think about structure too much and can just go for it. We are weak because other organisations find it difficult to see us as a real partner. We have to prove ourselves all the time.

'There is often a tension between the national and international levels. The International Secretariat is doing a wonderful job, but its demand on us national coordinators to contribute to the international level sometimes outweighs the support we need as national campaigns. When I do international work, like visiting Morocco to find potential partners, I want to integrate this in the national strategy – for example involve Moroccan communities in Belgium – but there is no time for that. We must be careful that the growth of the IS will not create more work for national coordinators.'

Successes

'We recently launched Traso, a new Belgian fashion brand. Traso stands for *travail soldé*, "discount labour". In shopping centres, activists distributed a Traso flyer that looked exactly like a commercial one. A closer look revealed information about the working conditions behind the clothes. Initially, people were keen to find Traso clothes because they were pretty cheap; then we told them that every shop sells them, and talked about their origins. Maybe in the future we'll even make a real Traso shop. It was a funny and new way of campaigning, and especially interesting because retail workers and their union joined in the action. Precarious employment is on the rise in Belgium too; Carrefour, for example, has announced closure of 16 supermarkets, with a possible reopening under franchise, which is never a good thing for workers. Unionists helped to make the flyer and informed the shop employees. They welcomed us, and some even put flyers in customers' shopping bags. It is a bit of a tightrope of course, because employees will not go against their shop or company. But Traso is a powerful tool to connect consumer and producer interests, in Belgium and globally. We will use it again.'

Distinctive Approach

'In our latest five-year plan, we have decided to work closely with other organisations in the upcoming "Better Bargain" campaign on giant retailers. It is useless to fight them as one small needle – we need a bundle of small needles. We want to join forces with groups that campaign on issues like food, toys, electronics, retail employment, the impact of supermarkets on small shops and on our lives. Not only on western lives; supermarkets have a huge impact in countries like China, India and Indonesia as well. Up till now, it has been difficult to get this approach accepted in the clean clothes network, because it touches on issues of consumerism and over-production. There is a fear that this line of thinking will endanger jobs in the garment industry, because in the end the question is: Who needs so many clothes? Another fear is that by widening our focus we'll lose in sharpness, which is one of our strongest assets. I think we can have a coalition while retaining a sharp focus. In the Beijing Olympics campaign, we've already had a joint action in Brussels with Amnesty, and with the Burma and Tibet movements. Each had its own demands and it was very powerful.'

Room for Improvement

'Urgent appeals are a strong weapon because they are concrete and effective in forcing companies to move. They are not merely "anecdotal" either. We can achieve structural results too. But the Belgian garment sector is small, which limits our work on companies. We have a pilot project on work-wear companies together with the Flemish CCC, and some urgent appeals, but mostly on transnational companies like Adidas or Nike. This means that, for us, there is usually an issue behind the direct issue, like getting Belgian Carrefour employees to participate in supply chain control. But when the direct goal is reached and the action stops, we sometimes lose grip on the "behind-the-scenes" issue.'

Personal Motivation

'The story of the clean clothes movement is a beautiful one, because it is characterised by respect. We all have very different walks of life, but we respect each other. I work with great people for great people, most of them women, and we all participate in our own empowerment. We can develop ourselves in a light structure, where actions and projects are more important than institutional identity or branding. I like our way of working. Our actions are based on facts, and they are not about destroying but about building. While they may seem small, in fact they are not. Three people offering a petition stand for 90,000 signatures. A mountain of 12,000 shoes on Adidas's doorstep stands for a year of work of many enthusiastic young people. We believe in awareness, and we are patient.'[2]

STEFAN INDERMÜHLE (44), CLEAN CLOTHES CAMPAIGN, SWITZERLAND

The Network

'In Switzerland the NGO, Berne Declaration, feels strong ownership of the campaign. It is an NGO with 20,000 paying members, working towards a just relationship between Switzerland and poor countries. The CCC board includes two church organisations, and we have about 25 supporting organisations with loose ownership. Unions are included, but due to 50 years of labour peace Swiss unions are weak, with very few people working on international relations. I much appreciate the international network, even if sometimes the process of reaching consensus almost kills us. The network empowers its members, not a leadership. We learn a great deal from one another, and because in the end responsibility lies with the participants, they tend to be reliable. There is no leadership to be corrupted by companies. I have seen companies grow uncomfortable because of this.'

Successes

'CCC Switzerland kicked off in 1999 with a pilot project on codes and implementation with giant retailer Migros and two other Swiss companies. Migros quickly accepted the CCC code for the entire non-food sector. Of course implementation lagged behind, and later Migros was one of the initiators of the industry's low-standard verification body BSCI. But at the time, the power of definition lay within the CCC. Our pilot resulted in ISCOM, a Swiss branch of the Fair Wear Foundation that became responsible for monitoring and verification of company code compliance. In 2007 it became the FWF's Swiss office. Our campaign is oriented towards getting Swiss companies to raise their standards and become members of FWF. If a sizable number of companies does not join in two, three years, the momentum may be lost and we'll have to rethink our strategies in depth.'

Distinctive Approach

'Ranking and rating of companies on code compliance always generates a big debate in the CCC, nationally and internationally, mainly because we might be seen to endorse companies that do a little better than others. I think dividing the good from the bad guys is an effective tool; it meets the public's need for guidance in ethical consumption, and it pressures companies to raise their standards because a bad report hurts them. Of course you have to be careful not to end up as companies' public relations department, but in my experience that just doesn't happen. It depends on communication. We defined the wording of the reports and after they came out, even the tabloid press wrote about the companies in a critical way. We've fought hard for the international CCC company database that is now almost finished. We contributed profiles of 30 Swiss companies.'

Room for Improvement

'Urgent appeals often make sense individually and can be useful for campaigning, but I miss a strategy. While they are laborious, I don't see how they make for real change. We should have less of them, and select the ones that can be embedded in the campaign for code implementation. With factory closures, for example, there is often little to gain. I fully understand that at this point workers need help and can ask for an international campaign; they have nothing to lose. But if results are not forthcoming we look helpless, and it's bad if that happens often.'

Personal Motivation

'Do I want to change the world? Of course! The gap between poor and rich is widening, even in our own countries. A major angle for change is human rights. I can dream of revolution, or work towards a society that upholds the achievements of the French Revolution: that all human beings are equal and human rights are enforced. In today's context of globalisation it is urgent to force transnational corporations to respect human rights. This makes me identify with the work I do as CCC coordinator. It even made me miss out on having a family – there was never enough time for the adventure of babies. The CCC has been my family.

'The work is value-driven. I don't need much money and a car; for me, a professional career and business success are not meaningful.

I have a sense of living in a community with the common target of a better world. I feel privileged. In fact, it is amazing how few people are going for this.'[3]

MAIK PFLAUM (38), KAMPAGNE FÜR SAUBERE KLEIDUNG, CCC GERMANY

The Network

'CCC Germany has 19 member organisations now, including two large unions who are also in the core working group of about five people. I am international coordinator; we also have a national one. The European CCC network is strong. It is where we discuss our political orientation and our joint activities. We can divide the work. And obviously a campaign in many countries is more effective than in one. The network also creates an overload of work. You have the national and the international agenda; communications between the two take time and energy. But this is necessary. For a strong movement, you need ownership. We have no bosses, and we wouldn't accept any. We need everybody's opinion, everybody's work. A major CCC strength is the global network, the exchange with people from Southern organisations. Their power and endurance, the risks they take, their clear view and sense of justice inspire me time and again. Their sense of fun too; we Germans are always so serious!'

Successes

'Many local groups are very committed, and we cooperate well with two unions. The network is growing, which means that it has a good image, even if it is difficult to stand out in the general information overload. If we do get through, the message is received well. For the 2006 World Football Championship, my NGO alone (Christliche Initiative Romero) received orders for 100,000 campaign postcards.'

Distinctive Approach

'Hermosa was a garment factory in El Salvador producing for big brands like Nike and Adidas. It was closed in 2005, after workers had formed a trade union. We found them sitting in front of the building to guard the machinery still inside. They had no money, no food, no shelter. We sent out an urgent appeal; we organised a worker tour in Germany; we convinced the Fair Labor Association to put pressure on its member brands; we sent stacks of letters to Adidas; we made materials for the media. We had some structural results: one of the women workers is now a national trade union leader; brands paid into an emergency fund; the factory owner was sentenced to two years' imprisonment; an ombudsperson was appointed to find jobs for the workers. But they are still blacklisted.'

Room for Improvement

'Germany is the seat of some of the largest garment traders and retailers in the world: KarstadtQuelle, Metro, Otto, and in later years Aldi and Lidl. It is also the home of Adidas and Puma. But work on pilot projects with companies on codes and compliance has been disappointing. In the last one, the Puma CSR department was willing, but the management refused to pay the 20,000 euros needed for the second project phase. A waste of time. We are not changing structures, and we should stop thinking we can change the companies this way. We have adopted a new orientation towards political regulation. We need government action, laws for transparency, for public procurement. Binding instead of voluntary regulation.'

Personal Motivation

'All people have the same rights, but this is not realised in our world. I think it is a worthy goal to try to provide for others what you want for yourself. I can't accept that a Puma CEO earns 12 million euros a year while others go hungry. I like to analyse what causes injustice and fight it. And I don't want to be trapped by the seductions of the "good life". I want to keep in mind what is really important.'[4]

FRIEDA DE KONINCK (42), SCHONE KLEREN CAMPAGNE, CCC FLEMISH-SPEAKING BELGIUM

The Network

'Our coalition is made up of trade unions, North–South NGOs and socio-cultural associations. Lately, trade unions are moving into the foreground because our work is shifting from awareness-raising towards confrontation and negotiations with companies and political action. As coordinator, I would like to be the potter's wheel in the middle of a group of artisans who are turning the wheel to make beautiful vases. But too often I find that I'm turning the wheel on my own. While "clean clothes" are well integrated in the work of our coalition organisations, their contribution to the national level could be better.

'Being in a European network works well. I like it that everybody works from different angles. Sometimes we can use other CCCs' work, like the educational and promotional materials the German CCC prepared for their campaign on Aldi and Lidl. The internet has moved network communications forward, but lately I find that, because e-mail knows no priorities or rules, there is a danger of chaos and saturation on the one hand, and distance on the other.'

Successes

'Our Belgian culture is one of clubs and associations, we like to do things together. The level of syndication is high; at Carrefour, for example, an unprecedented 90 per cent of the employees are union members. That provides good breeding grounds for awareness-building and mobilisation. Our campaign scores in this field; we have raised much popular support. Together with Vêtements Propres, we collected, for example, 90,000 signatures for the 2004 Olympics campaign. Clean clothes as a source for creative actions will never dry up. Clothes are so very near to people, they experience them as part of their personality. They are good campaign material.'

Distinctive Approach

'Employees in garment retailing are important to us. Together with the unions, we try to educate and mobilise them on global issues. Their experiences differ only in degree from those of workers in developing countries – many problems are similar, like precarious employment. They are always shocked to hear about global working conditions. It is not only a pleasure to work with them; we would also feel bad and stupid not to. We want them as our allies when we target companies. They can influence works councils and may facilitate contacts with companies, because they are already in a negotiating relationship.'

Room for Improvement

'I look upon the European expansion of the Fair Wear Foundation with hope. Mobilisation is not a goal in itself – it must result in improvement of working conditions, for which independent factory monitoring is an important tool. Over the past years, Vêtements Propres and the Schone Kleren Campagne have been trying hard to get Belgian work-wear companies to join the FWF. Only one has so far.'

Personal Motivation

'Clothes interest me. I like to spend time each morning choosing what to wear; I like to shop for clothes with friends; I dream about designing and making clothes myself. Another force drawing me into the clean clothes movement is the fact that I'm from a working-class family and have been active in the labour movement since I was 15. I owe much to the people I've met there. The problems and actions of workers affect me in a personal way, and I want them to have the same openings in life that I have had.'[5]

EVA KREISLER (35), CAMPAÑA ROPA LIMPIA, CCC SPAIN

The Network

'Our clean clothes campaign was launched in 1997, by the fair trade NGO Setem and Fundació Pau i Solidaritat, an NGO linked to a trade union. In the beginning, 80 organisations took part in the coalition, but mostly in a passive way. When funding stopped in 2002, the campaign fell into a coma. In 2005 it re-launched as part of Setem. We are now established in ten Spanish regions, with one consumer organisation, a research centre and about 20 NGOs as partners. The European network and the International Secretariat enlarge our reach, and because of all the cultural differences there is always some fresh air – a new way of working to question your own. We can for example learn from the UK media work. They may have as few resources as we do, but know how to concentrate on quality.'

Successes

'Urgent appeals are a good way to get involved in international work, to lobby companies and raise awareness; they combine major CCC strategies. The cases have names and faces, which is interesting for media and can wake up consumers. Sometimes they might have a structural impact – for example in the Spectrum factory collapse in Bangladesh, where a trust fund with company contributions is underway. If it becomes a reality, a precedent could be set for buyer responsibility.'

Distinctive Approach

'Fashion and clothes are big in Spain. There is Inditex-Zara, Mango, Mayoral, Cortefiel, and the department store El Corte Ingles with its supplier company Induyco, to name the major ones. With some we are in CSR working groups. Inditex is now a member of the multi-stakeholder initiative ETI, and Mango may be on the way. But is it a success? Corporate social responsibility is often just washing the company's face; actual progress is marginal. We also have to be careful that working with companies doesn't hinder our capacity to be critical. They claim that campaigning against them isn't fair, because we're collaborating. It often comes down to decisions about the time-frame: when does time expire for them to take positive action with regard to violations of workers' rights at their supplier? When is the time up for them to change?'

Room for Improvement

'As coordinator, I feel that we have to strengthen our network. Large NGOs like Amnesty and Oxfam rejected coalition membership – they have their own programmes. We try to cooperate on a case-by-case basis. With unions it is even more difficult. I would like to strengthen relations, but it's hard to find common ground for compromise, in order to reach a long-term alliance. Both NGOs and unions have to set aside prejudices. We have to be brave enough to explore new forms of collaboration.

'Our labour market is deteriorating; short-term contracts are on the rise. Work is losing its dignity. But it seems no longer self-evident that unions defend workers' rights – I am talking leadership, not grassroots. In Inditex shareholder meetings, unions are "throwing roses" at the company. Global workers' rights are often deemed to be a bridge too far.'

Personal Motivation

'I wanted to understand unequal relations in the world since I followed a course in international cooperation at 16. Now I think that not only economic or trade relations have to change, but also our mental model – the way we think, consume and behave. We can change things, and even marginal changes are worth the effort. We are impregnated with the idea of competition. Why can't we value a person for his efforts instead of his market value? Solidarity is a worn-out word, but still significant to me.

'*Mosca cojonera* is a Spanish saying that fits us: the "damned fly", also a fly "with balls" – the buzzing little pest that keeps escaping you. We have few resources, but using our network and the internet makes us rapid and flexible. Our fragility gives us strength.'[6]

BETTINA MUSIOLEK (45), KAMPAGNE FÜR SAUBERE KLEIDUNG,
CCC GERMANY

The Network

'After a few years of working in the German CCC, it seemed strange that we were focusing on developing countries while nearby garment workers were struggling to make a living in countries like Romania, Bulgaria and Poland. Since 1997 I have been trying to build a network in central and eastern Europe, and since 2000 also in Turkey.

'The European network is essential to our work in Germany and abroad. It taught me to think strategically. It is interesting to have an informal network that consciously refuses to build a power structure and is effective nevertheless, or maybe even because of it. People are fed up with power games – although we are only human, and of course not entirely free of it. Globally, Southern partners are an inspiration for my work. While their situation is often even worse than in eastern Europe, they provide examples of endurance and fighting spirit.'

Successes

'Progress comes in small steps. Eastern Europe is no longer a black box. The CCC as well as the public at large are now more aware of the situation in the eastern region, and of its similarities with developing countries. We have published reports, and developed partnerships with organisations in eastern Europe and Turkey. We have been able to help them build capacity and know-how about investigating working conditions and conducting worker interviews.'

Distinctive Approach

'In eastern Europe, people do not appreciate the confrontational role of NGOs. An independent civil society, so indispensable for capitalism and democracy, is only just in its infancy. The prevailing attitude is one of local compromise – maybe an inheritance from socialist times. Labour rights advocates focus on getting stakeholders together, to alert them to the problems and arrive at solutions in a national context. They are afraid – not without reason – that raising a big stink abroad will give them a negative image, which will block European integration. There is still much hope associated with joining the EU.'

Room for Improvement

'The formerly communist world is a region in despair and lethargy. People now have civil rights and freedom but have they lost their secure footing. Former Yugoslavia, once a cosmopolitan country with a mix of socialist and western experience, was bombed into the Stone Age. Many people fell into a deep black hole, and often still don't know how to deal with it. They lack the experience that it is possible to fight and change things. Although working conditions and the labour climate are usually a little better than in the low-wage countries of Asia, Africa or Latin America, they are bad enough, but organisations like unions and NGOs hardly ever stand up and fight. This makes network-building in the region a bit difficult. We must be patient, and take small steps at a time.'

Personal Motivation

'I'm from East Berlin. After the changes of 1989–90 and German reunification, the CCC has given me a political home. I have learned an enormous amount and have tried to bring in my experience from various social contexts. In the CCC I can work on economic, ecological, gender and development issues all at once. And I meet engaged and passionate women from all over the world.'[7]

NAYLA AJALTOUNI (29), L'ETHIQUE SUR L'ETIQUETTE, CCC FRANCE

The Network

'A couple of years ago, we landed in stagnant waters because the entire team had to be dismissed when European funding was lost, while at the same time the organisational structure was loose. Five organisations decided to rebuild the platform in such a way that members could be more involved. At the end of 2007, we became an association, guided by a steering committee representing the five organisations, and 28 organisations as platform members. Seven of them are trade union branches. Since then, things are looking up.

'Looking at the CCC as a global network, I sometimes find it difficult to harmonise the international and the national perspective. The need to focus on national priorities makes it difficult to be involved in the work on the international level. And because the national CCCs differ wildly in contextual aspects like type of government, lobbying methods, strategic priorities and coalition partners, we often spend much time and energy to reach consensus on wording, tone and tools of campaigns. But we get something in return: an exchanges of ideas, expertise, the media impact of an international campaign, better contacts with Southern partners, the legitimacy of an international platform that represents twelve countries.'

Successes

'Despite our new, much smaller structure, the response to our Olympic campaign has been very satisfactory. L'Ethique sur l'Etiquette has always had a strong legitimacy on labour issues in France, and apparently the public and media haven't forgotten that.'

Distinctive Approach

'We are different from other CCCs in that we have local clean clothes groups – up to 140 in the glorious years, still 35 now – that contribute to the national campaign by organising local events. They are a great strength of our campaign.'

Room for Improvement

'We stand before a huge challenge. We want to change a pattern of irrational overconsumption and irrational production that is not concerned with social and environmental damage. Multinationals create ever more riches without consideration of the human costs. We need to create an awareness of the interdependency of Northern consumption and Southern working conditions, and also of Southern and Northern workers. We need to strengthen solidarity between them. In France, the population often seems resigned when confronted with the exploitation of Southern workers: "It's the way it is, what can we do about it?" Or they think that causes are cultural: "In those countries it's normal for children to work." We need to make it clear that it is unacceptable that other people are exploited to satisfy our consumption needs.'

Personal Motivation

'I want people to think about the social costs of our consumption patterns, and I want to change them. I think that I can work towards this in the CCC because it focuses on human rights and on companies. Human rights are the subject of international treaties that all countries are committed to. Companies are supposed to take rational decisions, based on market laws and the consumer voice. It may be easier to obtain concrete and progressive results from them than from lobbying the authorities.'[8]

MICHAELA KÖNIGSHOFER (26), CLEAN CLOTHES KAMPAGNE, CCC AUSTRIA

The Network

'Our platform is made up of 13 organisations: solidarity groups, development organisations, church groups, and since 2007 one trade union. When our Polish partner Karat visited us and witnessed the participation of the church groups, they were impressed: in Poland Catholics had thrown stones at a Karat rally. Personal relationships are important. A good "click" with representatives greatly helps to motivate their organisations. This can be problematic, because I try to separate my private and my work life. But it's also cool when a platform functions smoothly and the CCK can use all the members' media, lobby work, knowledge, capacity and standing in society. One of our strengths is the large number of people in our database. Our newsletter reaches 12,000 people, and 5,000 receive the urgent appeals. Many will do something, when asked.

'I've been coordinator since 2006. It was quite hard in the beginning to get an orientation about our role and position in the international network, but I'm increasingly enjoying it. Facing an international industry, you simply need to have an international network. Sometimes the decision-making process is way too slow for me. I have to practice patience, and trust that there will be a decision, a process, a beginning, and a campaign in the end. Electronic communications are a real challenge for me. There are times when e-mail traffic swamps me. My friends get angry with me because I don't want to use e-mail in my personal life anymore.'

Successes

'Recently Shahida, a Bangladeshi trade union president, came to Austria for the campaign on the German retailer Tchibo; she said the impact of our work was noticeable, that factories were improving. That is a highlight for me.'

Distinctive Approach

'I would not call our house parties special, but others in the network think they are. They are a little like Tupperware parties. Somebody invites five to six people over plus one from CCK, for a basic workshop. They look at the wardrobe of the host, talk about buying clothes and about working conditions, play a game, and hopefully sign up to the network. We also throw larger parties to attract young people and raise some money.'

Room for Improvement

'I have to motivate the platform organisations more than they support me. Too much wait-and-see, and their contributions are mostly on campaign actions. I would like to discuss more on a political level and talk about strategy. On the strategic level we in Austria are not really confident. It doesn't help that we have to develop projects with an eye on funding, instead of working straight towards our goals.'

Personal Motivation

'During an internship in the second year of my studies I learned about the CCC and have wanted to work in it ever since. We have a joke that unfortunately is not just a joke: "We want to save the world but it is really hard!" I hope that we can at least improve it. It cannot be right that hedge fund participants earn billions, while others work all hours of the day and cannot pay their children's school fees. You try to do something about it, but you have to accept failure. I want to do something sensible, and I feel that the clean clothes movement provides the opportunity because the campaigns make sense.'[9]

CHRISTA DE BRUIN AND FLORIS DE GRAAD, SCHONE KLEREN KAMPAGNE, CCC NETHERLANDS

The Network

'The SKK and the International Secretariat formally split up in 2003. Currently the SKK consists of three coordinators with different tasks; we have a coalition of organisations that guides our policy and strategies, and a larger platform of about 25 organisations that exchange information and provide occasional support. Over the past five years, the coalition as well as the platform has been eroded. There is not one common denominator to account for this. Some organisations have a lack of capacity, and several other platforms active on globalisation and corporate social responsibility drain the available capacity. Maybe the novelty of the campaign just wore off. As coordinators, we prefer to represent a network that would guide and feed our campaign. We do cooperate with several organisations; in the Olympic campaigns, for example, we've had a terrific collaboration with the major union federation FNV as part of the platform. The international network functions very well. National and international campaigns reinforce each other.'

Successes

'One of our first campaigns was the one that forced the Swiss lingerie company Triumph to leave Burma. That was, well … a triumph! It was a coordinated campaign between many countries. In the Netherlands, we had an action in a nightclub hosting a big lingerie event attended by the Triumph CEO. Posing as paparazzi besieging a famous star, we arrived in a pink Cadillac and gave a speech denouncing Triumph's policies. The media loved it. The next day the branch association ranged itself on our side, and one week later Triumph withdrew from Burma.'

Distinctive Approach

'The 2007 Hema campaign was a fun campaign with good results. Hema is a department store so typically Dutch that it almost feels like part of our heritage. When its owner put it up for sale, we called on the Dutch people to buy it in order to save it, and improve supply chain working conditions into the bargain. Public and media responded immediately; we raised money pledges worth 340,000 euros. When a British equity fund outbid us, we had won 800 members for "Friends of the Hema", the first critical fan club of a department store. They love Hema products, but profess that they would love them more if they were made under certified, good working conditions.'

Room for Improvement

'Over the years, we've moved from awareness-raising into working on codes, monitoring and verification, and from there to companies' purchasing practices. When we do a sportswear campaign now, the demand package is extremely detailed. It is part of our policy to oppose and propose, but the technical nature of this work complicates communication with the public. Companies' use of our language without its content aggravates this problem. It is really hard to explain that a one-time consultation with a local union is not the same as a local partner network participating in monitoring and verification procedures. The same goes for urgent appeals. They can be effective in forcing a company to react, but it is not easy to report back to the public after the case has been dragging on for three years and shows only partial results. We should find a way to deal with this.'

Personal Motivation

'The issues are complex and challenging while the core idea is simple and close to your own life: Who makes our clothes, and under what conditions? Working together with activists and workers all over the world gives us a feeling of power. The solidarity, and knowing that strategies for change are developed together with workers and their organisations, motivates and inspires us. We are learning and doing many different things.'[10]

MARTIN HEARSON (26), LABOUR BEHIND THE LABEL, CCC UNITED KINGDOM

The Network

'LBL has six part-time staff, a platform of trade unions and NGOs, and over 200 individual members. I'm coordinator. Our platform is not big, and we haven't invested as much as we would like in affiliation, partly because we're short on time, partly because we can cooperate on a project basis anyway. It means that unless we cooperate with others, we don't have the campaigning infrastructure to organise big demonstrations or get more than a few hundred people to send postcards to companies.

'Although the European network functions well, it has some strains that I have seen in every network I've been part of. The International Secretariat is so dynamic, so ahead of the field, that it is not really a secretariat in the sense of following its membership. You get the typical tension of network members not feeling involved enough, while the centre feels it is not getting enough input. Ten years ago, European meetings were a four-person affair; now at least 20 people sit at the table. Given our growth, I personally would prefer more formalisation. Maybe it is a gender thing, a male attitude. Perhaps I tend to fall back more on rules and plans than women in the network do.'

Successes

'With few resources and without being able to mobilise large quantities of people, we've been able to generate a public debate and put pressure on companies through a series of research reports on high street companies and low-cost retailers that drew a great amount of media attention.[11] When, for example, the incredibly cheap clothes in the stores of Asda-Wal-Mart, Tesco and Primark were raising questions in society, we gave the answers as to who was paying the real cost, and provided the evidence. It moved the living wage discussion forward.'

Distinctive Approach

'The Fashion Colleges project emerged from requests from fashion tutors and students regarding ethical buying. For once we are responding to a demand instead of pushing one! We developed a website and teaching materials; we train tutors and students. We want the ethical discussion to penetrate the entire organisation, not just one department. The aim is to have a new generation of fashion professionals that understands the impact of its decisions on garment workers. Purchasing practices are the area of expertise of the fashion people, and the part they are able to influence. One of them told me that, by the standards of her company, she was terrible at her job, because she wouldn't negotiate on price and delivery times beyond what the supplier could deliver without hurting the workers. She performed badly against her targets that were based on getting the cheapest and fastest delivery. "So unless you influence the people who set the targets, you can't change anything", she said. But we think that if a new generation starts asking questions, there will be change. The programme has the added advantages of providing us with insight into the industry, and contributing to our credibility. The industry sees that we're not only interested in muckraking.'[12]

Room for Improvement

'We recently discussed three scenarios for the future. The first is consumer-oriented and aims at mobilising the public to pressure companies to change. The second is activism-oriented; it has a smaller reach but more depth, and a focus on urgent appeals and solidarity with partners in developing countries. The third is oriented towards public policy and trade agreements, and heading for binding regulation. Of course, all three are important – the question was what emphasis we'd prefer. We chose the latter. We grew up as a campaign thrashing brands. Their global fame made them vulnerable; their success was our opportunity, and we were in a sense parasitic on them. We've moved forward to define and ask for corporate social responsibility. So far this hasn't really solved the workers' problems. Now we should focus on things that are harder to get, even if it will not get us easy public support.'

Personal Motivation

'Somebody once described the CCC as "pragmatism with a radical edge". That is what I like about it. I did this kind of thing in my spare time for quite a while, and it actually made me quite uncomfortable when it first became my job. But the advantage is that I can cook and read and be in an orchestra in my spare time and work on something close to my heart, rather than having 40 hours a week taken up by a job that I don't care about so much, and then my activism squeezing everything else out. I think campaigners should have a life outside of their activism, so that they can bring in ideas and approaches from elsewhere. Especially in a campaign which so obviously plays on popular culture.'[13]

DEBORAH LUCCHETTI (39) AND ERSILIA MONTI (50), CAMPAGNA ABITI PULITI, CCC ITALY[14]

The Network

'Before 1995, Italian consumer organisations were mostly about consumer rights and better refrigerators. Then a new movement on ethical consuming tackled issues of transnational corporations, labour rights and the environment. An eye-opening garment campaign was the one against Benetton, the company that built its image on awareness of society's woes while making use of exploited labour in its Italian supply chain. These were the breeding grounds for Abiti Puliti. We are a coalition of ten organisations involved in fair trade, workers' rights and ethical finance. Through our affiliated organisations and like-minded magazines, we reach about 40,000 people. Unions have not been overly enthusiastic to work with us, but we think consumers and producers have common interests. Defending workers' rights means defending citizens' rights. Unions are growing weaker all over Europe, because production is leaving. They should try to organise consumers. Recently we've seen some progress; unions supported the Olympic campaign, and a union official joined the regional CCC meeting.

'We have set out to cooperate more closely with other CCCs in the region. It makes sense – we have something in common. Our companies are producing and selling in each other's countries. For the public procurement campaigns, Spain and Italy can benefit from each other's experiences in respectively clean clothes communities and fair trade. The global network is great – it is the reason we are strong and the only way to face globalisation. By trying to let

Southern partners have the lead, we have a global perspective that is missing in our political parties.'

Successes

'Our first urgent appeal case concerned workers' rights violations in the Bangladeshi factory A-One, which supplied retailer Coin-Oviesse through Tessival, the biggest Italian garment chain. Coin-Oviesse denied sourcing there, but contacts on the ground provided us with the company's orders in black and white. A journalist investigated and published the story. Now Coin-Oviesse has a code of conduct. Although the only thing that has been achieved in Bangladesh is payment of wages owed, the case empowered our campaign. Society considers us a stakeholder now; we were the only civil society campaign invited by the former government to prepare a workshop for a national CSR conference.'

Distinctive Approach

Ersilia: 'While companies like Armani and Prada relocate their cheaper fashion lines to low-wage countries, they rely on the craftsmanship of Italian workers for luxury goods. Despite relocations, 850,000 people still work in the Italian garment industry. Clothing production belongs to our country – it is part of our history. For 100 years, people in my mother's village made hats for all of Europe. My grandmother took part in strikes and demonstrations. We should try to recover this heritage, but on a new footing, with ethical production. I have written articles about past worker struggles in our newsletter, and I staged a couple of exhibitions of old dresses from our own homes, with photographs, artefacts and printed matter to match. It is an effort to unravel today's complexity by unwinding the long threads of family stories. The exhibitions end with stories of workers in global production chains and in ethical production.'

Deborah: 'My father was proud to wear clothes 15 years old. Back then it was crucial to take care of your clothes, instead of scoring the latest outfit. Clothes have always defined our identities; now brands are defining them for us. We should resist. But this kind of cultural struggle poses a dilemma. By questioning overproduction and overconsumption, you may endanger jobs, which is not on the CCC agenda! Some of us work on alternatives outside the CCC, like the construction of a new supply chain of small enterprises and cooperatives that produce with social and environmental standards, transparency, and a strong producer–consumer connection.'

Room for Improvement

'We fight for dismissed workers, then the factory relocates and we can't do a thing about it. Improvements in working conditions will in the end be annulled if we don't stop the worldwide liberalisation of trade rules. We must deal with institutions like the World Trade Organisation and the International Monetary Fund that are as important as the brands in causing global inequality and exploitation. But communicating these issues to the public is difficult. We have to be part of a broader movement that includes this wider perspective.'

Personal Motivation

Ersilia: 'My first job was in a transnational company. When I realised that I would never have an understanding of work if I didn't experience it at the bottom rung of the ladder, I resigned and became a cleaner, making ends meet by translation work in my spare time. In my perfect society, intellectual and manual work are not separated. Doing both gives you a perspective from both sides of the table. After that, I became a librarian and helped build a new union. When an ethical consumer movement emerged in Italy, I was glad to join it. I believe in the power of socially and politically aware consumers. My commitment to Abiti Puliti is part of a battle for a better society without suffering and injustice – and that includes plants and animals! The larger CCC network is built on giving and taking, and sometimes I feel at the heart of that. It is a privilege.'

Deborah: 'I'm from a proletarian family of immigrants that travelled from the south of Italy to Turin. At 13, I angered my father when he was looking for me and found me in the middle of the 1 May celebrations. At 15 I became an activist in the Young Christian Workers' movement. At 20 I was a metalworker, and unionised a small automobile factory of women workers in Turin. After several years of union activism, combined with university study, I became disappointed. The unions were not dealing with the challenges of globalisation, especially the injustices heaped upon workers in the global South. As a unionist in industrialised Italy, I did not feel close to them, not part of a global workers' movement. I decided to get to know "the enemy" from within, by working as a purchasing manager for a transnational corporation. When the movement against the negative impacts of globalisation found its voice in Seattle, I had a new arena for my political activism. My commitment has always been to workers' rights – women workers' rights especially, since they suffer most from the injustice caused by capitalism. When in 2005 the opportunity presented itself to collaborate with the CCC, this work seemed made for me, as if it had always belonged to my life. I could put my experiences to good use. This is my story. I think nothing is incidental.'[15]

THOMAS PETERSEN (37) AND BIRTE MOELLER JENSEN (51), CLEAN CLOTHES CAMPAIGN, DENMARK

The Network

Birte: 'As shop steward in a porcelain factory, I visited a Chinese export processing zone in 1996. The experience shocked me so much that, after my return, I started up an NGO because I wanted Danish people, and especially unionists, to know what was going on there. When it became clear to us that we can't solve labour issues on a national level anymore, that they necessitate a global approach, we began looking for a wider organisational perspective, and were glad to find the CCC in 2006. We are now the latest national platform, launched in 2007. Seven organisations have joined: the textile committee of Denmark's major trade union, a federation of retail worker unions, two labour NGOs, two consumer organisations, and one solidarity NGO.'

Success

Thomas: 'The first urgent appeal we took up was a case in Thailand. A garment factory had announced its intention to relocate production, and workers were anxious that they would not be paid the compensation due to them. We asked a Danish company sourcing at the factory to use its leverage, and after negotiations the Thai owner agreed to pay 75 per cent of the compensation due.'

Distinctive Approach

Birte: 'We have to face the fact that we are losing our jobs to people who work under terrible circumstances. We should not be afraid to share the work. It means that we have to create other jobs for ourselves, and at the same time check on labour conditions abroad. Our shop stewards should be made aware of the global situation and make connections abroad, so they can go to their companies and put the right standards in the code of conduct. We shouldn't just share the work, but also our experience with trade unions. People nowadays are so spoiled; they forget that trade unions are about solidarity.'

Room for Improvement

Thomas: 'We need to profile ourselves as a clean clothes movement in the public eye now. We need to get branded!'

Personal Motivation

Birte: 'The Danish expression for production relocation is "butterfly factories", and I've experienced firsthand what it means. My factory once had 4,000 workers; now 200 are left. The production of the Royal Copenhagen porcelain figurines was first moved to Portugal, then Mexico, China, Malaysia, Sri Lanka and back to Malaysia. I visited the Malaysian factory, where health and safety measures were disregarded altogether. No ventilation, hazardous paints, and workers sat in opposite positions, spraying paint in each other's faces. Wages were so low – the owner was stealing money from the workers. When I returned, I told the management of my factory that its code of conduct was just a piece of paper. In the next round of reorganisations I got sacked. I went on to study social science, and I am now delighted to have found a job as international development adviser with a trade union centre.'[16]

CARIN LEFFLER (44), KAMPANJEN RENE KLAER, CCC NORWAY

The Network

'CCC Norway was launched in June 2007. We have an employees' trade union and two NGOs in our coalition. They give advice and support, but are not yet so active in planning and carrying out our campaign. We are organising local groups that can follow up the CCC work in other parts of Norway.

'Although I find it hard to digest the amount of e-mail I get, I really like to work in the CCC network. It is interesting to see people from various backgrounds working together in multiple ways, but more or less with the same goals. I am surprised how efficient and consensus-oriented the CCC is. Some issues and questions are time-consuming, but I guess that is the cost of a level decision-making structure.'

Successes

'We're still quite young. So far we have done work on urgent appeals, a workers' tour, the Play Fair campaign, company research, report production, speeches and workshops, and street actions. I really hope that in a few years' time we will see more local groups acting in their communities according to the ideas of the international network.'

Distinctive Approach

'We have regional Scandinavian cooperation in which we share ideas, reports and information about companies – some retailers are established in several Scandinavian countries. We make plans together, discuss media strategies, and apply for funding for joint activities. CCC Sweden was invaluable for our launch.'

Room for Improvement

'It would be great to have a close colleague. I do miss someone that I could discuss problems and strategies with, for daily mutual support and inspiration. A minor challenge is translation. Within the CCC network there is so much valuable information, and translation can be time-consuming, believe me.'

Personal Motivation

'I have always been interested in solidarity work in an international context. I read about the CCC three years ago and immediately felt that I wanted to take part. For me the CCC offers the full package: idealism and activism in a professional framework, pooled knowledge, the grassroots perspective, close cooperation with organisations in producer countries, challenging structures and companies, lots of dynamics. I really feel that the work we do makes a difference.'[17]

Part 4

Debates and the Future

7
Support for Workers

The anti-sweatshop movement has achieved much in a short time. Worldwide, awareness has grown among citizens about the conditions under which their clothes are made. Many of them have formed and joined networks committed to changing these conditions. Most brand-name companies and retailers have accepted responsibility for conditions in their supply chains, in workplaces they do not own. Voluntary regulations have been developed and used in an effort to eradicate abuses and create space for decent work. Even some meaningful changes in national labour law have been accomplished.

Still, the facts on the ground are sobering. Overall, wages in the garment-producing sector in developing countries are stagnant or falling. The rights to freedom of association and collective bargaining have to be won again and again, and many battles are lost. Relocations within the industry are still rampant, leading to an informalisation of economies that undermines workers' lives, including the capacity to fight for a better one. Governments, adhering to the dogmas of export-led growth, neoliberal deregulation and global competition, fail to enact or enforce labour laws.

In its internal discussion paper for the 2007 International Forum in Bangkok, the CCC's International Secretariat concluded that new, creative strategies and alliances were needed to move forward and arrive at solutions to the regulatory vacuum created by the shift from nationally-oriented production systems to globally-organised production networks. To this end, the clean clothes movement is involved in a continuous process of strategy evaluation and development. Some debates date back 20 years and keep re-surfacing; new ones are launched every year. The following pages deal with the most important of them. They are grouped into the four focal areas of the CCC: support for workers; consumers; authorities and legal reform; and companies. This chapter focuses on the first – the fundamental issue of support for workers.

'Break the privilege of knowledge, break the North–South divide, break hierarchy and sameness, break the producer–consumer divide, organise and attack!'

181

These passionate words were addressed to the participants of the 2007 International Forum in Bangkok by J. John, executive director of the Centre for Education and Communication (CEC), an Indian partner organisation of the CCC. J. John is a stately man, proud of his heritage. He still talks with indignation about the British treatment of the Indian textile industry under colonial rule. 'We had thousands of artisans', he says.

> They produced twelve-meter-long saris that fit into a matchbox. When Manchester became a manufacturing centre, the British tried to destroy our industry. They took our raw materials to process them in Manchester; they invented protective measures to bar our products. But by the end of the colonial era, our industry had gained ground once more. From the competition angle, we have advantages over other countries. We grow cotton and we have artificial fibre; we have a technology base; we have both technical and artistic skills. And a huge cheap labour force.[1]

It is the emancipation of this labour force that drives his and CEC's activities today. The CEC supports labour organisation through research and campaigns, and tries to broaden the trade union approach by including social factors like tribal background and gender. It has been very involved in the Play Fair campaigns targeting the sportswear industry.

> We in Asia start with the workers. Their organisation will decide whether any change in the balance of production relations, any sustainable process of labour rights improvement, is going to happen. We have to be active subjects in the process, not just implementing bodies for other people's strategies.

Worker empowerment was high on the agenda of the first global network meeting in Barcelona in 2001, and in this context several issues surfaced that are still discussed today. While dissimilar in scope and character, these issues are alike in that they severely impact worker empowerment and continue to call forth debates among campaigners. Some – like gender and the relationship between Northern and Southern groups in the CCC – clearly overstep the boundaries of this chapter, and pervade most other fields of CCC activity. Because their impact on the subject at hand cannot be ignored, they are included here nevertheless.

URGENT APPEALS

The CCC cannot and does not want to represent workers, but it can support them. One of the tools at its disposal is consumer action targeting brands and retailers. Urgent appeals are doing just that: by mobilising public opinion, they pressure western companies into undertaking steps that will improve working conditions in the supply chain. Kelly Dent, a long-time labour activist in Australia and Asia and now working with Oxfam Australia, comments: 'In the early days, many people especially in the unions didn't understand what this consumer pressure was about. How could we change the world through shopping? It took time to figure out its place as part of an overall strategy.'[2]

In essence, the urgent appeals work has changed little since the first appeal was launched, 20 years ago. The CCC receives a call for action on a labour rights violation from workers or their representatives. After the violation has been validated, the CCC contacts brands and retailers ordering at the workplace in question, to try and solve the problem 'behind the scenes'. For example, a brand is asked to investigate the complaint and pressure the factory to remedy the problem. If this brings no result, the CCC mobilises its network to write protest letters to relevant brands, retailers, factory owners and authorities. This may develop into a full-blown campaign all over Europe, with street actions, worker tours and media exposure. The CCC network devotes a large part of its capacity to urgent appeals work.

What has change is the scale of such work. There are now 50 or 60 calls for support annually, and the CCC takes up approximately 30 of them. Between August 2007 and August 2008, two old cases were closed, 11 were ongoing, and 29 were initiated. Cases were mainly from Asia (Bangladesh, Cambodia, China, India, Indonesia, the Philippines, Sri Lanka), but there were also cases from Turkey, Morocco, Tunisia, Mauritius and Mexico. The core issue in most cases was freedom of association, but other issues were concealed behind them: there is always a motive for wanting to organise – starvation wages, forced overtime, sexual harassment, and so on.[3]

Cases are taken up according to criteria that have been developed over time. Tessel Pauli, urgent appeals coordinator of the CCC International Secretariat, describes the most important ones:

A case must be related to the garment and sportswear industries. There needs to be a brand or retailer involved that has a sizable market share or is headquartered in a country with a CCC because, for us to be able to use a brand or retailer image, public and media must recognise it as 'their own'. Good communication with the partner on the ground is essential. It must have actual presence in the factory and be in contact with workers. We always find ourselves in a field of contradictory information, and in the end workers are the only ones who can refute the information that factory management feeds to the brands.[4]

It is hard to quantify the success and failure of urgent appeals, because much of the gain and loss is immaterial – such as the increased confidence of a union that has seen itself propelled onto an international stage, or improved social accountability on the part of a company that has learned that routine audits may overlook critical data. On the other hand, victories may turn into defeats when wage raises have been won in factories that subsequently shut down. Nevertheless, some quantification can be – and in fact was – attempted in an assessment of the impact of urgent appeals, carried in 2005. The assessment showed that a little over 30 per cent of cases between 1999 and 2004 had seen full or partial success, measured according to workers' statements about whether or not their demands had been met. Contributing factors included strong organisations on the ground; a good working relationship between them and international campaigning organisations; a variety of tactics, tools and actions directed at multiple pressure-points; easy ways for consumers to express their support, and regular updates to motivate them.[5]

Although there is probably nobody in the CCC network who would like to go without the urgent appeals, there are different opinions about the degree of their power and efficiency. For example, Stefan Indermühle, coordinator of the Swiss CCC, thinks their results are disappointing, measured against the amount of time and energy they consume:

Urgent appeals are useful for campaigning, but I don't see how we are making a real change from all that work. It resembles a string of unrelated actions; they should be embedded more in large campaigns. Moreover, too many of them deal with factory closures. I can see how those are the cases where workers want a campaign because they have nothing to lose anymore, but the chance of success is small and that makes us look weak.[6]

Frieda de Koninck, of the Belgian Schone Kleren Campagne, agrees, but sees positive effects as well:

> Urgent appeals are seldom cost-effective. They generate so much work and you cannot roster them – an appeal is always an emergency. But maybe we shouldn't evaluate them only along that line. When we manage to make a difference, it feeds the courage and the will to fight, over there as well as over here. Appeals offer action perspectives to the western public and a concrete introduction into labour rights, globalisation and the CCC.[7]

Martin Hearson, of Labour Behind the Label, concurs:

> As a campaigner, you're always trying to find out where people start from and where you can get them. Consumers start from the question how to shop ethically; you want them to reach an understanding of worker empowerment, the importance of trade unions. Urgent appeals can do this. They start with the brand and take you to the more radical thing of worker empowerment.[8]

Martin's colleague, Sam Maher, is an ardent supporter of the urgent appeals system:

> It is bedrock of CCC campaigns and it strengthens the network. It allows for cooperation between North and South and between national CCCs. Urgent appeals are a good way to start a dialogue with companies, because they are about specific cases; companies cannot hide behind general answers.[9]

In order to preserve the assets and lose the liabilities, the CCC has come up with new approaches. Tessel Pauli comments that urgent appeals

> are by nature after-the-fact, which can be frustrating especially in cases of factory closures, when all is lost. We are encouraging partners to inform us about any early warnings that precede a closure, such as diminishing orders, dismissals or removal of equipment. Only when we are early do we have

a chance of salvaging some compensation for workers out of a bankruptcy.[10]

Nina Ascoly, urgent appeals coordinator at the International Secretariat from 1999 to 2008, is happy with two recent developments in the system.

> Increased funding has strengthened the national CCCs and facilitated the spread of knowledge and work, and broadened the scope for mobilisation. It embedded the work more on a European level and made for a well-balanced system. The second development comes out of the growing awareness of the fact that the industry is not going to be cleaned up one workplace at a time. This has been an impetus for the new 'strategic urgent appeal', which focuses attention on core problems occurring in a specific geographical area. We present such a 'strategic' or 'thematic' appeal to brands and retailers ordering in this area. We want them to acknowledge that core problems such as factory closures, informalisation of labour and absence of freedom of association are chronic in the sector. We want them to recognise the part played by their own business practices and request that they take preventive steps.[11]

According to Pauli,

> Getting companies to collaborate is one of the most challenging tasks. The corporate culture may be to blame, drenched as it is in competitiveness. They won't even write a collective letter to a supplier. This hampers the creation of the 'level playing field' they are all clamouring for.

The year 2008 saw the development of the first of these new appeals, focused on Indonesia. Consultations with partners to articulate the appeal are ongoing, while sportswear brands such as Nike, Adidas, Puma, Mizuno and Asics, plus several garment brands and retailers and the Asian transnational company Yue Yuen, have been presented with a document outlining a set of 'sector-wide solutions'. They also received a questionnaire that probes in detail their willingness to address the endemic problems of the sector.[12] It concerns solutions such as worker rights training programmes, formal employment contracts for all workers, long-term supply contracts, a living wage as a code standard, and incentives for factories to adhere to freedom of association and collective bargaining. Ascoly remarks:

> We targeted the sportswear brands in the 2008 Play Fair campaign. A number of them were willing to move ahead, and we had a meeting with them in Hong Kong to discuss prevention of rights' violations in Indonesia and elsewhere. Several brands committed to a roundtable discussion with the CCC, Oxfam Australia, Indonesian unions and labour rights groups in 2009. It's moving along, but still too early to talk about results, and it's nowhere near solving the problems in Indonesia. I think the forerunners of the industry are now about to recognise that sector-wide solutions are needed, but the significance of that phase should not be underestimated.

And Pauli expands on this point:

> Since the launch of the Indonesian strategic appeal, the proposed sector-wide solutions have provided context for two cases involving Adidas supplier factories that closed abruptly. The French, German and Spanish CCCs have taken it up and generated thousands of protest letters to Adidas, resulting in the rehiring of 870 dismissed workers by Adidas' new supplier factory in Jakarta.

THE INFORMAL ECONOMY AND MIGRANT LABOUR

Support for workers that is not intended as charity or neo-colonial arrogance must necessarily build upon the organisation of workers themselves. But globalisation of the industry has thrown a couple of obstacles in that path. It replaces steady jobs with informal employment, turning the labour market into a casino for workers and forcing them to grasp at straws. It has created a mobile workforce that consists largely of women and migrants – often both at the same time. They have little knowledge of labour rights, they have to keep moving, and most trade unions lack experience in organising these groups. These factors combine to make organisation of workers in the garment industry difficult.

Statistics on the informalisation of the economy are quite staggering. 'The bulk of new employment in recent years, particularly in developing and transition countries, has been in the informal economy', the ILO reported in 2002.[13] In 2004, the International

Confederation of Free Trade Unions calculated that 25 per cent of the world's working population was active in the informal economy, generating 35 per cent of global GDP – and that included western economies that were far more formalised than those of industrialising countries. The World Bank's World Development Report of 2001 listed the informal sector share of non-agricultural employment at 57 per cent in Latin America and the Caribbean, 78 per cent in Africa, and between 45 and 85 per cent in Asia.[14] Since then, the trend has been reinforced.

There are many types of work arrangement in the informal economy, from home-work to day-work, alongside steady jobs in the same factory. Informal economies grow inside formal ones. There are no 'model' informal garment workers, which, added to their mobile existence and generally low level of education, aggravates organisational difficulties.

For women and migrants, the informal economy is often the only option. Here they find, regardless of their skills, the infamous '3D' jobs: dirty, dangerous and degrading. Informal economy workers often have no wage agreements, earn below legal minimum wages, are not paid on time, have no employment contracts or regular working hours, are not covered by health insurance or unemployment benefits, and are not a priority for most governmental, political or labour organisations. An example from Indonesia:

> There are three types of employees hired in Batam's [export processing zones]. The most exploited worker is an outsourced worker. They are hired through a labour agency and usually sign a contract with the agency that holds them liable should they lose their job, sometimes at fees five to ten times their normal wage. These employees are traded like commodities, one step removed from human trafficking. Should they get ill, pregnant or hurt on the job, the company will immediately release them and the labour agency will likely fine the employee for breach of contract.[15]

Given the weak legal position of migrants, the stakes are high for those who try to stand up for their rights, and thus become visible. There are few legal or regulatory frameworks to protect them; often the factories they work in are not even registered. In some cases workers are not legally entitled to organise because they or their workplaces are not registered. Trade unions find organising informal workers difficult, and a drain on resources. They are confronted with down-to-earth problems like workers who are afraid to unionise and difficult to locate. They will often have limited access to phones and faxes, so that communicating requires personal visits. Migrants have no money for membership dues.[16]

On a positive note, labour organisations around the world are trying to address these problems. The ILO and the global union federation ITUC have invested in programmes to educate and organise informal workers.[17] Doug Miller of ITGLWF reported at the end of 2008 that his organisation was very active on migrant workers' rights in Jordan and Malaysia – two countries with huge numbers of migrant workers. It pressured Nike into formulating its new migrant worker guidelines.[18]

In the Netherlands, the major trade union federation, FNV, is committed to including informal workers in all its international work, and many unions respond favourably. FNV and the British GMB and T&G unions employ organisers from the language group or culture of the workers in question, in order to reach them more effectively. Interesting experiments are conducted to internationalise union membership. In the Baltic states, service station workers have been able to have their union membership recognised abroad – a kind of 'union passport'. When the British Trades Union Congress wanted to organise Polish workers, it invited Solidarnosc, its counterpart in Poland, to send organisers to lead workshops. Participants were keen to see the development of international union cards.[19]

Despite the obstacles, there are examples of informal garment workers who have either joined existing trade unions or formed their own organisations. A well-known example is India's Self Employed Women's Association, founded in 1972. At the time of writing it has 700,000 members, and it has been affiliated to the International Trade Union Confederation (ITUC) since 2006.[20]

A 2004 seminar on organising in the informal sector brought together members of the Irene network, which has been active on this issue since the 1980s, and the CCC. They concluded that campaigning efforts must have a multinational dimension, because migrant workers whose rights are violated need help from all sides: in the country where production is located, in countries where buying multinationals are headquartered and where the goods are sold, and in their country of birth. Various responsibilities must be considered carefully, especially because undocumented workers risk deportation in addition to job loss. Another important issue was that of competition between local and migrant workers – outbursts of xenophobia, especially in times of economic hardship, are only too familiar.[21]

Home-work is an important part of the informal economy, with pitfalls of its own for anybody who endeavours to organise the women – and a few men – involved. In 2009, ILO convention 177, which commits undersigning countries to promoting the regulation of home-work on the basis of equality with 'normal' employer–employee relationships, is ratified by only five countries.[22] In 2006, at a regional CCC conference in Delhi, participants from Thailand, Bangladesh, Malaysia, South Korea, Taiwan and India shared their experiences in organising home-workers and pushing their governments to ratify the convention. From the report, it appears that home-work was on the rise everywhere – in industrialising countries as well as in a country like Taiwan, where factory owners had moved production to the Chinese mainland but were still subcontracting to home-workers in Taiwan; or a country like Thailand, which, since wages began to rise in the 1990s, has been trying to compete by transforming factory work into home-work. The scattered workforce, the complex subcontracting chains and absence of production data, were identified as major organising constraints.

A number of recommendations were put forward. First, the gender dimension should be addressed. Organisational structures needed to be developed taking into account the specific character of home-based work. Worker education and capacity-building were important areas of work. Because home-workers are unable to bargain, their earnings can only be improved through better pricing. At the 'consumer end', the awareness-raising campaigns of the CCC should unravel supply chains all the way down to the back rooms of the home-workers. Its urgent appeals system must be alert to specific needs and demands of informal workers. Governments should be pushed to pass national legislation to protect home-workers, and to ratify convention 177. Monitoring of home-workers' conditions could not be done other than by local, independent NGOs; they would need capacity-building for auditing that would include informal workers. Ultimately, the report said, the goal was to build organisations that included informal workers.[23]

The Textile, Clothing and Footwear Union of Australia (TCFUA) and the Australian Fair Wear campaign are fighting abuse in home-work through an industry-wide national Homeworkers Code of Practice and a No Sweat Shop label. In Australia, 90 per cent of workers in the garment industry are home-workers, many of them migrants from Vietnam, China, and more recently from African countries.[24] The basic principle of the Homeworkers Code is that manufacturers make their production chains transparent, so exploitation can be identified and addressed. Manufacturers who want to use the No Sweat Shop label on their Australian-made garments undergo an accreditation process that entails 'mapping' the company's supply chain, and verifying that workers receive legal entitlements. The Code is voluntary, but once companies sign on, it is legally binding. A manual setting standards for sewing times ensures that manufacturers and workers have the same information, so every piece of work can have a known price.[25]

GENDER

Gender discrimination rests in part on the almost universal idea that women are merely supplementary earners, not 'real' workers, and that it is therefore justified to pay them lower wages and withhold formal working arrangements. The fact that pregnancy and childcare are seen as a liability is one more reason not to offer them steady jobs. Gender-based discrimination is a tool for labour-market flexibility.

While gender in itself is not an impediment to organisation – on the contrary, as history has often shown – in the present-day garment industry it works that way. Women wrestle with problems of multi-tasking, including raising children; after ten- or twelve-hour working days, they come home to the task of keeping the family fed, healthy and happy. Where will they find the time for union work, let alone to be a union leader? In factories and at home, they are confronted with sexual harassment and violence. The CCC urgent appeals impact assessment of 2005 recorded many examples of gender discrimina-tion: harassment of pregnant workers, sexual abuse, strip-searches, inadequate leave for a woman who miscarried, lack of maternity leave, denial of medical reimbursement to a pregnant worker, forced pregnancy testing, refusal of menstrual leave, refusal to include demands for pregnant workers in the collective bargaining process, forced overtime, rendering care tasks impossible, and failure to ensure the safety for women on their way home.[26] These problems are not sufficiently addressed – not by local trade unions, not by CSR schemes, not by the international labour movement.

Gender discrimination is universal, and is a tough nut to crack. Despite advances in women's education and almost universal ratification of the two ILO conventions essential to women's emancipation – number 100 on remuneration, and number 111 on occupational discrimination – women still earn less than men everywhere, and still carry the main responsibility for care of the family.[27] A report that investigated decent work and corporate social responsibility from a feminist angle concluded that neither core labour standards nor codes of conduct covered women's work in the informal economy. While gender discrimination 'forms an integral part of the market economy' and 'women are a central part of competitive strategies', their concerns are not embodied in the ILO core labour standards, and they have little access to the fora that define workers' rights. This is even more true for women in the South than in the North.[28] The core standards list should at least include the right to a safe and healthy workplace, limits on working hours, reasonable rest periods, and protection against abusive treatment in the workplace.

When women workers in Central America were asked to draw up their own ideal code of conduct, they came up with one that would safeguard their dignity and proper remuneration, prevent arbitrary and inhumane treatment, guarantee freedom of association and collective bargaining, and protect them from harm – in relation to both harassment and unhealthy working conditions. The code would also apply to home-workers – including protection and respect for pregnant women, the banning of enforced overtime, and the restriction of the working day to eight hours.[29]

Labour organisations are tackling gender discrimination: the ILO runs numerous projects; the global union federation ITUC has an 'action programme' on gender equality; and the ITGLWF runs gender projects and women's leadership workshops in several Asian countries.[30] International networks have also taken up the issues of women workers in the informal economy, and lobby for ratification of the ILO convention on home-work.[31]

According to Tessel Pauli and Nina Ascoly, the CCC itself needs to do more on the gender issue. Pauli remarks:

A common denominator of most urgent appeals is repression of workers' organisation, while gender-related rights violations are often the reason for the initial protests. When they lead to attempts to organise and this is repressed, the women's demands tend to be invisible behind that for freedom of association. We are changing our tack now; the headline of a recent case in Indonesia ran: 'Sexual harassment at supplier of Tommy Hilfiger' – which alerted the company immediately. I think we can use the new 'strategic appeals' to bundle women's problems in the workplace and present them more forcefully.[32]

And Ascoly comments:

Worker empowerment is at the heart of our mission, and these workers are mainly women. I can barely think of anything more radical or controversial than supporting women's empowerment. The gendered aspect of the rights violations epidemic in the garment sector needs all the attention it can get. Companies are obviously in need of awareness-raising on this issue. We must also prioritise it in our communication with the public and with partners. Sustainable worker organising must be gender-aware; a model of trade union organising that is male-dominated and sexist has no future. We need to put more effort into articulating the steps forward, in a very concrete way.[33]

TRADE UNIONS AND NGOs

In an essay titled, 'Who Built the South Korean Economic Miracle and Who are its Victims?', labour rights activist Cha Mi Kyung describes the history of garment production in her country as a fast-forwarding film. Garment production propelled South Korean industrialisation in the 1960s and 1970s – firstly on the fuel of foreign capital, but soon also Korean-owned. Severe exploitation of labour led to protests – a young garment worker set himself publicly on fire with a copy of the Labour Law in his hands – and to the birth of strong unions and rising wages. In the early 1990s production was relocated, and while Koreans lost their jobs, exploitation was exported to low-wage countries. The strong unions were helpless 'because there is not yet a long-term strategy of international solidarity on labour problems, no strategy of the workers' movement in the context of globalisation'.[34]

Irene Xavier, working in Malaysia for TIE Asia, an NGO working with unions and shop stewards, says:

Traditionally, unions have a national perspective, they are protective of their own labour force. With migrant workers, the initial call of unions has always been: 'Get rid of them, they are stealing our jobs.' The same is happening with contract workers. This mindset interferes with international solidarity.[35]

The same attitude can prevail in Europe. In the Flemish Belgian CCC coalition, NGOs and trade unions collaborate closely. According to coordinator Frieda de Koninck, unions are

> interested in consumer action, and involved in the public procurement campaign. Their engagement has grown. But they are also wary. They encounter multi-stakeholder initiatives in what used to be union terrain, and meanwhile they are losing power because the Belgian textiles and garment industries are going downhill. Employment in Belgium is their priority. While they engage with our campaign to introduce globalisation in their organisations, they have difficulty looking over the border. But change is never a straight line, is it?[36]

The Fair Wear Foundation, itself a multi-stakeholder initiative, does not want to crowd out trade unions. Director Erica van Doorn says that, normally, 'labour rights are the subject of tripartite negotiations between representatives of government, business and employees. The Fair Wear Foundation works in places where it fails, and we do everything in our power to strengthen the regular mechanisms.'[37]

Representation of trade unions in CCC coalitions is always pursued. CCC's Marieke Eyskoot remarks that trade unions

> represent workers; they have access to companies and can negotiate. Ideally, every national CCC has one or more trade unions in its coalition, and our cooperation with national and global unions in Play Fair campaigns is powerful. It can be frustrating because union structures are slow and cumbersome; on the other hand, they have a huge membership, press departments, designers and what not.[38]

And Pauli adds:

> In the Dutch CCC, collaboration between NGOs and the 'solidarity' department of the trade union federation FNV is excellent. A German and a Belgian union recently supported the urgent appeal of a dismissed union leader of the Triumph bra factory in Thailand; it intensified pressure on the brand. Of course there are tensions and differences of opinion about goals and strategies, but the common cause is more important. There are all kinds of unions – corrupt ones, undemocratic ones, good

ones. There are also all kinds of NGOs. Some take money from companies to knock together a useless report; some do pioneer work in worker education or legal innovation.

The love between unions and NGOs in CCC coalitions may not always be in full bloom, but neither is it one-sided. Doug Miller of the ITGLWF writes:

> Brands and retailers would simply not have engaged on supply chain rights violations if there had been no CCC – the old Milton Friedman definition of the social responsibility of business that is solely to make profit, would still have prevailed ... Strategically, the 'old' unions need to be part of alliances with other civil society organisations to campaign for change ... Most steps forward [in labour struggle] occurred in the last century, when collective agreements applied to the whole industry and established a rate for the job, and trade unions were able to organise those factories that were undercutting. International outsourcing pretty much put an end to that, so most [recent] gains have been piecemeal, based on urgent appeals, adverse media coverage and campaigns.
>
> Sector-wide solutions are important, but employers are fragmented and do not want to concede any authority to their associations, which are weak. So we have to target the industry leaders. Together with the CCC we are aiming for a sector-wide approach on precarious employment, hopefully beginning in Indonesia in 2009.[39]

Asia has its own examples of fruitful cooperation between unions and NGOs. In Sri Lanka, the trade union FTZ&GSEU organised women workers in the free trade zones through cooperation with women's groups. The union saw its membership multiply. Trade unions and NGOs, united in the Thai Labour Solidarity Committee, organised May Day rallies together and took up the issue of the minimum wage revision. The Play Fair campaign in India was successful mainly because of NGO–union collaboration. For the first time in India, garment workers' issues were raised in the mass media.[40] And Irene Xavier says:

> When unions have no other recourse, international campaigns are helpful. TIE Asia has learned that strategy through the CCC. In the beginning we were recipients of CCC campaigns. We would send information, they would run the campaign. Then union

leaders began to learn how to do it – how to substantiate the facts of a case, teach workers to notice the labels they were sewing into the clothes; how to trace the supply line to the brand in the North and apply pressure on it. Now many are able to send out good information when they want to campaign. They went on speaker tours in the North. They met with brand representatives and learned that kind of negotiating. They also learned a new, creative way of campaigning through international groups like the CCC, with colourful street actions and playful campaign materials. Coming from a traditional union background, labour leaders thought that was all children's stuff. But they found out that workers actually liked the fun and games.[41]

WORKER EDUCATION

Whenever labour rights activists from the South discuss organising, the education of workers comes up as a pivotal element affecting all other strategies. They have seen how a lack of self-confidence and knowledge, and a lack of experience in organising, in the long run weaken every attempt at corporate social responsibility, every unionising effort, and every international campaign. Another shared insight is that learning must be practical.

Education can take many forms. We will look at some that may serve as examples, for better and for worse.

The ILO Better Factories Cambodia programme combines monitoring of factories with capacity-building. It has the support of the Cambodian government, the US Department of Labor, international buyers, NGOs and trade unions. It combines unannounced audits with a series of training programmes and support for factories. Because it unites broadness of scope with in-depth, concrete action, the project is widely held in high regard. In fact, it is so effective that the *Source*, an international magazine of the textiles and garment branch, reported in 2008 that investors might be backing out of the surveyed factories, which were behaving increasingly better ethically. While many factories closed, new ones opened, and exports were maintained. The *Source* writes: 'Cambodia's much-praised Better Factories Cambodia programme covers less than 300 factories. As attention concentrates on these intensely monitored businesses, suspicion must remain that a growing proportion of Cambodia's manufacture is happening in the 200 that are not monitored.'[42] It is the old curse haunting this sector: workers whose lives improve lose their jobs.

Action research is a way of combining education with organising that many organisations have experimented with. Arnel V. Salvador of the Philippine Workers' Assistance Center writes:

In the middle of the 1990s, WAC investigated working conditions in Cavite export processing zone, the largest in the country and one of the four government-owned zones, south of Manila. The research led to the formation of unions in the zone, and we are still providing workers with the updated data. It is still the basic educational material for understanding why working conditions are what they are. Apart from illustrating the exploitative working conditions and absence of worker rights, it shows how everybody in the zone is organised: the investors, the government, the security forces – but not the workers. It also discloses the role of foreign capital and the working of the supply chain.[43]

As part of its campaign on home workers, the Textile, Clothing and Footwear Union of Australia (TCFUA) has set up English-language classes, and provides students with information on sewing skills and health and safety. The women work in 'study circles', and some receive leadership training. The union has also produced a video featuring the women in the programme, and some of them have since become union delegates. Because home-workers are difficult to reach, the union uses the media – especially radio – as well as word of mouth.[44]

In many countries, education is not only a prerequisite for organising, but also one of the few options open to labour-rights advocates. Chinese groups working on the mainland offer workers information about the labour law and help them make use of it. They also give 'pre-departure' training to rural migrants leaving for the cities. For training in factories, they are dependent upon multi-stakeholder initiatives, which provide access and a framework through provisions for worker training in their code of conduct.[45] Where entering factories is not an option, groups stage cultural events and visit workers' dormitories.

In Hong Kong, the Committee for Asian Women managed to unionise cleaning workers – women of the poorest section of society, with low self-esteem and no sense of belonging to the community. The programme began by building a sense of self-respect, instead of plunging headlong into labour rights.[46]

The CCC does not see providing education and training to workers as one of its missions. Nina Ascoly remarks:

Several CCC coalitions have organisations actively involved in support of worker education and other forms of training, and certainly our broader network includes organisations in production countries that are directly involved in worker education; but CCC staff are not sent out to train workers. We pressure brands and retailers to include worker education in codes of conduct. We do some capacity-building workshops and seminars where we provide resources – people or materials. But providing courses for workers is not our core business – not because we think education is not important, but because our resources are limited and our focus needs to remain specific. I think the general feeling is still that we want and need to be an action group.[47]

NORTH AND SOUTH

TIE Asia's Irene Xavier does not mince her words when she talks about the frictions that sometimes arise between Northern and Southern groups. 'There are many groups in Asia who have decided that international campaigns don't work for us', she says.

They accuse them of being oriented towards goals defined by Northern funding agencies instead of Southern needs. There is a feeling that Northern groups are aggressive and dominate the agenda. Not always without reason; but I have seen people from the North who have learned as much as we have, and Southern groups who have become more aggressive in articulating what they want. It is a learning experience for both sides. But it is really important to pay attention to these things. Northerners often don't understand how difficult it can be for us to obtain information. We cannot always depend upon e-mail, not everybody has a mobile phone, and sometimes you have to travel up-country to track someone down. Also, if you want workers and organisers to be involved in international meetings, you have to be sensitive to the issues of language, the complexity of information, and to culture. We always send out people to meet workers who come visiting us; many are travelling for the first time. We make sure they have some money, we offer them a meal. In the South, people like to see your face, meet your family, eat together before talking business. They need to feel at home.[48]

A Haitian labour-rights activist, participating in a workshop on the independent monitoring of company codes in 1998, expressed much the same feeling:

> Independent monitoring is a concept developed in countries with a long history of trade unionism and democracy. In countries without that, it is hard to grasp and you have to find organisations that are interested and capable to do it ... You need tools, like radio and cartoons, and to take it slowly.[49]

North and South may also find themselves at cross-purposes in urgent appeals. Sometimes a union negotiates a compromise, while the CCC would prefer to continue campaigning, as in the case of the dismissed union leader in the Thai Triumph factory. She was fired for wearing a T-shirt on national television with a text that displeased the Thai monarchy. At the end of a 45-day strike, the company and the union agreed to stop the campaign for the leader's reinstatement and leave the decision in the hands of the court. Tessel Pauli comments:

> We thought it was a pity. It was such a clear violation of freedom of expression; the goal was open and we couldn't score. But of course it is hard to continue a strike with 3,000 workers for any length of time – they can't go without income so long. We then made freedom of association the focus of the appeal, but it wasn't as strong. But of course we didn't want to operate on our own, and the risks for the union and the workers prevailed. It's not a question of who decides; you have to be able to carry a common strategy and bring it to a good end.[50]

Nina Ascoly stresses the value of stable relationships between organisations involved in a campaign:

> We can't work with partners on the ground unless there is trust. It takes time. Our long-term commitment is important; we're in it for the long haul. A second principle is that we don't operate in a hierarchical way. We are serious about making decisions together. I'm a professional optimist; I think the world can become better. You meet many cynical people along the way but our partners, who face repression and have sacrificed so much personally, are still working for change. I've always felt privileged to be involved in their struggle.

8
Consumers

'Where can I buy clean clothes?'

It is always the first question consumers ask when they are confronted with images of sweatshops and information about starvation wages and exhaustive working days in the garment industry. No wonder: when anti-sweatshop campaigns approach them as shoppers, they will ask questions about buying. No wonder, either, that they are confused when the CCC tells them that there are no clean clothes to be bought because, unlike coffee or bananas, clothes are not yet decently and sustainably produced in quantity. From there, the message becomes even more complicated, and it is amazing that clothes campaigns can be successful at all, dealing as they do with fun themes like production chains, multi-stakeholder initiatives and trade relations; denying the dazed consumers the gratification of a feel-good, cool and conscious brand, and asking them instead to pester retail and brand company management with questions about the origin of their merchandise.

Nevertheless, the efforts of the network to mobilise consumers are considered necessary and successful – by activists themselves, by governments and civil society that support the network financially, and not least by the brands and retail companies targeted. They find the links between themselves and the workers in supplying factories – so effectively blurred in the process of globalisation – laid bare by campaigns that use the internet, research reports, rallies, and other types of mass communication. In the words of one group of anti-sweatshop campaigners: 'globalisation enables manufacturers to shift their production sites to avoid militant workers, but they cannot so easily avoid militant consumers'.[1] Consumer pressure has proved to be a powerful weapon. Still, public interest in buying 'clean clothes' persists, and it is always difficult to answer this specific question without losing the public's interest and engagement.

FAIR TRADE

A well-known strategy that appeals to 'ethical consumers' is fair trade. Initiated in the field of agricultural products like coffee and fruit by non-profit importers, western retailers and small producers in the 1950s, fair trade has grown into a multimillion-dollar business. The basic idea is to support disadvantaged producers by paying them a fair and guaranteed price for their produce, plus a premium that enables them to build producer capacity and meet minimum social and environmental standards. Market access is provided through links with 'ethical consumers'; middlemen are eliminated as much as possible.

Initially, fair trade products used to be sold only in niche markets like Third World shops, charity shops and solidarity networks. To increase sales and expand distribution to mainstream retailers without losing consumers' trust, the Dutch fair trade organisation Max Havelaar introduced a certification label in 1988 that was followed by many others. In 1998, the Fairtrade Labelling Organizations International (FLO), and subsequently its Fairtrade Certification Mark, introduced in 2002, facilitated the next step: cross-border harmonisation and distribution. Fair trade coffee, bananas and a host of other products were now for sale in major supermarkets.[2]

Fair trade and the CCC have always been close, and have cooperated on many occasions. When Dutch fair trade groups became aware of the limitations of fair trade in the garment industry, they were instrumental in launching the 'original' Dutch Clean Clothes Campaign, and this was repeated by several European CCCs. Many of them, while prioritising the strategy of pressuring brands, have fair trade organisations in their platforms and work together in campaigns. Malin Eriksson, coordinator of the Swedish CCC *Rena Kläder*, says:

> Our member the Fair Trade Association has worked with the Fair Trade Cities concept, in which a steering group of politicians, companies, institutions and civilians tries to convince their city government to buy fair trade products. We are now expanding the concept and want people to look beyond fair trade products to ethical demands in everything the cities procure.[3]

Fair trade organisations make up a large part of the outer and inner platform of the Italian CCC Abiti Puliti. Two fair trade organisations support Abiti Puliti financially with part of their textiles sales, and Abiti Puliti is involved in awareness-raising and training organised by member organisations. In Switzerland, according to CCC coordinator Stefan Indermühle, fair trade is a characteristic aspect of the identity of Berne Declaration, the NGO that is in large part responsible for Swiss CCC strategy and activities.

> In the 1970s, Berne Declaration was an initiator of the fair trade movement in our country; the first fair trade coffee was poured in its offices. The fair trade organisation is a platform member of the CCC. Fair trade products have a relatively large share of the Swiss market; we're used to seeing fair trade as an alternative. In the garment sector we have had organic cotton since the 1990s; we are open to ethical alternatives in the entire supply chain.[4]

Despite these close ties, the CCC chooses other strategic paths. The fair trade label for shops, discussed in the first years of the CCC's existence, was abandoned when it became clear that fair trade in textiles and clothes invariably meets with the limitation that worker cooperatives – the production model on which fair trade labelling is built – are scarce in the apparel industry.[5] Virtually every garment worker is an employee, and improving employees' working conditions can only be successful if the industry itself reforms. Ineke Zeldenrust says:

> Creating a new, fair-trade brand takes an enormous investment, and it is a hard market to begin with. From a labour-rights activist's point of view, fair trade is a difficult and expensive strategy. Campaigns that target brands and retailers can have more impact, with fewer resources. Reputation damage is much more cost-effective.[6]

RATING AND RANKING

'Rating and ranking' of companies on their CSR performance is a way of raising awareness among consumers. It shows which companies are ahead and which are lagging behind. It is also an issue that has generated many debates in the CCC, revolving around the question of whether it is possible to profile and evaluate companies without seeming to endorse the best of them. Endorsing companies is not the role of the campaign, argue opponents of rating and ranking, and in this industry CSR performance is unreliable. Stefan Indermühle is of a different opinion:

> Dividing the good from the bad guys is a means of having impact. It satisfies the public and it puts pressure on companies.

Whether companies can use it in advertising depends on our own communication and wording. When we rated Swiss companies, we used the traffic light colours red, orange and green, and even green didn't mean the company was perfect. When we talk to the media, we emphasise what is wrong. No company ever used it in ads – it just didn't happen. We don't even rule out the possibility of a company label – a kind of quality-mark to signify that the company is transparent and accountable for complying with standards in its supply chain, and that local worker representatives are involved in verification of audit outcomes. I think this fits in with the CCC approach, and gives companies the stimulus they need.[7]

Several other European CCCs have used 'rating and ranking' in one form or another. Italy has a 'Critical Guide on the Garment Sector', based on brand research, which gives information about more than 90 companies and is very successful, according to Deborah Lucchetti of Abiti Puliti. Although the issue of public access and campaigning on rating and ranking remains controversial, at the end of 2008 most CCCs were feeding data from their national brand companies into a general European company database, parts of which are accessible on the internet.[8]

ETHICAL BRANDS

'Sweat-free' or 'ethical' brands are brands that order their products in the regular industry. Some of them certify only one or a few stages of production; some claim that the labelled clothes or shoes are completely sweat-free.

Parts of the anti-sweatshop movement, among them the CCC, do not endorse these labels, specifically when their claim is to be '100 per cent sweat-free'. According to them it is now still impossible to certify 'sweat-free' in any meaningful way in the regular industry, because this is so heavily subcontracted and 'footloose'. Clothes decently produced in Bangkok today may be subcontracted to home-workers in a village tomorrow. While any self-respecting brand these days wields a code of conduct and has auditing firms checking its implementation, general compliance with the core labour standards of the ILO is nowhere near being achieved, and neither is a sector-wide control structure in which workers are represented. Multi-stakeholder initiatives (MSIs), in which companies, unions and NGOs combine forces to develop credible control mechanisms, are considered to be a step forward, but intentions and reality are still too far apart for MSI member companies to be considered 'clean'. There is so far no basis for the credible certification of factories or brands, and to stick a label on them would serve the company and consumers' conscience, but not the interests of employees. Moreover, say the sceptics, even if a particular 'sweat-free' label succeeds in maintaining a supply chain with decent working conditions, business will continue as usual in the rest of the sector. 'One rack of clean clothes in a sea of dirty ones', says Ineke Zeldenrust, 'will lull consumers' conscience, while structural change recedes over the horizon.'[9]

Nina Ascoly, global campaign coordinator at the CCC's International Secretariat, sighs when the subject of ethical brands comes up.

> They are mushrooming and shaping the market we are working in. Some are multinationals with enormous PR machines and cutting-edge marketing techniques, some are small worker cooperatives, some are in between, and they all approach consumers with very different messages. Some genuinely support workers' rights, others are just after a niche market. We'll never, ever have a simple message like 'buy this'. In this we'll always be at a disadvantage compared to brands that offer consumers the easy way out of buying a responsible product. We'll have to accept that; it's because we want to see real change on the ground. Who said that was going to be easy?[10]

Most multi-stakeholder initiatives, though they would greatly benefit from product or company labels, have not yet launched them. Only Social Accountability International (SAI) certifies companies, using its SA8000 standards as a benchmark – but it does not allow a 'sweat-free' label on clothes. The UK-based Ethical Trading Initiative (ETI) explicitly rules out certification on the grounds of the extremely complex supply lines, and because inputs from governments and other legal bodies are indispensable but lacking. ETI also expresses the fear that companies in search of certification would shun the notorious countries, where as a consequence business would continue as usual. The American Fair Labor Association (FLA) accredits companies for having an adequate labour standards compliance programme in place – but no more. The Dutch-based Fair Wear Foundation (FWF) allows hangtags in clothes to certify that the brand company is working towards the FWF standards, although it does not rule out the possibility that a certified clothes label will one day be justified for companies with stable and short supply chains, provided that there is complete transparency and independent verification of their claims.[11]

Despite the challenges to credible certification, several 'sweat-free' initiatives have been launched. Some start up as small, alternative stores or brands that claim to have short and stable supply lines. Some echo the 'Look for the Union Label' campaign of the nineteenth-century American labour movement, and certify clothes that have been made in unionised workplaces. Interestingly Jeff Ballinger, an anti-sweatshop veteran and pioneer of the Nike Watch campaign, is now vice-president of the sourcing and policy department of Bienestar International Inc., owner of the No Sweat Apparel brand. It promises customers 100 per cent union-made, sweat-free shopping, and fair fashion at fair prices. Analogous to the 'open source code' in the computer world, it calls itself an 'open source' apparel brand, showing off its suppliers, which purportedly pay workers a living wage, are happy with unions, and provide decent working conditions.[12] Frustration made Ballinger change his tack, he said in an interview: 'Corporations will not get the message to their contractors that they have to reform. I've discovered that businesses that keep direct control of their production are nowhere near as exploitative.'[13]

Bienestar outsources production in the US, Canada and several developing countries. In 2005, despite its good intentions, an audit of one of its suppliers discovered the same non-compliance with decent work standards as occurs at 'normal' factories – which was to be expected, say critics in the anti-sweatshop movement, since it concerned a 'normal' factory, owned by the multinational Bata. The violations were published on No Sweat's website, and remedial steps were taken.[14]

Ballinger is not the only one disappointed at the results of voluntary regulation of the industry. Parts of the anti-sweatshop movement, especially in the US, are discussing fair-trade-associated ideas that might lead them out of the dilemmas raised by the strategies followed so far. Rattled by the eternal demand for sweat-free clothes, disappointed by the meagre results of codes and compliance mechanisms, and defeated by the flight of brands after the successful unionisation of factories, a number of organisations – including the International Labor Rights Fund (ILRF), Worker Rights Consortium (WRC) and SweatFree Communities – are considering other options. They are looking for models that enable certification of sweat-free suppliers, create 'parallel markets' for conscientious consumers, and establish links between producers and consumers that will guarantee producers a fair price and stable orders. Unlike the fair trade model, these concepts do not focus on disadvantaged producers. Their emphasis is on worker empowerment and union representation as the primary criteria for certification.

One of these new models was developed by Worker Rights Consortium, an organisation the CCC often collaborates with. WRC originated in the American organisation United Students Against Sweatshops, and was set up to monitor code compliance in factories producing logo apparel for American colleges and universities. Jeremy Blasi has worked for WRC since the beginning. 'The most common complaint WRC receives', he says,

> is firing or harassment of protest leaders who try to organise workers. It is amazing how that functions almost as a rule. It is important not just to undo the damage to the individual, but to show the workforce that they can exercise their rights, and the single best way to do this is have the fired leaders walk back into the factory.[15]

That, however, is not a regular outcome.

> The story most often told is the one about the Kukdong factory in Mexico. In 2001, it was the first case we worked on. After we got Nike and Reebok to use their leverage with the factory to reinstate workers who had been fired because of a strike, the workers founded the first independent union in the maquiladora sector.[16] A breakthrough. Just recently a second maquila factory got a functioning independent union that negotiated a collective bargaining agreement. In between, there has been a whole series of factories where workers tried to establish a union and companies closed down. That is why we have developed the Designated Supplier Programme.

Under this programme, university licensees would be required to source university logo apparel from supplier factories that had been verified to be in compliance with their obligation to respect the rights of their employees – including the right to organise and bargain collectively, and the right to a living wage. Licensees would have to enable suppliers to comply with the standards by paying them adequately, and by stable and sufficient ordering. At the end of 2008, WRC was gathering support for this programme among its 175 affiliated universities and colleges.[17]

The strategic preferences of the CCC concerning 'ethical brands' have led to controversies with organisations that set their sights on the development of a brand such as Solidaridad, a Dutch NGO with a fair trade background. Since the late 1990s, Solidaridad has tried to establish ethical labels for clothes in the Netherlands, as well as an organisation of ethical clothes companies, called Made-By. The aim is to combine the fair trade niche market with impact on mainstream companies.[18]

Nico Roozen is director of Solidaridad. Foremost in his mind are scale, volume, and getting mainstream companies to move towards decent standards.

> Sustainable production depends not only on standards; we consider the level of their acceptance in the sector to be at least as important. The ethical standard in itself doesn't say anything about effectiveness. In the end, it is the models that force the big players to commit that are relevant to our goals. You have to adapt to the specific situation, find the best starting point, set a bottom level for standards, and try to create upward pressure. We think that if you want everybody to join, you have to accept low initial standards.[19]

Clothes first appeared in Solidaridad's projects in 1998. One reason for that, says Roozen, is that cotton is one of the most important agricultural products, and as such is an obvious choice for Solidaridad, since the organisation focuses on sustainable agricultural development. But to involve consumers, you need an end product – namely clothes. There is also a historical reason.

> In spite of the fact that organic and fair-trade coffee had improved incomes and infrastructure in our first coffee farmers' cooperative, the younger generation was migrating to the cities. We began thinking about industrial development in the area, and since there was already some experience in sewing, several small clothes factories were set up. The idea was to produce for the local market and for export. We needed a fair-trade jeans brand.

This led to the foundation in 2001 of Kuyichi, conceived as a fair-trade clothes brand. After ten years, this has not yet been realised. 'The world of manufacturing is more complicated than I thought', wrote Roozen in 2001.[20] Kuyichi ran up against the hard facts of the fashion industry: to launch a brand, just one flagship jeans brand is not enough. Specialists say that a new brand has no chance of survival unless it positions itself in the top segment of the market, and has at least ten styles each for men and women, in 25 sizes, plus a collection of 120 'tops': sweaters, T-shirts, shirts, turtlenecks, jackets.

This went way beyond the scope of the Kuyichi production facilities, even when Brazilian and Guatemalan production locations were added. Apart from the problems raised by volume and quality demands, there were no integrated production chains. Without facilities for spinning, weaving and dyeing, without suppliers of accessories, everything must be imported, making the clothes expensive. In a world of fierce competition, this was almost a recipe for failure. 'Production in Latin America', says Roozen, 'is expensive compared to Asia. The textile sector in Latin America is struggling and can only survive in the high-quality niche market. We succeeded in Peru, not in Mexico.' Kuyichi clothes are now produced in Turkey, Peru, Tunisia, India, China and Italy. Almost half of them are made from certified organic cotton. On 'social certification', meaning compliance with labour standards, Kuyichi scores low – even lower in 2007 than in 2006, due to a reduction in the number of compliant suppliers, for various reasons.[21]

You can't change from black to white in one day. To be 100 per cent 'pure' right away is not the point; you must state your ambitions and be straight about progress. If we want consumers to play their part, we must develop models that give them a choice. Producers also need these niche markets with higher prices; without them they will not be able to increase wages or pay for better working conditions. They need the money, and the perspective that change is possible.

True to its ambition for an integrated approach, Solidaridad is also active on corporate social responsibility. Roozen comments:

With Made-By, an umbrella organisation of apparel brands, we are developing a model that aims to give consumers a choice, and brands the chance to work towards acting responsibly. At this moment 25 mostly small Dutch brands are affiliated. A blue button on the clothes' care label or hang tag communicates this to consumers.[22] I think it is inevitable that companies doing their best at corporate social responsibility want customers to know this. They need to take advantage of their effort. Enforcement and policing alone are not enough: companies must see added value. The CCC is always promoting the empowerment of workers, struggle, unions and so on; in my view that is only half the agenda.

The name Made-By, says Roozen, signals that the organisation does not present affiliated companies as fair or clean, just as companies with ambitions for ecological and social standards. It presents the level of realisation of these ambitions on the internet – in particular with its Track & Trace system, and with scorecards. Track & Trace is a database that (ideally) contains data about all production stages of particular pieces of clothing. A code on the label in the clothes gives access to these data on the internet, enabling consumers to follow the production chain backwards. Track & Trace, even if it is watertight (which Made-By's website says it will never be), has the drawback that consumers can only check the level of 'fairness' of the product after they have bought it, and only if they have a computer at their disposal.[23] A glance at the scorecards of the affiliated companies on the website shows that most of them still have a long way to go. Some of the world's giants, like Nike, H&M and Gap, do better – and they were confronted with full-blown campaigns based on ILO standards, not a stepping-stone, low-standards approach. 'I think that the level of compliance of our member companies is not the point', says Roozen, 'as long as we are transparent.'

The yearly scorecards of member companies on Made-By's website show what percentage of the collection of a brand is included in the Track & Trace database, plus the percentage of organic cotton a brand uses, plus the percentage of clothes made by 'certified' suppliers – although the term 'certified' is not quite justified since, for example, neither the Fair Wear Foundation nor the Ethical Trade Initiative feel confident that they can fully certify any one garment company. Made-By accepts all social codes, certification systems and memberships of social initiatives – even the ones scoring low on its own ranking list. It ranks them according to a benchmark that includes criteria like contents, multi-stakeholder character and transparency. Roozen says:

Fair Wear Foundation, Social Accountability and the Ethical Trading Initiative qualify among the best-in-class. The Business

Social Compliance Initiative ranks lower, while the Worldwide Responsible Accredited Production falls in the lowest category. Although BSCI is not a genuine multi-stakeholder initiative and has no independent verification, we will do pilot projects with it. I am even a member of its advisory board. I see a positive dynamic and I think BSCI can be a stepping stone towards SAI.

Solidaridad actively intervenes in production chains and builds partnerships with companies.

In India we have developed a new type of production chain by making a farmers' cooperative shareholder of the sewing factory that uses the farmers' organic cotton. We think it strengthens the farmers' position and assures the factory of a steady and good-quality supply of cotton. We support training of workers and management, and help companies when they have solvency problems. When a Peruvian factory owner couldn't raise the capital for improvement of social and environmental performance, we found a Dutch investor, a member of Made-By, willing to become a shareholder. We try to change the balance of power in the production chain by being partners in the process of change. Of course, you have to see to it that employees benefit. The CCC keeps telling us that helping individual companies is small beer, that it will have no impact on the driving forces behind the abuses in the sector. But I believe that enlightened entrepreneurs can set an example and generate upward pressure on standards in the production chain.

In recent discussions about ethical label strategies, the CCC continues to emphasise the importance of not lowering standards because, in their view, companies that perform poorly – or even well – against low standards should not be allowed a stamp of approval in the eyes of the public. The CCC professes always to push for the ILO standards, and is convinced that the strategies it employs leave companies ample room to get it right and set an example for the sector. It considers that supporting individual enterprises is not the task of an NGO.

SUSTAINABLE PRODUCTION

There is one urgent issue leading a rather shadowy existence in both the anti-sweatshop and fair trade movements: the consequences of unbridled economic growth for the earth's resources, for the natural environment, and in the end for people as well.

Garment manufacture may not be a highly energy-intensive industry in itself, but – to mention just a few points – its insatiable need for cotton, one of the most polluting and 'thirsty' agricultural products, and the daily hauling of tons of clothes across the globe cannot be considered sustainable. The speed with which clothes collections change on retailers' racks fills the observer with admiration for marketing departments: How on earth do they seduce people to buy all those jeans, sweaters and shirts? Whatever happened to the pride people used to have in taking care of their clothes and making them last ten years? Whatever happened to the love people felt towards that particular red dress, their black-and-white jacket, those warm gloves, and to the reluctance with which they parted with them after they had finally fallen apart?

Questioning pollution, overproduction and overconsumption raises a fundamental dilemma: it seems incompatible with improving the lives of Southern producers. Doug Miller, former head of research of the global union ITGLWF, and now professor of ethical fashion at the University of Northumbria, says:

> It is true that there is massive overconsumption in clothing, particularly in the buying countries, and there has been a response from some quarters – see Kate Fletcher's work on slow fashion and alternative fabrics. What of course is not thought through is the impact true sustainable fashion would have on employment levels in the sector.[24]

Kate Fletcher is a designer involved in sustainable fashion, primarily defined in ecological terms. On her website she writes:

> For too long environmentalists have treated fashion as an irrelevance, an unnecessary extravagance and the chief cause of escalating consumption levels. We think that this neglects the power and influence of fashion (for good as well as bad). And for too long the fashion sector has been indifferent to what happens to a garment beyond the point of purchase. We think that transforming people's relationships with their clothes can empower them, fuel personal creativity and reduce environmental impact.[25]

Carole Crabbé, coordinator of Vêtements Propres, puts it this way:

> In the 2009 Better Bargain campaign targeting giant retailers,[26] it will be difficult to include issues like the impact of big stores on small ones, the lifestyle aspect, and discussions about consumerism and overproduction. There is a fear that this line of thinking will endanger jobs in the garment industry, because in the end the question is: who needs so many clothes? There is a resistance to opening this debate; people are afraid it will lead to conflict with our partners in production countries. It also touches on the question whether we are part of the movement of 'alter-globalisation', which explores the relationships between reducing economic growth on the one hand, and reducing poverty and inequality on the other. That leads to all sorts of other questions. Is it good or bad that people in developing countries remain peasants? What about urbanisation and migration to the cities? It is a dangerous road for the CCC, because our sharp and singular focus has been important for our effectiveness. That is why, instead of expanding our scope in the Better Bargain campaign, we push for a coalition with the environmental movement, with campaigns on other products like food and electronics, and with the 'alter-globalists'.[27]

This is a strategic choice already outlined during the 2001 global CCC meeting in Barcelona. The report reads:

> At the Barcelona meeting it was confirmed that across the board there is a strong feeling that the CCC needs to take on environmental concerns in the context of garment and textile production, because these issues are linked to the social issues we currently tackle, and because this will broaden and strengthen the CCC's base of support. However, given the capacity problems ... and the importance of maintaining focus, the conclusion is that we will take up this work through cooperation with other, environmentally focused networks, and not as a central activity of this network. The work that is done on the promotion of organic cotton, involving member organisations of the CCC, is a good example.[28]

The Italian CCC Abiti Puliti explores yet another way to deal with these dilemmas. Coordinator Deborah Lucchetti comments:

A garment campaign is not only about labour rights, it is also a cultural struggle about who defines our identities. Do we give in to companies that need us to buy new stuff every month? Do the brands dictate what we wear or can we decide for ourselves? But we can't tackle this issue without concluding that the industry has to be overthrown, which doesn't go too well with labour-rights activism. So we work on alternatives, parallel to the fight for better working conditions.

Lucchetti is also president of FAIR, a fair trade organisation that is a CCC platform member. It supports the construction of a new supply chain of small enterprises in the Piemonte region that produces with social and environmental standards and a strong producer–consumer connection.

It started when a young entrepreneur called Gianluca Bruzzese, who had inherited his father's specialised tailor shop, contacted my fair trade organisation. He was fed up with producing for the big brands, which paid him 1 euro for a man's bathing suit they sold for 80. He felt he was losing out not only on money, but also on skills and dignity. He wanted to put his enterprise on a new footing. The Province of Novara was willing to supply funds and credit for a project that aimed to help small Italian textile and garment producers escape from the negative spiral of globalisation.

Our roadmap involved partnership with organic and fair trade farmers of cotton and other raw materials; the introduction of 'fair' criteria in the supply chain like fair and transparent pricing and producer pre-financing; a direct relationship between producer and consumers establishing the demand for clean clothes; sales through small shops, fair trade shops, solidarity groups and fairs; and the concept of consumption on the basis of daily and essential needs, not for reasons of growth. At the start of the project, in 2007, the CCC organised training on working conditions in the garment industry for all participants; you might say that the CCC has been an inspiring framework. We held at least 30 meetings with grassroots groups all over Italy to explain and promote the concept, and managed to involve over 100 'solidarity purchasing groups'. Most of them pre-financed production by paying 50 per cent of their orders in advance.

Of some importance was the establishment of a partnership with the Brazilian network of 'solidarity economy' Justa Trama, which consists of family cooperatives that produce textiles and garments for the national market. FAIR buys their organic cotton, and will provide them with access to the Italian fair trade market for their garments, allowing them the added value of finished products.

We established fair prices throughout the supply chain and, by cutting the costs of advertising, marketing and retailing, also for consumers. A woman's slip costs 7 euros. The families and consumer groups that order underwear directly at the workplaces – after having conferred with the artisans about materials and design – get it 20 per cent cheaper. In 2008 we began to sell 'clean' underwear, and by August, 30 per cent of Gianluca Bruzzese's turnover was produced and sold as 'clean'.[29]

9
Hard Law

Labour rights are human rights. Freedom of association and the right to collective bargaining, the right not to be discriminated against or exploited in forced or child labour, the right to decent work with a decent wage and decent hours, to freedom from occupational health and safety risks – they are all human rights. The international community agrees on this; the problem is implementation, especially in countries where political and civil rights are lacking.

At the turn of the century, a 'social clause' in trade agreements was proposed as 'hard' regulation. This clause, which would trigger trade sanctions against countries that violated labour rights, generated heated debate. In the CCC network, parts of the trade union movement were in favour, because the clause offered a chance to sanction labour-rights violations. Many Southern partners were adamantly against it. They used the metaphor of 'the knife in the bread': by eating the 'bread' of the sanctions, they would also have to swallow the 'knife' of the trade framework embedding the social clause. And they were not prepared to swallow, for example, the World Trade Organisation. J. John, executive director of the Centre for Education and Communication, an Indian CCC partner organisation, said:

> Even if we were to accept that the clause was not a protectionist tool of western industries and was meant to bolster labour standards against the effects of trade liberalisation, this is not the task of the World Trade Organisation. Its mandate is to make profit through trade. There are two agencies that should enforce the rights of workers: national government and the ILO.[1]

Internally divided, the CCC took a neutral stance in the debate. The social clause did not materialise in a significant way.

Decent working conditions are still not available for millions of people. Southern labour-rights organisations are sounding the alarm about the increasing deregulation of labour relations in the supply chain; about the growing number of workers with only short-term contracts, or none; about home-workers; about all those who get flipped in and out of production processes at the whim of corporations' ordering regimes. In the mantra 'People, Planet, Profit', which seems seamlessly to unite three forces that in everyday reality are generally at odds with each other, profit has a tendency to get the upper hand when there are no universally accepted rules of engagement, nor sanctions when those rules are broken – in short: hard law. While, in the long run, a 'level playing field' would benefit business, the prospects of short-term profits make the corporate world resist the international framework of dos and don'ts that would create it. In its 2003 study of CSR and supply chains, the World Bank concluded that

> government action has the benefit of rationalizing market forces by creating a 'level playing field'; it spreads costs across the breadth of society, provides a formal and public means of recourse when standards are not met, creates an environment in which other initiatives can be tried and can succeed, and should avoid the lowering of standards ... Systemic progress will not happen unless governments get involved more vitally.[2]

While the call for hard law and binding regulation has been a constant in the anti-sweatshop movement, progress is slow. Some successes have been recorded in the area of public procurement. In Belgium, the Netherlands, Sweden and Spain, for example, CCCs have convinced public authorities of cities, provinces and even whole countries to buy work-wear for their personnel from companies that verifiably adhere to fair labour standards. Carole Crabbé, coordinator of the Belgian CCC Vêtements Propres, says:

> We have been lobbying the European parliament on this and have gotten a strong Belgian position. Because the directives still leave too much room for interpretation and escape, we are launching a campaign with a Europe-wide organisation of cities to lobby authorities about implementation.[3]

In other areas, advances in labour legislation are sluggish. The main reason for this is the tough resistance from companies, as well as governments; another is the amount of time and resources that are needed even just to find a way into the legal fortresses erected to regulate society – let alone to redecorate some of their inner corridors and chambers. Nevertheless, the clean clothes movement has entered the fortresses and scouted the floors. The following pages are by no means exhaustive; they highlight those developments that are considered promising, and that have given rise to debates in the movement.

LITIGATION

The most attractive option in terms of catching public attention is perhaps that of indicting companies for breaking existing law. It is not a regular practice, however, and successes are few. The complexity of a subcontracted industry, the limited liability of companies, and restricted state jurisdiction combine to make it difficult – particularly when the abuse has taken place in production countries. Nonetheless, several cases have been brought before the court, mainly in Europe, Australia and the US. The aim is usually to win compensation for victims of labour-rights violations, and sometimes also to develop international law through precedent. Some examples follow.

In the US, a group called IRAdvocates has explored the possibilities of the Alien Tort Claims Act, a 200-year-old law also used in the famous Saipan case.[4] It gives US courts jurisdiction to hear cases of violations of customary international law occurring anywhere in the world, as long as the US courts have jurisdiction over the defendant. 'Customary international law' covers a limited range of charges of severe human rights abuses. Because this strategy has limits, IRAdvocates is also opening up new avenues, as in the case of *Jane Doe et al.* v. *Wal-Mart Stores Inc.* A suit was filed in September 2005 on behalf of workers from China, Bangladesh, Indonesia, Swaziland, and Nicaragua, who pressed their common claim that Wal-Mart knowingly used suppliers that systematically deprived workers of the basic provisions of Wal-Mart's code of conduct, including protection by their national labour laws. These workers were joined by employees of Californian enterprises that had lost business through Wal-Mart's unfair labour practices and felt cheated by Wal-Mart's false representations regarding compliance with its code of conduct. This group included trade union members who had been forced to make wage and benefit concessions to allow their employers to compete with Wal-Mart. This class of plaintiffs brought its claim under California's Unfair Business Practices Act. According to IRAdvocates, the case was based on an innovative theory that Wal-Mart's code of conduct created a contract, and that the workers at the supplier factories were third-party beneficiaries of that contract.[5] In 2007 the judge dismissed the claims.

In the context of the Australian Fair Wear Campaign, which took off in 1996, the trade union TCFUA took legal steps against 72 garment companies that violated Australian labour law. Most companies agreed to settle, Nike holding out longest. In 2000, Nike paid a fine of US$5,000 per violation.[6]

A legal standard used under British law is 'duty of care', which applies to individuals as well as organisations. It is used to win compensation in British courts for people living in countries where abuses have occurred, by holding the UK parent companies liable at home. The central issue in these cases is whether the parent company has a 'duty of care' to people affected by the operations of its subsidiaries overseas. Arguments in favour are that parent companies exercise control of operations from their home base; that practices unacceptable in the 'home' country are exported to other countries; and that profits are repatriated. If parent companies are aware of the dangers caused by their practices, but take advantage of lower safety standards in other countries to expose people to greater risks than would be acceptable in the UK, this is a failure of due care. Cases have been won on that basis, but they are very few; usually companies escape any sanction. They fight successfully not on the basis of the facts of the case, but on the technical questions of duty of care – particularly venue (they argue that the case should be tried in the country where the abuse has occurred) and jurisdiction. This use of loopholes in the law lends emphasis to the urgent need for international regulation of corporate accountability.[7]

In the apparel industry, supply-chain relationships between companies are usually less close than parent–subsidiary relationships, and consequently it is more difficult to connect the brand or retailer to the harm done. In these situations, consumer law might offer a way in. Some jurisdictions allow private enforcement action in the courts against companies that make false claims about their social and environmental credentials. The case launched at the end of the 1990s by Mark Kasky against Nike in the Californian courts is the best-known example. Kasky accused Nike of making a profit by telling lies about working conditions in Chinese, Vietnamese and Indonesian supplier factories. Nike settled by paying US$1.5 million to the multi-stakeholder initiative Fair Labor Association. Core, a British coalition dedicated to bringing about laws improving the environment and society at large, wrote:

Extending rights to complain about misleading CSR-related claims could also help deal with a related problem – the tendency of retailers to sign up to voluntary codes relating to supply chain management, and then not enforce them properly (if at all). While retailers can have all the reputational benefits that go with membership of a particular scheme, there is a lack of sanctions for non-compliance, not only with the substantive standards underlying a code, but also the monitoring requirements that go with it.[8]

Although, for workers in production countries, access to legal means is often just theoretical, there are local organisations that endeavour to provide them with it. In mainland China, so-called 'service centres' that are often set up with the help of Hong Kong-based labour groups, provide legal assistance and are sometimes quite effective in using existing law.[9] In the Philippines, which suffers under labour relations fraught with conflict, the Workers' Assistance Center (WAC) does the same. Deputy executive director Arnel Salvador says:

> Conflicts are increasingly accompanied by violence. Legal strikes are forbidden and strikers are beaten up and dismissed. There have been shootings and abductions. One of our missions is to offer free legal assistance to workers and unions that want to file cases against employers. Most of the individual cases we handle concern dismissal, and if employers are open for a dialogue, they are often settled at factory level. When whole factories close down, we have been able in some cases to get higher compensation than mandated by law.[10]

In 2007, WAC provided striking workers at the Chong Won Fashion garment factory – supplying Wal-Mart, among others – with day-to-day support, legal advice and a link to international campaign groups. Despite mass dismissals and police harassment, the workers maintained a picket line for nine months. The combined local and international campaign succeeded in pressuring Wal-Mart to admit that workers' right to freely associate had been violated, and that 117 fired union members should be reinstated. Although this cannot be filed as a legal victory, it serves as a precedent for brand company responsibility. In the end, the owner decided to close the factory rather than deal with the union.[11]

Litigation should not be embarked on lightly. The personal risks may be too much to bear for plaintiffs who find themselves up against powerful companies with money and lawyers to spare. Add to this the usual risk of factory closures and the amount of time and money needed by labour organisations to support plaintiffs, and it becomes clear that seeking justice in a court of law is not always an option.

NATIONAL LEGISLATION

Possibilities of national legislation concerning global impacts of multinational corporations are illustrated by the Belgian effort to establish a 'social label', by the British Companies Act of 2006, and by a type of legislation that raises import barriers for certain products, like a proposal for an American anti-sweatshop law that still has to be passed at the time of writing.

The Belgian law for the promotion of socially responsible production was passed in 2002. It created a product label that companies can apply for. Products that comply with certain social standards based on the ILO core conventions can carry the label, and thus have a commercial advantage.[12] The British NGO Core mentions labels as one of the options for CSR regulation in subcontracted supply chains, and states that a labelling scheme's chances are better when it is supported by consumer awareness – when it does not constitute an illegal trade barrier and is underpinned by international standards. In general, labelling schemes are limited to products, and do not point towards wider legal reform.[13] Carole Crabbé of Vêtements Propres recalls:

> We have created pressure for that law. In the first proposal, the label was based on certification of companies, which we endorsed, but in the parliamentary process that got lost. For the garment industry this was bad, because the complicated supply chain makes product certification impossible.[14]

According to Core, the Companies Act of 2006 constituted the biggest reform of UK company law in 150 years. Together with the Trade Justice Movement, Core contributed by staging a campaign that spurred over 100,000 people to write to their members of parliament calling for regulation of companies. The Act states that companies must consider their impacts on the community, employees and the environment. It links a company's financial performance to its social and environmental impacts. Key concepts are 'directors' duties', whereby company directors can be called to account for company performance, and 'transparency', which obliges publicly listed UK companies to report openly to shareholders on social and environmental risks and opportunities, as well as on employee matters and risks down supply chains.[15]

Some politicians endeavour to develop legislation that bars products from the country for environmental, social or other reasons. In the Netherlands, for example, every five years or so – usually after another child labour scandal has erupted – politicians propose import barriers against products made by children. Their efforts tend to founder on the rocks of trade vetoes. A new example of this kind of 'boycott' legislation is the Decent Working Conditions and Fair Competition Act, introduced in the US Senate in January 2007. The Act – co-sponsored by, among others, Barack Obama and Hillary Clinton, both senators at the time – states as its purpose to prohibit the import, export or sale of sweatshop goods in the US.[16] Such legislation, however, may serve to protect western industries more than production workers. It cannot but result in boycotts of products from developing countries, since western industries have largely transplanted the exploitative layers of production overseas. And how is a sneaker boycott going to help an Indonesian shoe-stitcher? As long as legislation does not explicitly address the balance of power in production chains, its outcome for sweatshop workers is dubious at best.

EUROPEAN LEGISLATION

Legislation on the global impacts of companies was on the European parliament's agenda for the first time in 1999, when it passed a resolution on the accountability of European multinationals. It was proposed by Richard Howitt, British Labour member of the European parliament, and it stated that voluntary codes of conduct should not be a substitute for international regulation. It called for a 'European Monitoring Platform', for hearings on the subject, and for legal measures to monitor multinationals. As history shows, parliamentary resolutions and their implementation are two different matters.

A first hearing was organised in November 2000. Evidence was presented on the sportswear industry in Indonesia, and on the marketing of baby-milk substitute in Pakistan. To the disappointment of the attending civil society representatives, the academic world and the UN, the invited companies Adidas and Nestlé failed to turn up.

In 2001 the European Commission published its views on CSR in a Green Paper. NGOs, trade unions and corporations sent in comments, among them the CCC. It had been appreciated, wrote the CCC, that the European Commission had taken into consideration such established principles of the international debate on corporate accountability as the complementary relationship between 'soft law' measures and legislation, the necessity of addressing supply chains in their entirety, systems of verification, transparency and reporting, and the involvement of new stakeholders in verification systems. Issues not addressed were also pointed out, including binding regulation on a sector-wide scale, mandatory reporting, and the necessity of adapting national law to allow for jurisdiction over transnational corporations.[17] The Directorate-General for Employment and Social Affairs published all reactions on its website. Richard Howitt, now appointed CSR spokesperson for the European parliament, wrote:

> I have been astounded by the level of support from NGOs and campaigning individuals. Last year Amnesty International organised demonstrations in favour of my resolution across Europe for international Labour Day. Baby Milk Action and the Clean Clothes Campaign have consistently promoted the resolution and EU activities in this field on their websites and in newsletters ... Greater public pressure is the fuel and food of a more socially conscious Europe.[18]

In 2002, Howitt proposed a second resolution. In his accompanying speech, he said:

> Next, CSR really must be built into all EU policies and programmes. It is quite breathtaking that the European Commission and the European Investment Bank commit billions of euros of European taxpayers' money each year to the private sector – through contracts, regional aid, investment promotion – yet do not have simple contractual clauses to respect basic labour and environmental standards, nor clear monitoring and complaints procedures to enforce them ... Full, comparable and verified corporate information; an inclusive dialogue for all stakeholders; consistent support across EU policies; genuine responsibility from Europe for the global supply chain of European business; these

are the elements that will truly forge a European framework for corporate social responsibility.[19]

The European parliament agreed, and passed Howitt's resolution that asked for a 'Framework for Corporate Social Responsibility' that would include, among other things, mandatory reporting on the social and environmental performance of companies, and personal liability of companies' board members for that performance. Business should only be awarded financial assistance if it was in compliance with basic standards. Trade and development programmes should tackle abuses committed by companies in developing countries.[20]

The European Commission's answer was disappointing. In July 2002 it chose to emphasise the voluntary nature of CRS. It did not even support mandatory reporting. Instead it extolled the advantages of CSR for companies. It focused on means of sharing best practice, on the promotion of CSR management skills, and on the introduction of an ethical dimension to European procurement policies. As a tool for accomplishing this, a 'multi-stakeholder forum on CSR' is proposed, with representation of businesses, trade unions, consumer groups and NGOs.[21]

After two years of working, this forum proposed a combination of voluntary and binding measures that, if implemented, would have taken corporations a couple of rungs up the ladder of accountability. But the European Commission took two years to respond, and when it finally did, in 2006, the multi-stakeholder approach appeared to have been abandoned. In a communication called 'Implementing the partnership for growth and jobs: making Europe a pole of excellence on corporate social responsibility', the Commission launched a European Alliance on CSR that included only representatives of the business community.

In 2005, in an effort to pool knowledge and resources and formulate a common strategy, over 250 civil society organisations across Europe launched the European Coalition for Corporate Justice (ECCJ). Its mission is 'to promote an ethical regulatory framework for European business, wherever in the world that business may operate', and it coordinates the CSR work of, among others, the Fédération Internationale de Ligues des Droits de l'Homme, national chapters of Oxfam, Greenpeace, Amnesty International, Friends of the Earth, and CSR networks like the German CorA, the British Core and the Dutch CSR Platform.[22]

The ECCJ criticised the new European Commission's stance on CSR:

[T]he Commission has shifted from improving [CSR] performance to increasing competetiveness ... While the Alliance provides the member companies with a European Union stamp of environmental and social excellence, its actual credibility flounders because of a lack of standards, transparency, multi-stakeholder participation and credible monitoring and verification.[23]

A number of policy recommendations advocated the transformation of corporate responsibility as a toothless ideal into a regulated, sanctioned system.

At the end of 2006, the European Commission reconvened the multi-stakeholder forum. Civil society representatives, disappointed about the outcome of the multi-stakeholder process, decided not to attend. In 2007 the European parliament, with an overwhelming majority, passed a third Howitt resolution. It pushed for a combination of voluntary and regulatory approaches to CSR, for multi-stakeholder participation, and for a mechanism by which victims, including third-country nationals, could seek redress against European companies in the national courts of the member-states.[24]

In May 2008, the ECCJ wanted to jump-start the European discussion again by organising, together with the Socialist group of the European parliament, a conference on 'smart regulation'. It published two reports[25] that proposed law reforms intended to create an improved regime for corporate liability in Europe, and which would resemble the British Companies Act described above: extending parent-company liability; establishing duty of care onto parent companies, including company–subcontractor relationships; and mandatory social and environmental reporting. Liability would apply to companies as well as to their directors. In his opening speech at the conference, Richard Howitt commented that the European Commission had

decided to adopt a definition of CSR as 'beyond compliance', which – by definition – excludes regulation ... No-one ... that I know suggests taking companies to court can be the principal way to regulate corporate behaviour. But 24 years after the Bhopal disaster in which at least 18,000 people died, and where still no one has ever faced a judge, who can deny that resort to litigation must be present for the very worst violations? And for those that argue exterritorial jurisdiction ... is both legally and politically unacceptable, let me remind you it is a matter of political will.

We've done it for over 100 years on maritime law. Of course we do it on war crimes. More recently we've chosen to do it in fighting corruption and in combating so-called sex tourism ... The ultimate aim of campaigners must surely still be to get an international convention on corporate accountability.[26]

After a promising beginning, the European road revealed itself to be a long and winding one. Ineke Zeldenrust comments:

While we consider 'hard law' on labour rights an urgent necessity and working towards it is one of our missions, the work is frustrating because processes are mostly slow and unfruitful. Since about 2003, we see little political will in the European context to give CSR a basis in law. But as long as this continues and parliamentary resolutions are not implemented, they at least have public-relations value. [The unimplemented resolutions] serve to bolster our arguments in the media.[27]

OECD GUIDELINES

The complaint we filed under the OECD Guidelines cost an inordinate amount of time and energy and had very disappointing results. The process is slow and bureaucratic, has no binding consequences for the company involved and we were pressured into confidentiality – while we are a campaigning organisation. Keeping the public informed is one of our main missions.[28]

Christa de Bruin, coordinator of the Dutch CCC, will think twice before embarking on that path again.

The OECD Guidelines for Multinational Enterprises, adopted in 1976 and revised in 2000, are a set of voluntary principles and standards jointly addressed by governments of OECD countries to multinational enterprises operating in or from their countries.[29] The Guidelines cannot be described as 'global' because they do not apply to multinationals based in non-adhering states – including, for example, China, Malaysia, Russia and India. The 30 member-countries and nine non-members that have adopted the Guidelines are nevertheless home to the majority of privately owned multinational companies.

The Guidelines cover an array of issues, including the environment, science and technology, consumer protection, disclosure of information, anti-corruption, human rights, employment, and industrial relations. ILO standards underpin all four fundamental labour rights – namely freedom of association and the right to collective bargaining, the effective abolition of child labour, the elimination of all forms of forced or compulsory labour, and non-discrimination in employment and occupation. The employment chapter includes clauses such as training, handling of complaints, and prior notice to workers in cases of major changes, but has no provisions on working hours, employment contracts or living wages. The revisions of 2000 highlight the responsibilities of companies when doing business internationally, like the guideline that says a company should not threaten to transfer production from a country to influence negotiations between employer and employees unfairly, or hinder the right to organise.

The OECD has two advisory committees, one from the business world and one from the international trade union movement.[30] While there are no sanctions against companies violating the Guidelines, each endorsing government must set up a national contact point (NCP) to oversee implementation, and in this respect the Guidelines are a step towards binding regulation. NCPs differ in structure, but are often located in trade or foreign ministries. They are responsible for publicising the Guidelines, promoting adherence, and reviewing complaints against companies – euphemistically called 'specific instances'. Once an NCP has received a 'specific instance' and deems it admissible, it first sets out to mediate between the complainants and the company. If a violation is established, the NCP must offer recommendations to remedy the problem. If the parties cannot agree upon a resolution, the NCP is expected to publicise its findings.[31]

The German CCC ran a complaint against Adidas in 2003, concerning violations of the Guidelines in two Indonesian supplier factories. Although the outcome was disappointing, the German CCC considered it a 'useful exercise'. The acceptance of the complaint set a precedent for corporate responsibility in the supply chain, and Adidas's acknowledgement of the allegations about wages and working hours set another. The CCC argued from the beginning that the Guidelines should follow the ILO conventions on wages and hours of work, since low wages compel workers to work overtime, thereby leading to cases of de facto forced labour.[32]

Of course, every 'useful exercise' ends with recommendations, and the German ones found their way into the evaluation of OECD Watch – an international network that, among other things, tests the effectiveness of the Guidelines. Its 2005 Report, *Five Years On*, assembled the lessons learned by NGOs since the 2000 revision. Since that time, NGOs had registered 45 complaints; in only one of them had the timely intervention of an NCP averted conflict.[33] Its general conclusion was that

> there is no conclusive evidence that the Guidelines have had a positive, comprehensive impact on multinational enterprises. Furthermore, there is no evidence that the Guidelines have helped to reduce the number of conflicts between local communities, civil society groups and foreign investors. As a global mechanism to improve the operations of multinationals, the Guidelines are simply inadequate and deficient. Without the threat of effective sanctions, there is little incentive for companies to ensure their operations are in compliance with the Guidelines. Therefore, OECD Watch believes that governments must establish legally binding, international social and environmental standards and corporate accountability frameworks.[34]

Southern civil society groups, especially, appear to be sceptical – not only because of the lack of sanctions, but also because their access to the complaints procedure is poor. Where western NGOs complain about the time and money needed to gather evidence and be involved in a procedure that takes years, for Southern groups these restrictions are multiplied by the thousands of miles between them and the NCP offices, and between them and multinationals' headquarters. Still, many are interested in using the Guidelines as a potential tool of empowerment, and Friends of the Earth Netherlands has put together a toolkit that explains how the complaint procedure can be used.[35]

Governments have done little to promote the Guidelines. Transparency International Germany states that 'the German NCP and the OECD Guidelines are one of the country's best kept secrets'.[36] The OECD's own efforts to analyse implementation of the Guidelines have been hampered by the unwillingness of NCPs to share information. Not until 2004 was the OECD Secretariat permitted to set up a central register of cases, and even then many NCPs withheld names of companies, and even the nature of the complaints. The victim is transparency, especially since NCPs demand confidentiality once mediation has started.[37]

It seems that, despite the lack of sanctions, companies balk at the prospect of a 'specific instance' being raised against them, and NCPs are not strong enough to overcome their resistance. According to John Ruggie, special representative to the UN Secretary-General for business and human rights:

> The housing of some NCPs primarily or wholly within government departments tasked with promoting business, trade and investment raises questions about conflicts of interest. NCPs often lack the resources to undertake adequate investigation of complaints and the training to provide effective mediation. There are typically no time frames for the commencement or completion of the process, and outcomes are often not publicly reported. In sum, many NCP processes appear to come up short.[38]

So it seems that, if the OECD Guidelines are to benefit workers in any significant way, there will have to be a radical overhaul of the NCPs' modus operandi. OECD Watch recommends strengthening of NCPs' capacity, enabling them to investigate and independently assess complaints; strengthening of the scope of the Guidelines to include supply-chain issues; and improvement of performance through reviews by parliamentary committees and peer NCPs, among other measures.[39]

In 2007, at their annual meeting, NCPs themselves agreed that they could do better. At the time of writing, NGOs continue to have few positive experiences with the handling of their complaints, although it is encouraging that the Netherlands, the UK and Argentina have strengthened the independence and fact-finding capacities of their NCPs.[40] The efforts to give the Guidelines more sway received a boost when John Ruggie, in his 2008 report on human rights and multinational enterprises, made specific reference to the potential of the Guidelines, while acknowledging the current shortfalls in their implementation.[41]

THE RUGGIE PROCESS: DO NO HARM

The International Labor Organisation is the United Nations agency dedicated to bringing about decent working conditions for all. The ILO conventions are widely accepted as global standards for such conditions. But it is also obvious that they do not fill the global regulation gap. It is, for example, rather stunning to realise that conventions 87 and 98, which deal with freedom of association and the right to collective bargaining, are ratified by 149 and 159 countries, respectively – but that leaves about half the world's workers in the dark, because countries like Brazil, China, India, Mexico and the US have not ratified either one or both conventions.[42]

And then there is implementation. In the 1970s, the United Nations' human rights mechanisms began to address the fact that many of the problems they dealt with had their roots in corporate conduct, and work began on a 'UN Code of Conduct for Multinational Enterprises'. In a 2008 speech, John Ruggie encapsulated what had happened since then:

> I was appointed in July 2005, to pick up the pieces of a Geneva train wreck produced when an expert subsidiary body of the then UN Commission on Human Rights proposed a set of draft Norms on transnational corporations and other business enterprises. This sought to impose on companies, directly under international law, the full range of human rights duties that states have accepted for themselves – from respecting rights all the way up to fulfilling them … Human rights NGOs were uniformly in favor; business was vehemently opposed. Governments did not approve the proposal, establishing my mandate instead – essentially, to start all over again. Now fast-forward to 2008. Just last week the UN Human Rights Council adopted a resolution by acclamation welcoming the policy framework for business and human rights that I proposed in my most recent report, and asking me, in a renewed mandate, to translate its general principles into operational terms. My proposal was supported by the major international business associations and leading human rights organizations.[43]

The NGOs that had lobbied hard to make the UN Code of Conduct happen were of course severely disappointed at the 'train wreck'; nor were they happy with the way Ruggie interpreted his mandate – excluding binding regulation and sanctions for multinational corporations that violated human and labour rights. Most nevertheless decided to make the best of it and to contribute to the stakeholder consultations set up to feed Ruggie's mandate.

The CCC is one of these stakeholders. In 2000, in a conference on corporate liability, it had summed up the tasks for those intending to tackle the legal fortress: gather evidence about victims of corporate abuse; build coalitions, especially with Southern partners; share information; develop tools to track and check corporative practices; research existing law; file test cases and OECD complaints to build a body of evidence; and use 'the development of a body of norms as contained in codes of conduct as a basis for reporting and cooperation with the UN Subcommission on Promotion and Protection of Human Rights'.[44]

In the spring of 2007, the CCC wrote a letter to Ruggie with suggestions about how to proceed from voluntary to binding regulation, and especially on the functioning of multi-stakeholder initiatives:

> While valid attempts [at collaboration between MSIs] are made ... the process is painfully slow, and at the same time new, typically industry-controlled initiatives continue to emerge ... Also, even with key initiatives working together, they lack the institutional power to develop a sector-wide approach that includes governments. It is unlikely that, in the absence of an outside force or event forcing the pace and the process, the current roster of stakeholders and initiatives will manage to sort themselves out to the point of developing a collective program of work that would manage to overcome the current deficiencies.[45]

The CCC pleaded for a broad regulatory framework that would include governments, and asked for guidance on guarantees for freedom of association and complaints mechanisms. It suggested putting control of purchasing practices and transparency high on the agenda. John Ruggie's answer was clear about the limitations of his mandate:

> After a decade of experience we have come full circle to realize that we can't get the job done without states, for only they have the capacity, at national and global levels, to bring relatively small voluntary initiatives to a scale where they can constitute systemic interventions that lead to sustainable change ... The trick will be to ensure that any recommendations from me facilitate and act as a catalyst for more specific initiatives that others may undertake ...[46]

The name of the 2008 Ruggie report is *Protect, Respect and Remedy: A Framework for Business and Human Rights*, and a wonderfully simple sentence on page 9 describes the message it sends to the corporate world: Do no harm.[47]

The report highlights examples of the existing imbalance between states and business – such as the European mining company that challenged South Africa's black empowerment laws because these allegedly damaged the company's interests. At the time of its publication, 2,500 bilateral investment treaties permitted investors to use international arbitration to challenge laws intended to improve domestic social or environmental standards. At the same time, states lacked the capacity to enforce national laws against transnational firms – or they refrained from doing so for fear of losing investment. Multinational companies could still shrug off allegations of abuse by subsidiaries because, legally, parent companies could 'disown' their daughters.[48]

Ruggie proposes a common conceptual and policy framework, organised around three core principles: the state's duty to protect against human rights abuses; the corporate responsibility to respect human rights; and greater access to effective remedies. On state duty, Ruggie concludes that, while governments are supposed to make the balancing decisions required to reconcile different societal needs, it can be questioned whether they have got the balance right. Human rights are often neatly tucked away on a shelf, while trade and industry operate out of an entirely different cabinet – a pattern that is replicated internationally. Human rights should be integrated into every trade agreement, every investment treaty, and every export credit for overseas projects.[49]

The framework's second focal point is the corporate responsibility to respect human rights. No company in its right mind would say that it does not respect human rights, but relatively few have systems in place to back up the claim that they do. Ruggie outlines a 'due diligence process' that would guide the establishment of such systems.[50] It implies, at a minimum, that they should be underpinned by the international bill of human rights and the ILO core conventions; and consists in a detailed human rights policy including a human rights impact assessment before starting any commercial undertaking, the integration of the policy throughout all departments, the tracking of performance by monitoring and audits and confidential complaints mechanisms, and the exchange of best practices. The intricacies of supply-chain responsibility are tackled by the concept of 'complicity', which must legally be interpreted as 'knowingly providing practical assistance or encouragement that has a substantial effect on the commission of a crime'. Non-legally, says Ruggie, complicity is widely accepted as a benchmark by public and private investors, and by companies and campaigning organisations. 'Claims of complicity can impose reputational costs and even lead to divestment, without legal liability being established.'[51]

Both state protection and corporate respect are powerless when victims of labour rights violations have no access to means of redress and remediation – the third core principle of the framework. Access to formal judicial systems is often most difficult where the need is greatest; non-judicial mechanisms like MSI procedures and OECD Guidelines are incomplete and flawed, and victims keep falling through the holes.[52] States should strengthen judicial capacity and address obstacles to access to justice, including for foreign plaintiffs. Non-judicial complaints mechanisms should be legitimate, accessible, equitable, transparent, predictable, and rights-compatible.[53] Ruggie concludes that the United Nations 'is not a centralized command-and-control system that can impose its will on the world – indeed it has no "will" apart from that with which Member States endow it. But it can and must lead intellectually and by setting expectations and aspirations.'[54]

NGOs involved in the Ruggie process agree on the general direction and analysis of the framework, but cannot but be disappointed by the lack of binding regulation. In a 2008 letter to Ruggie, they continued to push for global standards for corporate responsibility and for mechanisms to hold companies to account. They pleaded for the further development of international law to include the liability of corporations; the special representative was asked to move beyond existing frameworks, and to consider what the law should be.[55]

In January 2009 the British NGO Core began energetically to flesh out the Ruggie framework by proposing the establishment of a new national body to investigate, sanction, and provide remedies for abuses committed by UK companies abroad. It continued to explore possibilities for using and expanding national and international law, and presented two options: a Commission for Business and Human Rights and the Environment, with a broad mandate including regulatory, policy-making, investigatory and dispute–resolution functions. It also proposed a Business and Human Rights and Environment Ombudsman service, with the more limited mandate of helping to resolve disputes.[56]

10
Companies

While the clothing industry had set off on its journey around the world, national unions and governments stayed behind in the regulatory vacuum created by the relocations. International bodies like the International Labor Organisation had pinned labour-rights standards on the world's notice-boards, but was unable or unwilling to undertake their realisation. The clean clothes movement was born out of the awareness of that vacuum. It wanted to hold transnational corporations accountable for the grim labour conditions in their supply chains. The strategy of the first years, in which campaigns targeted companies unlucky enough to be caught dirty-handed, soon proved to be insufficient, and made way for an approach that took aim at the roots of labour-rights violations.

The predominant strategy in the last decade of the twentieth century was the development and promotion of corporate accountability, focusing on the implementation of a generally accepted, effective code of conduct for the garment industry. After the first storm of civil society protests against the sweatshop conditions in the industry, brands had started to work with an immense variety of weak and vague codes, which confused the issues and did not really achieve anything. The CCC's 'Code of Labour Practices for the Apparel Industry Including Sportswear' was to unite the clean clothes movement behind a set of well-defined standards for decent work, and challenge the industry's codes. The starting point was the set of core ILO conventions on child labour, forced labour, discrimination, and freedom of association. Years of intensive deliberations and consultations in the CCC network followed; the labour and women's organisations in the Philippines, Hong Kong, Indonesia and India had an especially vital input, advocating standards on wages, hours of work, job security and health and safety. They argued that, without them, the code would not cover the primary needs of garment workers.

The CCC presented its model code in 1998. It advocated freedom of association; the right to collective bargaining; freedom from discrimination; an end to forced labour; an end to child labour; a minimum employment age of 15; a living wage; a maximum working week of 48 hours, and maximum voluntary, paid overtime of 12 hours; the right to a healthy and safe working environment; security of employment; and independent code-monitoring.[1]

AUDITS

Code implementation needs a control structure, and to this end a huge commercial 'social auditing' industry sprang up in the 1990s. It conducted the tens of thousands of audits commissioned by brands and retailers every year. Although codes and auditing constitute an improvement on the previous flat denial of responsibility, today even the commissioning companies themselves admit that their auditing is inefficient, and is not effectively battling labour rights violations. Factory owners present auditors with falsified records and complain of 'audit fatigue'; auditors fail to perceive even the most crass abuses – the collapse of the Spectrum factory in Bangladesh happened despite the codes and audits of companies like Carrefour and Inditex-Zara.[2] A 2007 research report that compared ethical trade in the US and the UK found that

> an 'audit heavy' approach to ethical trade was widely believed to be expensive and inefficient. A representative from a US clothing brand stated: 'The average number of visits a factory gets in a year from monitors is anywhere from 20 to 25 ... We need to refocus that because we are really spending 80 per cent of our time basically duplicating efforts ...'

The report quotes the head of the CSR department of a UK retailer saying: 'We need to shift away from spending 5 per cent of our time on solutions and 95 per cent on data gathering, to 5 per cent on data gathering and 95 per cent on tackling the solutions.'[3]

After 2000, the annual CSR reports of some of the world's largest brand companies became increasingly candid about the failures of auditing. The Gap's and H&M's 2004 reports and Nike's 2005 report admitted that labour-rights violations persisted in their supply chains, that audits were failing to point out code violations such as abuse, extreme overtime, non-payment of minimum wages and the absence of freedom of association and collective bargaining agreements, and that unions and NGOs were more effective in that respect.[4]

The anti-sweatshop movement had by then been criticising the practice of commercial auditing for a decade. In an effort to substantiate and summarise the arguments definitively, the CCC published the research report *Looking for a Quick Fix: How Weak Social Auditing is Keeping Workers in Sweatshops* in 2005.[5] After having interviewed social auditors, managers and 670 workers at 40 factories in eight countries, the researchers concluded that audits showed many shortcomings, due to the way they were conducted: in minimal time, and sloppily – by auditors lacking knowledge of local circumstances. Many of them were insufficiently trained, especially on subjects like freedom of association; subcontracting was often not detected, leaving entire layers of production in the dark; if workers were interviewed, this usually took place on factory grounds and in the presence of managers; workers had sometimes been instructed by management on what to tell auditors; visits were announced beforehand, giving management the chance to produce a clean façade. This way of working resulted in audit reports that might identify health and safety risks and mention quantifiable code violations like working hours or pay levels, but were weak in detecting issues such as discrimination and obstruction of freedom of association. If they found violations, they often failed to identify causes. More often than not, effective correction was not on the agenda. Auditing reports were not publicly available.[6]

The one compelling question that arose was: Where is the voice of workers in all this auditing that is meant to protect them? Worker interviews seemed to be no more than items to be ticked off, along with testing the fire extinguishers. Even from the point of view of efficiency, this made no sense: who better than workers could inform auditors about the conditions on the shop floor? Consequently, almost all the recommendations of the *Quick Fix* report were geared towards creating a space for workers to be heard. They included credible complaint mechanisms, the involvement of local organisations, education and training for workers and management personnel, transparency regarding audit results, the active promotion of unions and other forms of worker organisations, and the remediation of violations.[7]

Two of the report's recommendations went beyond criticism of faulty audits: companies were urged to join multi-stakeholder initiatives, and to take a hard look at their own purchasing practices.

MULTI-STAKEHOLDER INITIATIVES

Some leading brands and retailers are seeking to redress the inefficient audit-avalanche through the use of databases on the internet to allow the sharing of audit data, and through supplier ownership of the audit process and the data it generates.[8] Although these approaches may work towards improving efficiency, harmonising standards, and lessening the burden for suppliers and securing their cooperation, they do not address the absence of workers' representation within the systems that are supposed to benefit them.

Systems that try to involve workers in the process of upholding labour standards on both ends of the supply chain are the so-called multi-stakeholder initiatives (MSIs). There are five leading MSIs in the apparel industry, of which three are headquartered in the US: the Fair Labor Association (FLA), Social Accountability International (SAI) and Worker Rights Consortium (WRC). The UK has the Ethical Trading Initiative (ETI); and the Netherlands the Fair Wear Foundation (FWF), which is generally considered to have the highest standards, and to pay most attention to worker representation.[9] Many of the world's largest clothing and sports shoe companies are now members of an MSI.

While MSIs differ considerably in their methods and standards, they agree on the necessity of the company-independent control of code implementation, and towards this end they bring together companies, unions and NGOs. In this, MSIs differ fundamentally from business-driven initiatives such as Worldwide Responsible Accredited Production (WRAP), the Business Social Compliance Initiative (BSCI), and the Global Social Compliance Programme (GSCP), which, though they may have unions and NGOs on their advisory boards, never treat them as equal and responsible partners at the organisation's core. Independent verification is not on their agenda; they hire commercial auditors and, the audit reports remain company property.

Harmonisation of code content and of multi-stakeholder initiatives is considered increasingly important by all involved. Not only have the clothing and sports shoe sectors been the main source of the proliferation of codes and audits since the early 1990s; the simultaneous activities of MSIs in factories and countries add to the confusion. In a meeting of American and European MSIs in 2002, Ineke Zeldenrust of the CCC asked: 'Do we really have the luxury of not working together? Must consumers and civil society groups in the North and worker rights' organisations in the South confront as many multi-stakeholder code initiatives as they do company codes?'[10] In the same meeting, MSIs agreed on the necessity of a common language and common benchmarks in code implementation, and on improving monitoring and verification by comparing practices. Civil society groups in production countries would also welcome better coordination and consistency among the various multi-stakeholder initiatives, if only to avoid multiple demands on themselves for information and collaboration – although there is also a fear that harmonisation might lead to the crowding out of local initiatives and experiments.[11]

FAIR WEAR FOUNDATION

Erica van Doorn, director of the Dutch Fair Wear Foundation, is all for collaboration between MSIs. 'It is necessary', she says in the FWF office, high on the thirteenth floor of the World Fashion Centre in Amsterdam.[12]

> Working conditions in the garment industry still leave much to be desired, and we can use all resources. We see an increasing convergence of MSIs, and companies are asking for it. We collaborate with the Fair Labor Association, if only to prevent our auditors from meeting on factory doorsteps. Some of our member companies overlap; Liz Claiborne, for example, is an FLA-member; its daughter-company, Mexx, is with us. We are pooling resources such as audit teams because we both have too much work and little money, and because we share principles. Like the FLA, we think it is important that an MSI is a no-advocacy zone. To gain the trust of employers and employees alike, an MSI needs to be a neutral place, different from the CCC or unions. Their task is to challenge companies and point out abuses; our task is to support code implementation and remediation of violations. While the CCC's motto is 'We not only oppose, but also propose', the FWF says: 'First propose, then maybe oppose'. In that sense our respective fields of work have become more clearly defined over the years.

The FWF is not averse to a dialogue with business-driven initiatives like the BSCI.

> We talk with them every couple of months. They don't offer independent verification of the monitoring activities of their

member companies, but some of their members are interested. We can also learn from them; they have developed useful monitoring tools and are strong on acquisition of member companies. They organise roundtables on all kinds of subjects in various parts of the world. You may criticise them for weak and vague standards or implementation methodologies, but they are a reality that we have to deal with.

An important collaborative MSI effort is the Joint Initiative on Corporate Accountability and Workers' Rights – Jo-In for short. In 2003, the ETI brought together the CCC, FWF, ETI, FLA, SAI and WRC, to try to settle the confusion of the multiple codes and code-related initiatives. From 2004 to 2007, Jo-In conducted a pilot project in Turkey to chisel out best practices, involving eight multinational brands – Adidas, Gap, Gsus, Otto Versand, Marks & Spencer, Nike, Patagonia and Puma – and focusing on the improvement of wages, working hours and freedom of association.[13] Of the 15 factories invited to join the project, in the end only six agreed to cooperate. At the end of 2008, there was still no concluding report, but interim reports showed that tensions existed between the six organisations:

> [T]here are varying views among the six as to how to best overcome the endemic workplace violations – both in practical and philosophical terms. As a result, compromise and a clear common vision for the project have been difficult to achieve, and, in a few cases, have not been reached. Public disclosure, effective methods for worker interviews, living wages, management systems, the role of trade unions, campaign tactics, and pricing and sourcing policies were other topics where differences in approach arose.[14]

Nevertheless, some important steps forward have been reported. The draft Common Code is used by brands, MSIs and other initiatives as a model. Another accomplishment has been the development of the 'wage ladder' as a way out of a stalled debate about the living wage. A living wage is broadly defined as a wage that covers a family's basic needs and provides some discretionary income. The CCC specifies 'needs' as including nutritious food and clean water, shelter, clothes, education, healthcare and transport, allowing workers and their families to participate fully in society and live with dignity. The living wage has been the subject of many debates. Although most of the organisations involved in Jo-In advocate paying workers a living wage, most codes of conduct do not specify what 'basic needs' are, or identify which methodology for calculating living wages is best, what data should be used, or what sort of household the living wage is meant to support. Without greater clarity and consensus on these questions, provisions calling for a living wage may prove difficult to enforce. To prevent this from obstructing the Jo-In pilot project, the wage ladder was designed. It is a benchmark for charting factories' progress in increasing wages, and focuses on the question of how to arrive at a living wage rather than on the definition of the sum of money it should amount to. Departing from existing wage levels, different strategies of raising them are explored, such as increasing the prices paid, improving productivity, improving management systems, and applying cost-sharing schemes.[15]

This outcome was the result of stiff negotiations. According to the CCC and the WRC, some topics relevant to the payment of a living wage were kept out of the limelight: the lack of political will, unequal income distribution, and especially the pricing and purchasing practices of companies. CCC and WRC suspected that companies were using the argument of technical measurement complexities as a shield against positive action. The ETI, FLA, SAI and FWF acknowledged these were relevant topics, but they maintained that they wanted to give due attention to productivity, competitiveness, and trade union negotiation.

In 2008 Jo-In was transformed into a forum focusing on a definitive common code, on collaboration on complaints registered by workers in factories where several MSI members were sourcing, and on a common approach to freedom of association. Van Doorn commented:

I think the draft Common Code and the wage ladder have been good results of Jo-In. The important thing now is to improve the purchasing practices of our member companies in such a way that factory owners can respect the ILO standards. We need to convince buyers and producers to cooperate in this.[16]

The FWF is a relatively small organisation in terms of the combined size of its member companies. At the end of 2008, it had 44 member companies, owning 56 brands between them. Some of them were work-wear companies – the result of the CCC's successful public procurement campaign. While the number of Dutch companies has increased, so has the number of international brands. The FWF now had members in Switzerland, Germany, Belgium, Sweden, Denmark, the Netherlands, and the UK. Van Doorn remarks:

> Annually, we have been growing by an average of ten companies; we are aiming for 25 new members in 2009. We need to grow to make an impact. Expansion in Europe has been on the agenda for years now, and we hope to have our roadmap finished in 2009. It means we'll have to internationalise the Board and the Committee of Experts, but it doesn't necessarily imply that we'll have a representative in an office in every capital. That would probably not be cost-effective, and with our limited means it would be difficult to manage. Switzerland and Germany have stakeholder platforms in which companies, unions and/or NGOs are represented. I think we should move in that direction for the other European countries as well. These platforms discuss code implementation and national developments in the field of social accountability. They provide a space for information exchange between participants and can suggest improvements of FWF policies and procedures to the Board and the Committee of Experts.

Such an arrangement would ask a lot of the European CCCs, many of whom are eagerly awaiting the establishment of the FWF in their country. Swedish CCC coordinator Malin Eriksson, for example, reported that companies that have been awakened to the necessity of CSR need a platform from which to be able to improve, and that, in the absence of the FWF, many join the BSCI.

Until 2008, the FWF's work consisted essentially of the auditing and verification of member companies' production locations, with an emphasis on the representation of local stakeholders. To this end, it developed networks in the production countries involved; it commissioned country studies into the industry, local labour law, the local minimum wage, workers' organisations and working conditions; and it trained local audit teams. It is a challenge to find the right people to do worker interviews, says Van Doorn, '[n]ot only because they have to know local languages and customs, but also because they are assigned to receive and handle complaints. They are vulnerable and sometimes exposed to intimidations and threats.'

In 2008 the FWF introduced a new tool: the management system audit. It is designed to address buyers' responsibility for code implementation:

Improving working conditions requires commitment from both producer and buyer. In a work plan, they disclose their supply chain and describe what they intend to undertake to get the FWF code implemented. After a year they write a 'social report' that describes the progress made. We then do a management system audit, focusing on issues like purchasing practices, coherent monitoring, complaints procedure, remediation, transparency, and internal communication between the CSR and other departments. Auditing sourcing companies themselves is inescapable. We have seen factories in Thailand that did really well after years of improvements, and subsequently lost all their clients to cheaper producers. If buyers are not committed, we will not succeed. We see distinct differences between members experienced at CSR, and ones with hardly any trained CSR staff. The ones with a good CSR record have preferred suppliers whom they will guarantee orders if, for example, improvements are carried out, and whom they allow to produce in advance when business is slow. Those are real changes, and the management system audits will make them visible. When they are fully functional, we will publish the results.[17]

PURCHASING PRACTICES

Corporate social responsibility and its avalanche of codes, audits and multi-stakeholder initiatives can be tools to keep the debate with companies going and improve workers' lives. They bring solutions for individual cases of abuse – 80 per cent of complaints handled by FWF are solved – and they have raised health and safety standards in the industry. But disappointment grows as it becomes clear that CSR is not raising wages or preparing the ground for freedom of association. The purchasing practices of brands and retailers have been mentioned by many as one of the key obstructions – they have a negative impact on the shop floor in three different ways.

First, the downward pressure on prices translates into lower wages, since for factory owners this is the most obvious way of reducing costs. Second, the volatility of ordering – these days there are even online auctions of orders – causes an increase in factory closures, precarious work, and unemployment. Finally, short and irregular delivery times and unpredictable order volumes force workers into extreme overtime.

Companies are aware of this. As early as 2004, the Gap CSR report mentions geographical shifts in production following the expiration of quotas as a root cause for weak CSR, along with brands' pricing, quality demands and unrealistic order deadlines.[18] In a well-researched article on social auditing in China, *Business Week* reporters quote a Taiwanese manager of a shoe factory in mainland China:

> [W]e can't ask Nike to increase our price ... so how can we afford to pay the higher salary? By reducing profit margins from 30 per cent to 5 per cent over the past 18 years, Shoetown has managed to stay in business and obey Nike's rules.

The report concludes:

> Ultimately, the economics of global outsourcing may trump any system of oversight that western companies attempt. And these harsh economic realities could make it exceedingly difficult to achieve both the low prices and the humane working conditions that US consumers have been promised.[19]

MSIs try to tackle pernicious purchasing practices. In the Netherlands, the FWF developed its management rating system. In the UK the ETI launched its Purchasing Practices project, after an impact assessment over the period 2003–05 had shown that no progress had been made on precarious employment, the living wage, or freedom of association. Each company participating in the project – including Asda, Debenhams, Gap, Marks & Spencer, Pentland and Sainsbury's – was partnered with an NGO or trade union, and they collectively examined case studies on purchasing practices to find out how they could be improved.[20]

The CCC campaigned on purchasing practices for the first time in 2004, when the Play Fair Olympic campaign explicitly addressed the sector as a whole. It had become clear that systemic changes in the sector would not occur through the CSR efforts of individual companies. More often than not, factory closures and relocation of orders offset positive results of CSR and worker organisation. In an industry addicted to the lowest possible production costs, raising them through better purchasing practices would be perceived by companies as a recipe for failure – unless improvements were made across the sector. When companies bring the lack of a 'level playing field' to bear as a reason for doing nothing, it is a logical step to propose change for everybody involved.

The Play Fair campaign has tried to awaken consumers to the incredibly small percentage of the selling price of sports shoes that ends up in workers' pockets: not even 1 per cent.[21] When people realise that labour accounts for so little of the price they pay, they always wonder why wages aren't doubled immediately, since that would obviously mean a lot to workers, while neither buyers nor consumers would feel any pain. It may be a simple question; it certainly doesn't have a simple answer. It involves an explanation of the downward pressure on prices through the many links of the subcontracting chain, until finally the weakest link at the end foots the bill; it involves an explanation of prices in the clothing and sports shoe sectors, which have remained stagnant for over a decade, while competition between retailers is fierce and markets are close to saturation.[22] The perpetual sale that makes for happy shoppers in all corners of the world is a sign of this profit-squeeze at the retailer end; of course, this translates into lower manufacturing prices. A report written for the 2004 Play Fair Olympics campaign mentioned that, since 1997, there had been an annual 5 per cent decrease in the wholesale price of shoes that left the factories of the world's biggest sports shoe manufacturer, Pou Chen/Yue Yuen, which glues together the Nike Airforce 107, the Reebok Freestyle Hi Punk, the Asics Gel-Kayano 14, the Puma Motorazzo, the adiSTAR Revolt, and many others. But while Pou Chen is able to compensate for lower prices with larger orders and higher productivity, smaller manufacturers cannot follow suit. Instead, they try to cope by squeezing the only costs they know how to squeeze: labour costs. Gains made in the field of CSR suffer accordingly:

> It is expected that continued drops in retail prices in key markets will have serious and detrimental long-term effects on CSR and the various codes of conduct. The main problem is that workers seldom have any recourse for defending themselves, because they are restricted in their right to organize and bargain collectively.[23]

It is easy to see how difficult it is to get complicated information like this across to the public at large. And while consumers are easily moved but difficult to enlighten, companies are not very forthcoming with information about purchasing practices. They are secretive about buying strategies and consider them essential to their competitiveness; it is very hard to get them to expose their prize assets to the competition.

Campaigning on purchasing practices is further complicated by the enormous impact on the market of two relatively new types of player: Asian transnational corporations and global retailers.

ASIAN TRANSNATIONAL PRODUCTION COMPANIES

Globalisation has not only divided the clothing and sports shoe industry up between western and Northern brands on the one hand, and eastern and Southern producers on the other. Some eastern brands have become global players, like the Japanese Asics and Mizuno. Eastern trading companies like the Hong Kong-based Li & Fung have developed into supply-chain managers with multibillion-dollar turnovers. Li & Fung dispatches orders for retail clients at the touch of a button to a network of thousands of factories around the world. If brands and retailers do business through agents like these, it is more difficult to hold them accountable for production conditions.

Probably most influential has been the emergence of a new type of enterprise that can best be described as a production transnational. Often from humble beginnings, these Asian corporations – originating mainly in Taiwan, South Korea and Hong Kong – grew so big in the 1990s that their earnings today outbid those of some global brands. They have formed a new concentration of capital and power, and changed the dynamics of the supply chain. Like the brands, the Asian corporations are always heading for the most cost-effective production locations, including favourable trade conditions.

The most colourful example is maybe the Taiwanese Pou Chen company that started out as a family workshop making canvas and rubber sandals, and today is the single largest producer of sports shoes for the US sneaker industry, churning out 100 million pairs of shoes each year through its Hong Kong subsidiary Yue Yuen.[24] Pou Chen produces mostly in China, Vietnam and Indonesia. Some of its factories are gigantic walled-in compounds, housing tens of thousands of employees.

Another Asian production transnational is Nien Hsing, a Taiwanese clothing manufacturer that operates factories as far away as Africa and Central America. A company like Nien Hsing operates as follows: a western brand orders a batch of jeans; the company ships fabric from China to Vietnam, where factory workers produce the garments that are then exported back to Taiwan (or South Korea or Hong Kong), or directly to the EU or US buyer. The company supplies not only materials and labour, but also research and development, machinery, managerial resources, capital and distribution. Nien Hsing's immense power is illustrated by the example of its withdrawal from Nicaragua in 2008, which annihilated 15,000 jobs out of the 19,000 in the country's Free Exporting Zones. The withdrawal took place after a series of minimum wage increases and a government decision to ban a double-shift system.[25]

Production transnationals are advanced along the trend towards 'one-stop shopping': they offer to handle the entire process, from order to distribution. They are able to deliver cheaply and quickly. On top of that, some are vertically integrated: they not only produce the finished product, but supply yarn or fabric as well, which makes them more competitive.[26] Not only do these companies relieve brands from complicated and troublesome aspects of the garment business; they are also very efficient in squeezing profit out of production – the part of the industry that brands have discarded to concentrate on the profitable end-consumer markets. The Asian companies are successful at this because they are good at organising, disciplining and exploiting the labour force in developing countries. In this role they have an acute interest in keeping wages down and suppressing workers' organisations, and thus they play a large role in the industry's purchasing practices. But because, unlike the branded companies that have placed themselves in the spotlight, they keep a low profile, it is difficult for campaigners to zero in on them and get them to take responsibility for working conditions in their supply chains.[27] There are only a few examples of successful campaigns – including the one against Nien Hsing in Lesotho, which involved strong local organisation and support from international consumer and labour-rights organisations, in East and West.[28] It is a form of 'triangular campaigning' that is not easy to accomplish, but may be the only way of tackling the new power dynamics in the supply chain.

GLOBAL RETAILERS

In the 2004 documentary *Is Wal-Mart Good for America?* American sociology professor Gary Gereffi explains how the big-box price-fighting retailer Wal-Mart succeeded in becoming the world's biggest company.

Wal-Mart's growth in the mid-to-late '90s is one of the great success stories in American business. They were more single-minded in terms of global cost-cutting and internal efficiency than any other US retailer. And that helps us understand how and why they were able to pass companies like Kmart and Sears that were the early leaders in US retailing and offshore sourcing.[29]

The documentary shows how Wal-Mart's use of information technology involves suppliers all over the world in the management of Wal-Mart's inventory and logistics. Sophisticated computer programmes inform suppliers about store prices and manage distribution globally with unparalleled efficiency. In China, in particular, this succeeded in marrying a high-technology system of transportation and delivery of goods with low-cost production in Chinese factories.[30]

By the mid-1990s, Wal-Mart was the dominant US company in global sourcing, and the largest retailer in the US economy in virtually all consumer goods categories. It fashioned the company into a gateway to US consumers and, following the global expansion of its stores, to consumers all over the world. In 2006 it served 100 million shoppers a week. This gave the company unprecedented power over a great many industries, among them the clothing and sports shoe sector. Wal-Mart is the number one supplier in the US of clothing and sporting goods. Its purchasing practices have an exceptional impact on suppliers and their employees.

In the documentary, a Hong Kong entrepreneur who used to supply Wal-Mart relates how he was called to the company's headquarters and, together with other suppliers, was seated in a row of negotiating booths, where a Wal-Mart buyer laid a product before them. They were asked to bid on its production costs per piece, in a kind of reverse auction. Bidding on inexpensive products, in most cases the winner bid only one cent less than the others – which goes a long way towards explaining workers' wages.

Wal-Mart claims to benefit Americans, because it provides them with the goods they want for the lowest possible price and because it keeps Americans in jobs, as the biggest US employer after the federal government. Still, objections to these claims come from all sides, and they are getting louder. Not only does Wal-Mart fuel unemployment by crushing small retailers and driving US manufacturers out of business or overseas, it is also a notoriously bad employer.

Wal-Mart is pushing wages down to a level where the people that work in Wal-Mart stores are going to be forced to buy in

Wal-Mart stores, because they can't make enough money to buy goods elsewhere in the economy.

The traditional model of American capitalism from the mid-twentieth century was that American corporations were respected because they were globally efficient, but they also paid their workers a good wage so that they could become consumers and part of the middle class of American society. I think we've lost that model today, because globalization has pushed Wal-Mart and companies like them towards global efficiency, where consumer prices are the only things that matter ... Wal-Mart is doing fine for Wall Street. It's one of the most profitable companies in America. But Wal-Mart is not doing fine for Main Street ... Wal-Mart is also very well known for being a non-union company and pushing non-union conditions on its workforce ... It pays its workers at a minimum pay scale with very few fringe benefits. Because Wal-Mart is the largest private employer in the United States, whatever Wal-Mart does in terms of the labor market, all other businesses have to follow. So Wal-Mart is really determining the direction in which the US labor market is moving.

Rubbermaid [a former Wal-Mart supplier that went broke after Wal-Mart had refused a price hike] represents an innovation-oriented, high road towards US competitiveness. Wal-Mart represents a cost-driven, low-price low road towards US competitiveness. And in a sense, they're two dramatically different styles in which the US economy can be organized. The Wal-Mart model – the global sourcing efficiency model – is winning out over the innovation-oriented model to a large degree. And that becomes a real challenge for the US workforce.[31]

Of course, Wal-Mart is not the only retailer working in the 'global sourcing efficiency' mode. Europe has its Carrefour, its Lidl, KiK, Aldi and Tesco. In eight EU countries, five giant supermarkets are responsible for 70 per cent of all grocery sales, and they have expanded into clothes, pharmaceuticals and banking.[32] These companies generally have very weak codes of conduct, and company-controlled systems of monitoring implementation. In 2006, the supermarkets Carrefour, Metro, Migros, Tesco and Wal-Mart launched their Global Social Compliance Programme (GSCP), which, because of their huge buying power, may eclipse all the MSIs. But it is inconceivable that a company like Wal-Mart would actually implement the right of, say, Cambodian workers to freedom of association (as referred to in the GSCP), when it hands its own managers a *Manager's Toolbox to Remaining Union Free*, which states that:

> Staying union free is a full-time commitment. Unless union prevention is a goal equal to other objectives within an organization, the goal will usually not be attained. The commitment to stay union free must exist at all levels of management – from the Chairperson of the 'Board' down to the front-line manager ... The union organizer is a 'potential opponent' for our center.[33]

Historically, the CCC has always campaigned against giant retailers – take Auchan, H&M and Carrefour. Early in 2008, the German CCC organised a campaign on its national supermarkets Aldi, Lidl and KiK.[34] The British CCC Labour Behind the Label has been part of the Tescopoly alliance, launched in 2005, which exposes and fights the detrimental effects of Tesco's practices on labour conditions in the supply chain, on small businesses, and on communities and the environment. The alliance combines the forces of large international NGOs and local pressure groups, and its website offers visitors all kinds of angles on campaigning to curb 'supermarket power'.[35]

In 2009, the CCC launched the global 'Better Bargain' campaign, which targets the purchasing and sales practices of a special group of giant retailers: companies with multiple products, and operating on a European scale. Because of the size and power of these companies, and because they sell multiple products and operate in non-branded, low-cost segments of the market, the campaign will pool the resources of European organisations in the fields of labour rights, farmers' rights, the environment and development. It is felt that this initiative will provide a good opportunity for global campaigning, uniting consumers with workers in both production and retail. Supermarket employees have to deal with short-term contracts, low wages and anti-union company policies, just like the factory workers whose products they sell. This offers a potential basis for cross-border solidarity. Sometimes exchanges between factory and retail workers are very revealing; through their unions or workers' councils, retail workers can ask questions about the purchasing practices of their employer.[36]

The campaign is not only about labour conditions in the garment industry. It is an opportunity to collaborate with campaigns targeting other product sectors experiencing the same kind of supply-chain problems, like the electronics and toy industries – the big retailers sell those products as well. The 'Better Bargain' campaign also draws attention to the destructive impacts of giant stores on local small businesses and communities, and on the environment. Farmers, for example, often complain that the downward pressure large buyers are able to exert on prices for agricultural products leads to an industrial way of farming that violates ecological principles vital to healthy food production.

A preliminary step in the campaign has been to attract the attention of the European parliament. In January 2008, a majority of MEPs signed a document asking the Directorate General of Competition to investigate the impacts of the concentration of buying power in the supermarket sector on small businesses, suppliers, workers and consumers. It asks the European Commission to think of ways to protect these groups against any negative impacts. In 2009 the 'Better Bargain' alliance continues to build up pressure by involving the organisations of all those affected by the practices of the giant retailers.

NEW CAMPAIGN PERSPECTIVES

After almost 20 years of campaigning, the CCC International Secretariat takes stock of what has and has not been achieved in its discussion paper *The Structural Crisis of Labour Flexibility*.[37] It analyses the obstacles to systemic change, and poses the question of how to continue in the next decade of anti-sweatshop campaigning. Many of its insights have been developed in close cooperation with global partners. The 2006 Delhi conference, for example, which brought together over 50 participants from 15 Asian countries with campaigners from Europe and the US, produced a host of facts and analyses that fed into the strategic paper. The paper outlines three complementary paths to be explored: local, regional and sector-wide.

The local path concerns the urgent appeals system. To make it more efficient and effective, a 'thematic' approach is proposed that focuses on core problems for workers in a specific geographical area. All complaints that fit that general pattern can be gathered and brought to the attention of the brands, retailers and governments involved. This strategy might lead to a more structural approach to labour-rights violations.[38]

The second and third paths both lead to the heart of the problem: the relocations that keep annihilating local labour successes. Both aim to fight the race to the bottom – the regional strategy by uniting the labour movement in a geographical region and demanding a floor to wages in that region; the sector-wide strategy by targeting the industry in its entirety. A first example of the regional strategy is the Asia Floor Wage campaign. An alliance of 34 trade unions and NGOs in 14 Asian garment-exporting countries, supported by European and US labour advocates, has proposed a campaign to prevent wage competition between Asian countries. The campaign website does not beat about the bush:

> Workers are afraid to fight for better wages, because they might lose their jobs. The Asia Floor Wage Campaign is a response to this problem. We propose a floor wage for garment workers in Asia. The Asia Floor Wage is different in each country's national currency, but has the power to buy the same set of goods and services in all countries. An Asia Floor Wage for the garment industry will help us fight poverty, develop economically with decent labour standards, and improve the lives of workers who are mostly women.[39]

The odds are that circumstances will favour such a campaign, say its proponents. In the first place, about two-thirds of the total global trade in readymade garments is carried out in Asia, and although relocations occur between countries, the continent as a whole is not likely to lose much business. Second, as we have seen, Asian transnationals represent a trend towards concentration of production. These companies assemble thousands of workers in one place, and often have direct relations with brands and retailers. Third, there is also a concentration on the buyers' side, as we have seen in the case of Wal-Mart. These circumstances may provide leverage when bargaining for a more equal distribution of profits between factory owners and workers, on the one hand, and between manufacturers and buyers on the other.[40] The larger the factory, the more difficult it is to relocate, while at the same time strikes may have a huge impact, especially because orders are large and usually on a tight schedule. Because the transnational production companies invest not only in pure garment assemblage but also in design, pattern-making and quality control, the effect of a wage increase on the company's overall costs may be relatively small. Finally, they might be vulnerable to a demand for better labour standards expressed by brands and retailers because of their close relations with them. The Asia Floor Wage campaign is an attempt to unite Asian workers behind the demand for a doubling of the regular wage level in each country, which ranges between $1.50 and $2.50 per day.

In 2006 three countries – China, India and Bangladesh – produced 60 per cent of garments in the region and 42 per cent of the garments in the world. These countries are also pools of the worst-paid labour in the world. By giving a bottom to the wage level for these workers, the campaigners believe that a global effect can be achieved.[41] This, of course, implies a change in the purchasing practices of brands and retailers. Because labour costs make up only 2.5–5.0 per cent of the retail price of items of clothing, it should be possible for buying companies to increase the prices they pay.

Both local and regional paths presuppose a sector-wide approach. Only the participation of a large number of companies will provide enough weight to tip the scale: in individual factories, on a country level, on a regional, and most assuredly on a global level. But how to convince the majority of unwilling and highly competitive enterprises of the fact that such an approach would be productive? The Play Fair 2004 and 2008 Olympic campaigns made efforts in that direction, but results were meagre – even if leading companies like Reebok, Nike, Adidas, New Balance, Umbro and Speedo agreed that CSR would benefit from cooperation, and convened a working group with the Play Fair coalition to explore incentives for trade unionism, collective bargaining, and improving wages across the sector. The Play Fair campaigns proposed a 'sectoral framework agreement' between the International Textile, Garment and Leather Workers Federation (ITGLWF) and the World Federation of Sporting Goods Industries (WFSGI), which would promote freedom of association and collective bargaining. As it happened, the WFSGI appeared to be an association without any real power, while its members retained their own CSR programmes. According to Doug Miller, then head of research of the ITGLWF: 'Sector-wide solutions are important but the employers are fragmented and do not want to concede any authority to their associations, which are weak. So we have to target the industry leaders.'[42]

The sector-wide approach will continue to play an important role in future anti-sweatshop campaigns. In 2008, Oxfam Australia and the CCC published a document called *Sector-Wide Solutions for the Sports Shoe and Apparel Industry in Indonesia*, which combines the local, regional and sector-wide approaches. It focuses on issues most detrimental to Indonesian workers: the lack of freedom of association and collective bargaining, short-term contract labour, and factory closures.[43] It addresses all buying companies, and calls for their collective action on demands detailed in the document. Consultations have begun with local Indonesian partners about how to translate words into actions. Companies sourcing in Indonesia have received a questionnaire asking about their willingness to engage in improving specific labour standards. Although not all companies had sent in answers at the time of writing, it seems that there is a fair measure of willingness to address worker training on labour rights and the curbing of precarious employment. The development of transparency in purchasing practices and creation of the conditions for freedom of association are less popular. These two issues are going to be discussed in meetings of the new working group established by brands and the Play Fair coalition. CCC staff member Jeroen Merk says: 'Interestingly, the sector itself shows signs of moving in a collaborative direction, either within or outside of MSIs, either formally or informally. Those are developments we need to be in touch with.'[44]

While bad purchasing practices are a root cause of bad working conditions, correcting the former will not necessarily lead to improvement of the latter. Although, in all probability, steady ordering will lead to greater job security, a supplier does not have to translate a fair price into a living wage and fair contracts. Moreover, it is difficult to determine what a fair price or a living wage is, without the input of workers themselves.

And that is what it comes down to, when all is said and done. Whatever the strategy, whatever the angle or the source, there is only one basis for fair and decent working conditions: workers themselves. There will be no respect for labour rights in the garment industry unless workers are able to organise and express themselves freely. The clean clothes movement is not done yet.

13. (left) Barbed-wire bra – image used in the campaign that convinced lingerie company Triumph to withdraw from Burma, 2001. © Clean Clothes Campaign

14. (below) South African union leader Jabu Ngcobo meets garment workers in Lesotho, 2001. © Clean Clothes Campaign

15.   Yunya 'Lek' Yimprasert, founder of the Thai Labour Campaign, Bangkok 2007. © Liesbeth Sluiter

16.   Protest against the closure of the Gina Form bra factory that supplied brands such as Victoria's Secret and Calvin Klein, Bangkok 2006. © Clean Clothes Campaign

17.   The Greek god Zeus launches the Play Fair campaign at the occasion of the Athens Olympic Games, Amsterdam 2004. © Clean Clothes Campaign

18.   Ineke Zeldenrust during an action for Indonesian PT Busana Prima Global workers in Amsterdam, 2003. © Clean Clothes Campaign

19. (left) Françoise Rabary Harivelo, leader of garment union Syndicat Textile Malagasy, and Hanta Adrianasi, doctor and labour-rights advocate, Bangkok 2007. © Liesbeth Sluiter

20. (below) CCC International Campaign Forum, Bangkok 2007. © Liesbeth Sluiter

21.   (left) 'Help the Hema' campaign of the Dutch Clean Clothes Campaign, Amsterdam 2008. © Clean Clothes Campaign

22.   (below) Marieke Eyskoot of the Dutch Clean Clothes Campaign tries to convince bus drivers to ask their employer for 'clean' uniforms in public procurement campaign, Utrecht 2006. © Liesbeth Sluiter

23.   Clean Clothes Campaign Austria stages an action in the context of the Play Fair at the Olympics Campaign, Vienna 2008. © Klaus Bock

24.   Press conference for the pre-launch of the Play Fair Beijing Campaign 2008, Hong Kong 2007. © Clean Clothes Campaign

25. Emine Aslan sits outside Desa factory for months after being fired for trying to organise her co-workers, Istanbul 2008. © Clean Clothes Campaign

Epilogue

A last look backwards; a glimpse into the future. Who better to share them with than Ineke Zeldenrust, who took part in the very first 'clean clothes' protests in Amsterdam, and is still immersed in the daily cut-and-thrust of network dynamics? 'OK,' she says, 'but only if I can check with a few colleagues afterwards. One of the reasons that we have a network is that collaboration usually brings better results.' So be it.

Is it possible to gauge the consequences of the economic crisis that began in 2008?

We see a great many factory closures. On the other hand, a branch publication reports that global clothes sales in 2008 have reached an all time high once again; it blames overcapacity and bad loans for the closures. For sure, many companies will now go for the bottom line, but I just hope that the responsible ones will fight the crisis by building stable supply chains with better transparency and accountability. I hear many people saying that this crisis is a chance for more sustainability all around. I wish governments could respond in the same way to a social crisis as they do to this economic one. They appear to be able to line up support budgets and new laws incredibly fast.

Several figurehead companies say they work with fewer suppliers in order to rationalise and better control their supply chains. Do you think this is a trend, and does it represent progress?

We think the metaphor of the hour-glass still holds: many orders will go to increasingly fewer suppliers, who subcontract to a great many workplaces where working conditions are poor and control is lacking. Whether this is rationalisation is hard to say as yet, because we keep seeing proof of counter-trends: informalisation of labour, pressure on delivery schedules, pressure on prices. Those trends all feed the lower end of the hourglass. Also, we can still surprise even forerunner companies by pointing out violations in a supplier factory they didn't know they had. Nevertheless, serious company commitment to 'preferred suppliers' who adhere to labour rights would create space for better working conditions.

Fewer factories often implies fewer jobs. Not exactly the CCC's mission.

One of our enduring dilemmas. If you really take into account the consequences of this crazy showpiece economy for the environment and for communities, you have to start thinking about alternative production systems: less, but better. But what does that mean for labour? Our primary responsibility lies with garment workers. For them a bad job may be better than none. On the other hand, even in Bangladesh, which has the worst jobs in the world, some union leaders never stop emphasising that the fight is not about employment at any price, but about good jobs. In 2006 Bangladeshi workers burned down 200 of their own factories; have you ever seen a more explicit message?

I think there are ways to reduce production volume without hurting workers. Think: if the present average working week of 70–80 hours were to be shortened to 40–50 hours, you'd kill two birds with one stone – or rather, feed three with one piece of bread: you'd reduce production, reduce working hours and overtime, and save jobs. Wages would remain insufficient, so additionally profits would have to be divided more justly. Of course this is an oversimplified scenario, but there is truth in there.

Is the CCC developing a vision of a new economy that encompasses issues like the environment and the welfare of communities?

The urgency of fighting rights violations, of finding adequate strategies, of working together in a worldwide network – these things take up all of our time. I think we should not stop doing them; they are needed, and are the reason why we exist as an organisation. But I do think that a next chapter should be the development of a long-term vision, as a foundation for the urgent work. What is a sustainable garment industry? What type of enterprises would fit it? What does a stable supply chain look like? I think our proposals for a sector-wide approach are a first step on this direction.

In this context, there have also been some informal brainstorming sessions about an economy on a regional scale. Such an economy might strengthen the grip of workers on the supply chain, because it will no longer be so scattered, and this will fortify workers in negotiations with management. You'd have to ask whether and how this could harm those who are most vulnerable in the present-day global economy – women in the South; but I think there are ways to do it that will not hurt workers. Still, we have no idea about the form regional economies could take, or which strategies of the labour and solidarity movement could take us there. It presupposes a grip on economic design that we don't have. Our work on the purchasing practices of companies, the Asia Floor Wage campaign, the discussion about fair trade and ethical brands, about worker-owned cooperatives – they touch upon the subject; but for the moment our agenda is improving working conditions in supply chains, not designing new ones. On the basis of what workers want, we can indicate the direction, but we are not managers, nor do we want to be. They know about business; we know about labour rights.

What shifts do you see happening in CCC strategies?

In all our network evaluations, our four mainstays endure: the work on consumers, on companies, on authorities and legal reform, and on support for workers. But within these, changes occur. Some CCCs, for example, approach consumers more as citizens who do not only buy but also vote, have families and jobs. Although it is important not to lose consumer power as a tool to pressure companies, this perspective offers possibilities for action other than in the consumer sphere.

We also see that people are less inclined to become members of organisations. Traditionally, we 'collected' organisations in our coalitions; now you see that, for example, the Swedish and Austrian CCCs approach people individually, and use Facebook or similar networking tools to communicate with and organise them.

Are consumers interested in the CCC's message?

There are many studies to prove it, and there is a lot of interest in the subject, judging from the requests for information that reach us. We don't have to explain anymore that Clean Clothes is not the name of a dry-cleaner, and I think it is partly our achievement. The challenge has always been to provide them with channels for action, and to bundle together and amplify their voices. The network model implies that every affiliated organisation can do its own thing: write letters, organise a street action, have a religious service – whatever works best for its constituency. It's good when companies hear about it from various angles.

Do you see shifts in the company work as well?

We have done a lot of work on corporate accountability, and have reached its limits. We now need to find ways to apply pressure to the many links in the supply chain: the retailer, the brand, the agent, the Asian production company, factory management. Formerly, we just put pressure on Nike; that won't do anymore. We've already done some work on a multiple-pressure-point strategy, and need to extend that – not only into actions, but also into a vision on a sustainable supply chain, including ways to organise workers along such a chain.

How about new themes in company work?

Wages will remain important, and women's issues, and supporting freedom of association. All these killings of trade unionists in Cambodia and the Philippines – repression is fierce and the economic crisis will reinforce it. We are going to collaborate more with human rights organisations on this. Labour rights are human rights: that is what we want companies to realise. They need to respect human rights, not after the fact of a violation, but before they place an order, by making sure that in the factories they work with, workers have a contract and are paid a decent wage, and that social insurance contributions are paid.

I've heard many CCC members say that more work should be done on authorities and legal reform.

We have a resource problem there, but I think there are groups working in this field that we can support, like the European Coalition for Corporate Justice and Amnesty International.

Apart from that, the question is always what leverage we have with authorities. We've done well indirectly, through our collaboration with, for example, John Ruggie of the UN and Richard Howitt of the European parliament, but it remains to be seen how much of what is in their recommendations will be realised.

Is it all right for companies to exert pressure on governments for progressive labour law and its implementation?

In the ILO they have ample opportunity to address governments, together with the trade union movement, but they don't. Second, they often do just the opposite: they pressure governments to relax labour law. In this context, admonishing them to use their influence in a positive way can be dangerous, because it sets a precedent. In a meeting with Southern partners we've come to the conclusion that we can ask companies to support local organisations in their demands to their governments. In the 2008 Play Fair campaign, Nike was asked to stick its neck out, and agreed to ask the Chinese government to ratify the ILO convention on freedom of association.

Will the CCC continue to grow?

As a network, yes; in terms of engaged citizens who link up, yes. The International Secretariat – that's a different matter. We're six to seven people now, and the balance between the smaller national CCCs and the IS can be problematic. We serve the network, and people pose all kinds of questions that we need to be able to answer; on the other hand, we sometimes overcharge the national CCCs with work we ask them to do. Internally, growth would change us as an organisation. As things stand, we can still sit around the table to confer, and we know what everybody is up to even with all the travelling going on. We'd lose that if we continued to grow. It's an ongoing discussion.

It has always been important to us to take on young people. They can come up with ideas that I've never dreamed of, like the campaign 'Buy the Hema', which later turned into 'Friends of the Hema'. I personally would never have considered buying one of our targeted companies, let alone becoming its 'friend', but it is one of the most successful campaigns the Dutch CCC has had in years.

What is a CCC weak spot?

In large campaigns like Play Fair or Better Bargain, and also in urgent appeals campaigns, we must be able to organise public pressure with the speed and force of an avalanche, but it is my impression that this is not as easy as it used to be. Network partners can no longer take it for granted that the troops will promptly react to a roll-call. Maybe the fact that people don't easily join organisations anymore is to blame – there is certainly no lack of interest.

And its strength?

Our strategies are subjected to daily reality checks, because we always have one foot on the shop floor through our urgent appeals work, and because the demands and experiences of workers guide whatever we do. In today's world, it is amazing that, despite all barriers, people who wear clothes can still hook up with people who make them, and I think that if we keep doing it, in the end we will wear cool jeans and warm socks that are made under good working conditions.

Notes

INTRODUCTION

1. Naomi Klein, *No Logo*, Harper Perennial, 2005, p. xviii.
2. Charles Kingsley, *Cheap Clothes and Nasty*, 1850, available at <www.historyhome.co.uk/peel/economic/sweat.htm> (accessed 17 January 2007).
3. Ibid.
4. See <www.fashioninganethicalindustry.org>, fact sheet 1 (accessed 10 November 2008). Even after production of clothes was largely relocated to low-wage countries, parts of it remained in western Europe – notably clothes that needed a high level of craftsmanship, or very short delivery times.
5. Matthew Brunwasser, *New York Times*, 2007, translated as 'Roemenië loopt leeg', *NRC Handelsblad*, 17 April 2007.

1. A FOOTLOOSE ENTERPRISE

1. Personal conversation, Amsterdam, 29 October 2007.
2. Rudie van Meurs, 'Confectie. Als je hun inkopers een sigaar aanbiedt zeggen ze: wij presenteren hier de sigaren', *Vrij Nederland*, 3 January 1981.
3. Marijke Smit and Lorette Jongejans, *C&A: De Stille Gigant, van kleding-multinational tot thuiswerkster*, Amsterdam: SOMO, 1989, pp. 2–3; <www.c-en-a.nl/aboutUs/company/history/>, accessed 6 April 2007; 'C&A, une enseigne originale et performante', Information Presse, C&A France, undated.
4. Rudie van Meurs, 'Confectie. Het verborgen geldcircuit achter C&A', *Vrij Nederland*, 10 January 1981.
5. C&A is certainly not the only company to pressure manufacturers. But it is the market leader, and extremely secretive at that, which made it a preferred target for journalists and the anti-sweatshop movement alike.
6. *NRC Handelsblad*, 13 August 1975.
7. Rudie van Meurs, 'Een geheime C&A nota over emotionele reclame', *Vrij Nederland*, 24 January 1981.
8. Smit and Jongejans, *C&A: De Stille Gigant*, p. 64.
9. Ward Bezemer, 'De Prijs is het Bewijs', *Hervormd Nederland*, June 9, 1990.
10. Ibid.
11. Smit and Jongejans, *C&A: De Stille Gigant*, p. 76.
12. 'Beknopt overzicht diverse activiteiten', communication C&A Nederland, February 1993, p. 2.
13. Personal conversation, Amsterdam, 29 October 2007.
14. Smit and Jongejans, *C&A: De Stille Gigant*, pp. 39–40.
15. 'C&A. Een boekje open over onze mode-inkoop', C&A brochure, Amsterdam, 1990.
16. Edith Tulp, 'Opening in gesloten C&A-cultuur', *Textilia*, 1 May 1997.
17. Export processing zones (EPZs) or free trade zones are a mainstay for an export-oriented, foreign-investment-led economy. They are industrial areas

producing for export where taxes, tariffs and regulations are minimised and infrastructure optimised, in the hope of attracting foreign investment. They are criticised for giving companies a free rein in social and environmental matters, while failing to fulfil the promises of technology transfer and of helping local industries along. Because their low wages are a major incentive for companies to establish themselves in EPZs, their production is always labour-intensive and low-tech. They typically offer assembly work; materials are shipped in from wherever they are cheapest. According to a 1998 ILO report, approximately 27 million people then worked in about 850 export processing zones around the world; in Asia alone there were 225 zones. The leaders were China, with 124 zones; the Philippines, with 35; and Indonesia, with 26 zones. 'Labour and Social Issues Relating to Export Processing Zones', ILO, Geneva, 1998, p. 3.

18. *De Schone Klerenkrant*, October 1990, p. 4.
19. Personal conversation, Amsterdam, 29 October 2007.
20. Ibid.
21. Jan Bom, 'Waar C&A zijn voordeel haalt', *FNV Magazine*, 12 December 1990; *De Schone Klerenkrant*, October 1990, pp. 3–5.
22. *De Schone Kleren Brief*, January 1990.
23. *NN* magazine 62, July 1990.
24. Personal conversation, Amsterdam, 29 October 2007.
25. Financial support concerns emergency money only – for example, a strike fund in the absence of union funds. The CCC does not conceive of itself as a development organisation that subsidises its partner organisations – along the lines of Oxfam, for example.
26. *NN* magazine 62, July 1990.
27. After having evolved into an international campaign, the name 'Clean Clothes Campaign' stands for the movement as a whole and for the International Secretariat, while 'Schone Kleren Kampagne' is the Dutch branch. In this book, for English-speaking readers, I have also used 'Clean Clothes Campaign' or CCC for the movement's early years, when in fact the group was using only the Dutch name.
28. Personal conversation, Amsterdam, 29 October 2007.
29. Ibid.
30. Van Meurs, 'Confectie. Als je hun inkopers een sigaar aanbiedt'.
31. *Koopkracht* 7/8, July–August 1990. The judge found that it would have been better to publish C&A's defence together with the article containing the accusations, but no fine was imposed.
32. Bert van den Hoed, 'C&A vindt actie onrechtvaardig en onaangenaam', *Utrechts Nieuwsblad/NZC*, 12 November 1990.
33. Johan van Rixtel, 'Lage lonen: goedkope kleding', *NN* magazine 68, October 1990; Theo de Valk, Peter Custers and Pit Gooskens, 'Kledingindustrie', *De Schone Kleren Krant*, October 1990; *De Schone Kleren Brief*, March 1991.
34. De Valk et al., 'Kledingindustrie'. It is interesting to compare garment sector figures for the Philippines, Bangladesh and India with more recent ones (the following figures are rounded). The Philippines appear not to have been able to keep up with the expansion of the other two countries. In 1991, the Philippines had 14,000 clothes factories that employed 204,000 workers. In 1999, those figures had risen to 19,000 factories with 208,000 workers (indicating that small factories were still the norm); then a slow decline set in. In 2005, a little over 16,000 factories were registered, employing 213,000 workers. The number

of women working in the sector had fallen from 154,000 in 1991 to 150,000 in 2005 (<www.bles.dole.gov.ph/2007%20Publications/2007%20PIYB/Employment%20Statistics/LFS_Coverage.htm#lfsparta>, accessed 12 December 2008). Exports did not grow much either. Taking into account the devaluation of money in general and of the dollar specifically, they grew from US$1 billion at the end of the 1980s to US$2.646 billion in 2006 (<www.census.gov.ph/data/sectordata/sr07284tx.html>, accessed 12 December 2008). Developments in Bangladesh have been much more explosive, with 759 factories employing 335,000 workers in 1989, and 4,740 factories with 2.4 million workers in 2008. The value of clothing exports was US$0.6 billion in 1990 and US$10.1 billion in 2007 – representing a jump from 38.5 per cent to 80.8 per cent of total exports (<http://bgmea.com.bd/index.php?option=com_content&task=view&id=56&Itemid=175>, accessed 2 February 2009; *WTO International Trade Statistics 2008*, Table II.70, p. 115; <www.wto.org/english/res_e/statis_e/its2008_e/its2008_e.pdf>, accessed 2 February 2009). The Indian textiles and garment industry has experienced a 'mega-bonanza' since the end of the MFA quota regime, employing about 35 million people in 2001, about 3.5 million of them in garment factories. While textiles and textile products as a share of total exports had diminished compared to 1990, this was due to the growth of other sectors; actual exports had grown to US$13.2 billion in 2003/04 (*Background Note on Ludhiana's Garment Industry*, Fair Wear Foundation, January 2006, p. 1; <www.fairwear.nl>, accessed 4 February 2009). Tirupur, the most important garment-production region, showed extreme growth. The value of textile exports between 1984 and 2002 multiplied by a factor of 60 (Background Study Tirupur, Fair Wear Foundation, June 2004, pp. 4–6; <www.fairwear.nl>, accessed 4 February 2009).

35. Cock Rijneveen, 'Oosters geploeter voor westerse zomerjurkjes', *Haagse Courant*, 3 March 1994.
36. Nick Buckley, 'Why I'll never buy a pair of Levi's again', *Mail on Sunday*, 27 November 1994, pp. 37–41; Nick Buckley and Nick Fielding, 'Now C&A is accused in "sweatshop" labour row', *Mail on Sunday*, 4 December 1994; Nick Buckley and Nick Fielding, 'C&A cancels £5m-a-year deal in child labour row', *Mail on Sunday*, 18 December 1994; Nick Fielding, 'For 40p, this girl works 13 hours a day making C&A clothes. And shoppers in Britain spend millions buying them', *Mail on Sunday*, 8 January 1995, pp. 5, 37–9.
37. Personal conversation, Amsterdam, 12 November 2007.
38. Ineke Zeldenrust, personal conversation, Amsterdam, 21 November 2007.
39. Complaint by C&A to the Press Complaints Commission, February 1995.
40. Nick Fielding's statement to the Complaints Commission, 1 March 1995.
41. Adjudication, Press Complaints Commission report, 30 August 30 1995.
42. Code of Conduct for the Supply of Merchandise, C&A, 1991.
43. Socam 1997 *Annual Report*, Brussels, May 1998.
44. C&A paper for the LATC London conference, 21 October 1997.
45. Socam 1997 *Annual Report*, Brussels, May 1998.
46. Chapter 6 deals with the expansion of the European network.
47. Jenny Luesby and William Lewis, 'Rag trade probes work practices', *Financial Times*, October 1996.
48. De Vré, 'C&A speelt open kaart', *Trouw*, 9 February 1999; René Bogaarts, 'C&A has clean clothes', *Volkskrant*, 26 April 1997.
49. Personal conversation, Amsterdam, 12 November 2007.

50. *Case file: The Multinational Retail Trading Company C&A*, CCC International Forum, Brussels, April–May 1998.

51. Dieuwke Grijpma, 'De Max Havelaar-broek komt!', *NRC Handelsblad*, 9 October 1997.

52. In 1919, the International Labour Organisation was founded as part of the League of Nations, which in 1945 became the United Nations. In the course of its existence, the ILO passed a number of 'conventions' that set the standard for just and fair labour relations the world over. They are a work in progress. The first one, dated 1919, concerns hours of work. All ILO member-states must respect the 'core conventions' concerning child labour, forced labour, discrimination, and freedom of association. These conventions, plus five standards on the living wage, health and safety, maximum hours of work, security of employment, and collective bargaining form the basis of the Clean Clothes Campaign Code of Conduct (<www.ilo.org/ilolex/english/convdisp1.htm>, accessed 18 August 2007; <www.cleanclothes.org/codes-of-conduct>, accessed 18 August 2007).

53. Socam 1998 *Annual Report*, Brussels, May 1999.

54. 'C&A opposes illegal sweatshops as well', communication Board of Directors, C&A Netherlands, December 1988.

55. De Vré, 'C&A speelt open kaart'.

56. 'Top shops use Europe's "gulag" labour', *Sunday Times*, 27 September 1999.

57. Claudia Tellegen, *Clemens en August* (documentary), NCRV Document, 2000.

58. Edith Tulp, 'Opening in gesloten C&A-cultuur', *Textilia*, 1 May 1997; 'C&A krijgt European holding structuur met basis Brussel', *Texpress*, 7 March 1998; Gerrit de Jager-Mollema, 'Van "geen commentaar" tot een beetje commentaar', *Groene Amsterdammer*, 7 November 1998; Cor Hospes, 'Opruiming', *Management Team*, 29 January 1999.

59. A living wage means that wages and benefits paid for a standard working week must always be sufficient to meet the basic needs of workers and their families – such as housing, clothing, food, medical expenses, education – and must additionally provide some discretionary income. A living wage must reflect local conditions and may therefore vary locally. Clean Clothes Newsletter no. 20, December 2005. See also Chapter 10, the section on the Fair Wear Foundation.

60. Tellegen, *Clemens en August*.

61. C&A, *Corporate Social Responsibility Report*, Brussels, 2006, p. 43.

62. <www.cleanclothes.org/component/content/article/8-urgent-appeals/53>, accessed 1 June 2009.

63. C&A, *Corporate Social Responsibility Report*, Brussels, 2006, p. 44.

64. Ibid., p. 45.

65. Marques Casara, 'Que moda é essa?' *Observatório Social Em Revista*, May 2006.

66. From the report of the São Paulo City Council Investigative Committee, cited in 'Que moda é essa?'.

67. Stijntje Blankendaal, 'Kleding C&A uit illegale ateliers', *Trouw*, 16 June 2006.

68. 'C&A gaat samenwerken met website Wehkamp', *NRC Handelsblad*, 1 March 2007; Frits Baltesen, 'Omzet C&A groeit bovengemiddeld', *NRC Handelsblad*, 3 March 2007; Frits Baltesen, 'C&A breidt uit naar China en Texel', *NRC*

Handelsblad, 25 April 2007; <www.fashionunited.nl:80/nieuws/cna.htm>, accessed 25 March 2008; Anne Huschka, 'C&A op zoek naar de bodem van de kledingmarkt', *NRC Handelsblad*, 19 March 2008; <www.quotenet.nl/quote500>, accessed 10 November 2008.

69. *Acting Responsible*, C&A Europe, Düsseldorf/Brussels, April 2008, <www.c-and-a.com/aboutUs/socialResponsibility/report>, accessed 3 January 2009.
70. Global social compliance programme. See the section in Chapter 10 on global retailers.
71. The Fair Wear Foundation is a Netherlands-based multi-stakeholder initiative in which businesses, unions and NGOs collaborate to improve working conditions in the garment industry. See the section in Chapter 10 on the Fair Wear Foundation.
72. Personal conversation, Amsterdam, 20 February 2009.

2. DESTINATION ELSEWHERE

1. In her book *No Logo*, Naomi Klein vividly describes the rise of the global brands. In *Threads of Labour*, a volume of essays about garment industry supply chains from workers' perspective, Jennifer Hurley and Doug Miller use the term 'merchandisers' to describe brand owners that divest themselves of their manufacturing capacity in favour of offshore outsourcing, and concentrate marketing, design and finance at their headquarters in western countries. Angela Hale and Jane Wills, eds, *Threads of Labour*, Blackwell, 2005, p. 21.
2. SOMO/CCC, *Kleding in Bedrijf, de wandel van de handel*, 1996, updated 1998, pp. 4–13.
3. In 2006, after many protests from workers against abusive working conditions and low wages, Tri-Star left Uganda without repaying any of its debts, owing wages and severance pay. 'Footloose Garment Investors in Souther and Eastern Africa', *SOMO paper*, March 2008, p. 4 (available at <http://SOMO.nl/publications-nl/Publication_2477-nl/view>, accessed 3 January 2009).
4. The MFA was replaced by the Agreement on Textiles and Clothing (ATC) under the WTO in 1995. When quotas were phased out in 2004, other regulatory mechanisms became important, like trade agreements with import tariffs and non-tariff measures. Considerable impact on trade and investment is also exerted by so-called Rules of Origin, which define the percentage of goods and services in the exported product that must originate from the exported country. SOMO, 'Footloose Garment Investors in Souther and Eastern Africa', *SOMO paper*, March 2008, p. 2.
5. China, for example, was hit with extra quotas restricting its exports to European countries in 1995, when economic reforms were transforming China into a power that was making stunning advances on western markets (<www.eurocommerce.be/content.aspx?PageId=40956>, accessed 7 May 2008). From 2005 to 2008, after the MFA phase-out, China was the only member of the WTO subject to quota restrictions on its textiles and apparel products (<www.brookings.edu/testimony/2001/0425globaleconomics_lardy.aspx>, accessed 7 May 2008).
6. Duncan Green, *Fashion Victims: Together We Can Clean Up the Clothes Trade. The Asian Garment Industry and Globalisation*, Cafod, 1998, pp. 19–20.
7. SOMO, 'Footloose Garment Investors in Southern and Eastern Africa', *SOMO paper*, March 2008, p. 4.

8. International Labour Organisation, *Globalization of the footwear, textiles and clothing industries*, Geneva 1996, p. 25.
9. ILO, *Decent Work and the Informal Economy, Report VI, International Labour Conference, 90th session*, 2002.
10. Private conversation, Amsterdam, 12 November 2007.
11. Research results were compiled by CCC in three booklets, presenting facts and background in an accessible way: *Kleding in Beweging, het werk achter het merk*, CCC, 1995; *Kleding in Bedrijf, de wandel van de handel*, SOMO/CCC, 1996, updated 1998; *Ethiek in de Fabriek*, CCC, 1998. *Kleding in Bedrijf* was translated into English in 1997 as *Of Rags and Riches* (<www.cleanclothes. org/component/content/article/9/7-publications-overview>).
12. *Kleding in Bedrijf*, pp. 7–16.
13. The European expansion of the CCC will be the subject of Chapter 6.
14. For a full overview of CCC principles, see <www.cleanclothes.org/the-principles-of-the-clean-clothes-campaign>, accessed 1 June 2009.

3. ASIA

1. Fair Wear Foundation Background Study Bangladesh, January 2006 (<www. fairwear.nl>, accessed 29 March 2008).
2. Nils Klawitter, 'Blood in the supply line', *Spiegel Online*, 13 December 2005, www.spiegel.de, accessed 30 March 2008.
3. Fazlul Hoque, president of the Bangladesh Garment Manufacturers' and Exporters' Association, quoted in 'BD eyes $15bn textile exports by 2011' (<www.dawn.com/2006/09/03/ebr12.htm>, accessed 31 March 2008).
4. Data compiled from <www.cleanclothes.org>, accessed 28–31 March 2008.
5. Klawitter, 'Blood in the supply line'.
6. <www.cleanclothes.org>, accessed 31 March 2008. In 2009 the CCC partner-organisation AMRF reported that at least the process of payment had started. Some seriously injured Spectrum workers had received a one-time compensation payment from the fund, although it was not clear how many people received how much money, nor whether family members of the deceased were included (e-mail communication, 6 January 2009).
7 Personal conversation, Bangkok, 30 November 2007.
8. Barely two months after this conversation, factory investigator Mehedi Hasan, working for the American NGO Worker Rights Consortium, which is part of the CCC network, was arrested and imprisoned. He was one of many who fell victim to the ban on political and trade union activities during the state of emergency called in January 2007. Thanks to a worldwide protest-letter campaign and other pressure, Mehedi Hasan was released after two weeks (<www.cleanclothes.org>, accessed 4 March 2008).
9. War on Want, *Fashion Victims: The True Cost of Cheap Clothes at Primark, Asda and Tesco*, 2006, available at <www.cleanclothes.org/pub.htm>, accessed 10 February 2008.
10. Duncan Pruett, with Jeroen Merk, Ineke Zeldenrust and Esther de Haan, *Looking for a Quick Fix: How Weak Social Auditing is Keeping Workers in Sweatshops*, CCC, November 2005, available at <www.cleanclothes.org/component/content/article/9/7-publications-overview>, accessed 1 June 2009. The report is discussed in more detail in the section on audits in Chapter 10.
11. Personal conversation, Bangkok, 29 November 2007.

12. *Disrobing Nama: Non-Agricultural Market Access and its Implication on* [sic] *Women Workers in the Garment Sector and Domestic Industrial Policy*, MSN and CAW, Thailand, April 2007, p. 98; *Trade Union World Briefing* 19, ICFTU, August 2006.

13. *Trade Union World Briefing* 19.

14. *Disrobing Nama*, pp. 98–114.

15. *A Brief Report on the Conference Global Campaigning – Local Action*, CCC internal document, p. 32, written for a conference organised by the Clean Clothes Campaign and Centre for Education and Communication, 19–21 January 2006.

16. *Trade Union World Briefing* 19; Kelly Dent, *Brief Background on Sri Lanka*, 1999, available at <www.cleanclothes.org/component/content/article/9/7-publications-overview>, accessed 1 June 2009.

17. Salman Kelegama, 'Ready-Made Garment Industry in Sri Lanka: Preparing to Face the Global Challenges', *Asia-Pacific Trade and Investment Review* 1: 1, April 2005.

18. This happened, for example, with the Fine Lanka company, which produced for, among others, Sears Roebuck, J.C. Penny and Jeep. In 2000, 858 Fine Lanka workers lost their jobs after they had formed a union. *CC Newsletter* 15, June 2002.

19. The FLA was incorporated in 1999 as an American NGO, uniting companies, NGOs, colleges and universities in a multi-stakeholder organisation with the mission of ending sweatshop labour and improving working conditions worldwide. It engages in monitoring to assess whether affiliate companies are in compliance with FLA standards. Multi-stakeholder initiatives are discussed in more detail in Chapter 10.

20. An urgent appeal is a request for people to take action, usually in the form of protest letters addressed to the brands, employers and authorities involved, on a specific case of labour rights violation. The urgent appeals system is one of the tools the CCC uses to inform western consumers about production circumstances, while at the same time supporting workers and their organisations. It is discussed in more detail in Chapter 7.

21. In February 2008, the footloose nature of the industry asserted itself once more. In the article 'The earliest labour newspaper in the Free Trade Zone', *Dabindu*, February 2008, p. 2, the closure was reported of Jaqalanka Garments, due to a fall in orders. At that time, the 200 workers remaining out of a workforce of 470 were still awaiting full payment of wages and severance.

22. It is not without significance that the 'miracle' of these 'Asian tigers' came at the price of political oppression and abuse of human rights. The countries to be swept up by the global spinning wheel after the 'tigers', had authoritarian regimes of their own: Thailand, Malaysia, Bangladesh, Indonesia, the Philippines, Pakistan, Cambodia, Vietnam, Laos, China and Burma.

23. *Disrobing Nama*, pp. 63–80.

24. 'Nike Company Profile', compiled for the CCC Brussels 1998 Forum (<www.cleanclothes.org/component/content/article/9/957-nike-archive>, accessed 1 June 2009); Nina Ascoly and Ineke Zeldenrust, *East and South-East Asia Regional Labour Research Report*, CCC, December 2003 (<www.cleanclothes.org/component/content/article/9/7-publications-overview>, accessed 1 June 2009).

25. Ascoly and Zeldenrust, *East and South-East Asia Regional Labour Research Report*, p. 10.
26. Duncan Green, *Fashion Victims: Together We Can Clean Up the Clothes Trade. The Asian Garment Industry and Globalisation*, Cafod, 1998, p. 20; Marvin J. Levine, *Worker Rights and Labour Standards in Asia's Four New Tigers*, Springer, 1997, p. 184.
27. Timothy Connor, *We Are Not Machines*, Oxfam Community Aid Abroad et al., March 2002. Menstrual leave might be considered a luxury under western working conditions; in Indonesia women are not allowed to go to the toilet for more than a restricted number of minutes per day, cannot afford tampons or pain medication, and regularly work between 10 and 15 hours a day, sometimes standing up. For some women, menstrual leave may also be a religious requirement. Leslie Kretzu, 'Labour rights in Indonesia: What is menstruation leave?' *CC Newsletter* 13, November 2000, p. 12.
28. *Workers' Voices: An Interim Report of Workers' Needs and Aspirations in Nine Nike Contract Factories in Indonesia*, Center for Societal Development Studies, Atma Jaya Catholic University, Jakarta, 2001, pp. 31–2.
29. Leslie Kretzu, 'Labour rights in Indonesia: What is menstruation leave?' *CC Newsletter* 13, November 2000, p. 12.
30. Urban Community Mission Jakarta and Ingeborg Wick, *The Knot in the Thread: Indonesian Garment Production for German Fashion TNCs*, Südwind Institute of Economics and Ecumenism and the German CCC, Südwind Texte 11, Siegburg/Germany, May 2000, p. 5.
31. Ibid., p. 9.
32. 'Nike Company Profile'.
33. In 2005, Nike became the first major brand to disclose its global supply chain publicly. In 2007, China headed the Nike list, with 132 production locations among a total of over 700. Thailand came in second, with 63 companies, while Indonesia had 37 (<www.nike.org>, accessed 9 March 2008).
34. *CC Newsletter* 16, February 2003, pp. 8–9 and back cover.
35. Associated Press, 29 July 2002.
36. *Jakarta Post*, 22 November 2002; CCC's Nike archive, <www.cleanclothes. org>, accessed 7 March 2008.
37. The appearance and importance of these Asian multinational producers is discussed in Chapter 10, in the section on Asian transnational production companies.
38. Ascoly and Zeldenrust, *East and South-East Asia Regional Labour Research Report*, pp. 17–18.
39. *Decent Work and the Informal Economy*, ILO, Report VI, International Labour Conference, 90th session, 2002.
40. Personal conversation, Bangkok, 29 November 2007.
41. *Internationally Recognised Core Labour Standards in Indonesia*, ICFTU, report for the WTO General Council Review of Trade Policies of Indonesia, Brussels, 2003, pp. 2–4.
42. In 2008, the CCC, Oxfam Australia and Indonesian trade unions published the document, 'Sector-wide solutions for the sports shoe and apparel industry in Indonesia', that outlines a set of measures to counteract the effects of factory closures and informalisation of the economy. The document is sent to brands sourcing in Indonesia and to multi-stakeholder initiatives (<www. cleanclothes.org/documents/080320_Sector-Wide_Solutions_in_Indonesia.pdf>,

accessed 1 June 2009). See also the section on new campaign perspectives in Chapter 10.

43. Personal conversation, Bangkok, 28 November 2007.

44. 'Action in Bangkok by former Nike employees', <www.cleanclothes.org>, accessed 26 March 2008; Voravidh Charoenloet, *Thailand After the Economic Crisis of 1997: Labour Issues*, Faculty of Economics, Chiangmai University, n.d.; Ascoly and Zeldenrust, *East and South-East Asia Regional Labour Research Report*, p. 9.

45. *Workers' Story Thailand, 1996: Eden*, TIE-Asia, <www.cleanclothes.org>, accessed 19 March 2008; *CC Newsletter* 7/8, February and September 1997.

46. In Thailand, as in other southeast Asian countries, unions are often established on factory- instead of sector-level. While this facilitates grassroots organisation, it does not make support from factories in the same line of work easy or automatic. Philip S. Robertson Jr and Somasak Playioowong, *The Struggle of the Gina Workers in Thailand: Inside a Successful International Labour Solidarity Campaign*, Working Papers Series 75, City University of Hong Kong, November 2004, available at <www.cleanclothes.org>, accessed 26 March 2008.

47. Junya Yimprasert and Suthasini Kaewleklai, 'Par Garment – Endless Struggle', Thai Labour Campaign, 17 May 2000, available at <www.cleanclothes.org/component/content/article/4-companies/1040-par-garment-endless-struggle>, accessed 1 June 2009; 'Runaway employer at Thailand's Par Garment', available at <www.cleanclothes.org>, accessed 19 March 2008.

48. Robertson and Playioowong, *Struggle of the Gina Workers*.

49. <www.betterfactories.org>, accessed 15 March 2008.

50. Ibid.

51. Ascoly and Zeldenrust, *East and South-East Asia Regional Labour Research Report*, pp. 29–30.

52. <www.icftu.org/displaydocument.asp?Index=991218896>, accessed 28 December 2007.

53. Personal conversation, Bangkok, 26 November 2007. In May 2004, Ros Sovannarith, union president at the Trinunggal Komara factory, was murdered in a manner similar to Chea Vichea. In March 2006 Hy Vuthy, union president of the Suntex garment factory, was shot dead while riding his motorcycle home after finishing his night shift at the factory. He had just successfully negotiated a one-day holiday for Suntex workers for the Khmer New Year. Hy Vuthy's murder was preceded by at least five incidents of violence against union officials at Suntex and the neighbouring Bright Sky factory, both owned by the Singapore-based Ocean Sky Group (<www.cleanclothes.org/component/content/article/8-urgent-appeals/63-justice-still-needed-in-chea-vichea-murder-case>, accessed 1 June 2009). In December 2008, after nearly five years in prison, the two men convicted of killing Chea Vichea were provisionally released, pending a retrial. The Supreme Court called for a new investigation into the case (<www.cleanclothes.org/component/content/article/8-urgent-appeals/1258-good-news-release-of-born-samnang-and-sok-samoeun>, accessed 1 June 2009).

54. Personal conversation, Bangkok, 2 December 2007.

55. <www.oxfamsol.be/nl/article.php3?id_article=385>, accessed 2 January 2008.

56. The River Rich factory case is one of them. In 2006, after the factory management had failed to honour the agreement that had been reached in

a labour conflict and the ensuing strike had been violently repressed by the police, an international campaign built up pressure. In the middle of 2007 a satisfactory agreement was signed between the company's main buyer, Inditex, the management, and the unions, *CC Newsletter* 24, 2008.

57. Micha X. Peled, *China Blue* (documentary), Teddy Bear Films, 2006.
58. The ratio of men to women workers in Dongguan, one of the industry's hotspot cities in the South, is approximately one-to-three (*China Labour Bulletin* Research Series 2, 'Falling Through the Floor: Migrant Women Workers' Quest for Decent Work in Dongguan, China', September 2006, p. 5, <www.clb.org. hk/en/files/File/research_reports/Women_Workers_Report.pdf>).
59. Personal conversation, Amsterdam, 27 September 2006.
60. *Conditions of Women Workers in Special Economic Zones and Labour Standards in Supplier Factories of German Garment Retailer Companies and Brands in China*, Hong Kong Christian Industrial Committee, September 2004, pp. 1–4.
61. 'Stitched up', in *Codes Memo* 20, December 2005, pp. 17–19 (<www. maquilasolidarity.org>, accessed 28 February 2009; <www.pbs.org/wgbh/pages/ frontline/shows/walmart/interviews/gereffi.html>, accessed 14 March 2008).
62. Nina Ascoly and Ineke Zeldenrust, *Challenges in China: Experiences from Two CCC Pilot Projects on Monitoring and Verification of Code Compliance*, SOMO, October 2003, pp. 5–7.
63. David Barboza and Elisabeth Becker, 'Free of Quota, China Textiles Flood the USA', *New York Times*, 10 March 2005.
64. 'Er dreigt een omgekeerde, ongewenste immigratie', *NRC Handelsblad*, 7 November 2008; Hans Moleman, 'Een tsunami aan goedkope waren', *Volkskrant*, 15 December 2007; speech of Dutch ambassador to China, Dirk Jan van den Berg, at the FNV conference *Made in China*, 3 March 2007; 'Shoppen tot je erbij neervalt in Shenzhèn', *NRC Handelsblad*, 30 June 2007.
65. *Play Fair 2008: No Medal for the Olympics on Labour Rights*, ITUC, ITGLWF, CCC, pp. 8–9, available at <www.playfair2008.org>, accessed 29 February 2009; *Whose Miracle? How China's Workers are Paying the Price for its Economic Boom*, ICFTU, December 2005.
66. China Labour Bulletin, 'Falling Through the Floor', p. 14.
67. China Labour Bulletin, 'Wages in China', February 2008, <www.clb.org.hk/ en/node/100206>, accessed 14 January 2009.
68. 'Stormloop op goedkope bakolie Chinese supermarkt: drie doden', *NRC Handelsblad*, 12 November 2007.
69. *Washington Post*, 14 May 2002.
70. Au Loong-yu, Nan Shan and Zhang Ping, *Women Migrant Workers under the Chinese Social Apartheid*, Committee for Asian Women, May 2007, p. 4.
71. China Labour Bulletin, 'Wages in China' and 'Falling Through the Floor'.
72. <www.europarl.europa.eu/sides/getDoc.do?pubRef=-//EP//TEXT+TA+P6-TA-2006-0346+0+DOC+XML+V0//EN&language=EN>, accessed 14 January 2009.
73. China Labour Bulletin, September 2007, 'Small Hands: A Survey Report on Child Labour in China', p. 32, available at <www.clb.org.hk>, accessed 13 January 2009; Rao De Juji, Wei Xing, Liu Huilong, Li Ming, Kou Jinming, Shi Xisheng, Cheng Xi, Wei Xuejun, 'Authorities attempt to play-down Dongguan child labour scandal', *Southern Metropolitan Daily*, 28 April 2008 (<http:// www.china-labour.org.hk/en/node/100247>, accessed 21 May 2008).
74. <www.ituc-csi.org/spip.php?article2141>, accessed 14 January 2009.

75. <http://survey08.ituc-csi.org/survey.php?IDContinent=3&IDCountry=CHN&Lang=EN2007>; <www.clb.org.hk/en/node/100014> – both accessed 16 January 2009.

76. Han Dongfang, 'Collective Bargaining and the New Labour Contract Law', China Labour Bulletin, 26 February 2008 (<www.clb.org.hk/en/node/100210>, accessed 13 January 2009).

77. <www.ituc-csi.org/spip.php?article2141>, accessed 14 January 2009; *FNV Company Monitor*, FNV Bondgenoten, October 2006, p. 15.

78. ITUC et al., 'Play Fair 2008: No Medal for the Olympics', pp. 9, 26.

79. Dexter Roberts and Pete Engardio, with Aaron Bernstein in Washington, Stanley Holmes in Seattle, and Xiang Ji in Beijing, 'Secrets, Lies and Sweatshops' (<www.businessweek.com/mediacenter/podcasts/cover_stories/covercast_11_16_06.htm>, accessed 13 January 2009).

80. Han Dongfang, 'The state of the labour movement in China' (<www.china-labour.org.hk/en/node/100349>, accessed 28 February 2009).

81. CCC *China Strategy Meeting*, September 2006, internal CCC document.

82. ITUC et al., *Play Fair 2008. No medal for the Olympics*, p. 5.

83. <www.playfair2008.org/docs/Clearing_the_Hurdles.pdf>, accessed 10 January 2009. See section on sportswear campaigns in Chapter 6 for more details of the Play Fair 2008 campaign.

84. In 2009, Staphany Wong left the IHLO to live and work in Germany.

85. Personal conversation, Bangkok, 29 November 2007.

86. Personal conversation, Amsterdam, 19 May 2008.

87. See beginning of the China section for a description of the NGO Worker Empowerment.

88. Interestingly, a garment branch report analysing developments in 2008 states that global garment sales in 2008 registered at an all-time record. The report maintained that factories worldwide were collapsing not because westerners have stopped buying clothes, but because of overcapacity and financial weaknesses throughout the industry, and because of the increasing reluctance of banks to incur risks by further lending, causing weak companies to weaken further. *The Source: The Clothessource Digest of Sourcing Intelligence* 12, 2008, p. 1. This 'survival of the fittest' mechanism gives rise to the speculation that the crisis serves the industry by cutting the dead wood, while workers are left without jobs and compensation.

89. In 1995, 15 per cent of China's exports to OECD countries were high-tech in nature; in 2007 this had increased to 35 per cent, while the nominal total increase was three times as high. Speech of Dirk Jan van den Berg, 3 March 2007.

90. 'Er dreigt een omgekeerde, ongewenste immigratie', *NRC Handelsblad*, 7 November 2008; 'Chinees protest tegen ontslag', *NRC Handelsblad*, 26 November 2008.

91. 'China telt 20 mln nieuwe werklozen', *NRC Handelsblad*, 3 February 2009; 'Miljoenen Chinezen hopen op nieuw werk', *NRC Handelsblad*, 4 February 2009.

4. AFRICA

1. Personal conversation, Bangkok, 2 December 2007.

2. The Friedrich-Ebert-Stiftung is a German political foundation close to the German Social Democratic Party. It works in over 80 countries, and has been in Madagascar since the 1960s.

3. Personal conversation, Bangkok, 1 December 2007.
4. A recent survey of the textiles industry estimates that this sector represents 20 per cent of the employment in the formal private sector, with 84,544 workers, of which 54 per cent are women, in 80 enterprises. The main labour issues are overtime; low wages which, even if they are within the legal framework, do not meet basic needs; high risks to health and safety; lack of a vocational perspective; and the weakness of unions in collective bargaining. Conditions have deteriorated because Madagascar has a high rate of unemployment, and its industry is a high-cost one in comparison to other countries. *Etude sur les entreprises franches textiles à Madagascar*, Cabinet Miara-Mita, Friedrich-Ebert-Stiftung, November 2008.
5. Personal conversation, Bangkok, 30 November 2007.
6. SOMO is a Dutch organisation that has researched multinationals since 1973.
7. The Lomé/Cotonou agreements, introduced in 1975, regulated an economic partnership between the European Union and 73 former colonies of European states, whereby certain products could enter the EU free of duty or quota restrictions. In 2008 they were replaced by economic partnership agreements (EPAs). The African Growth and Opportunity Act (AGOA) is an eight-year agreement, signed in 2000 as an extension of the US General System of Preferences. It arranges for the duty- and tariff-free export of more than 6400 products, including garments, from almost 40 sub-Saharan African countries to the US. In return, AGOA demands that African countries remove trade and investment barriers, give US firms equal treatment with African firms, and further privatise and open up markets in the service sector.
8. Personal conversation, Amsterdam, 4 February 2008.
9. Esther de Haan and Gary Phillips, *Made in Southern Africa*, CCC 2002, p. 46, <http://www.cleanclothes.org/documents/Africa-report.pdf >.
10. Personal conversation, Amsterdam, 4 February 2008.
11. SOMO, *Footloose Garment Investors in Southern and Eastern Africa*, March 2008, p. 5, <http://somo.nl/publications-nl/Publication_2477-nl>.
12. Michael Koen works for the South African Civil Society Research and Support Collective. He has been educational secretary of an affiliate of Cosatu, the Congress of South African Trade Unions, lectured at university, and worked for several labour services organisations.
13. Personal conversation, Bangkok, 28 November and 2 December 2007.
14. de Haan and Phillips, *Made in Southern Africa*, pp. 50–1.
15. Esther de Haan and Michael Koen, 'Action Research in the Garment Sector in Southern and Eastern Africa', March 2005, p. 9, <http://www.cleanclothes.org/component/content/article/9/7-publications-overview>, accessed 1 June 2009.

5. EUROPE'S NEIGHBOURS

1. Personal conversation, Amsterdam, 20 February 2008.
2. Unless otherwise stated, data in this chapter are compiled from the report *Made in Eastern Europe*, CCC, March 1998 (<http://www.cleanclothes.org/component/content/article/9/7-publications-overview>, accessed 1 June 2009); *CC Newsletter* 11, August 1999, pp. 11–12; *CC Newsletter* 15, June 2002, pp. 6–7; Regina Barendt, Kerstin Ewald, Vanja Lesić, Katerina Milenkova, Bettina Musiolek, Danica Pop-Mitiç, Bilge Seckin, Tim Zülch , ed. by Chantal

Duval, *Workers' Voices: The Situation of Women in the Eastern European and Turkish Garment Industries*, CCC and Evangelische Akademie Meissen, 2005, <http://www.cleanclothes.org/documents/05-workers_voices.pdf >, accessed 28 February 2009.

3. *Made in Eastern Europe*, CCC, March 1998. Solidarnosc is the Polish trade union established as an alternative to the communist union in 1980, and temporarily banned by the communist government in 1981. It was the first non-communist trade union in a communist country.

4. Duval et al., *Workers' Voices*.

5. Personal conversation, Amsterdam, 20 February 2008.

6. Personal conversation, Bangkok, 29 November 2007, and e-mail communication, 20 October 2008.

7. Karat Coalition, *Fair Play, Always in Fashion*, project report 2008, available at <www.karat.org>, accessed 28 February 2009.

8. Poland is also one of four countries involved in the CCC's Fair Fashion project, which tries to inspire teachers and students of fashion colleges to care about social standards in clothes production.

9. Fair Wear Foundation, 'Background Study on Turkey', July 2004, p. 29, available at <www.fairwear.nl>, accessed 29 February 2009; Duval et al., *Workers' Voices*.

10. <www.wto.org/english/res_e/statis_e/its2008_e/its2008_e.pdf>, table II.69, p. 114, accessed 6 January 2009.

11. FWF, 'Background Study on Turkey', pp. 3–4, 12–14.

12. Dr Jason Heyes, ed., *Tackling Unregistered Work through Social Dialogue: Final Report of the 2005–2007 EU–ILO Project*, ILO, 2007, p. 37.

13. FWF, 'Background Study on Turkey', p. 32.

14. Ibid. pp. 16–18.

15. <http://www.cleanclothes.org/component/content/article/8-urgent-appeals/64>, accessed 1 June 2009.

16. Women's Rights at Work Association; the trade unions Disk-Tekstil and Teksif; Türkoder Consumers Organisation, Working Group on Women's Home-Based Work, and Avcilar Home-Working Women's Cooperative. Duval et al., *Workers' Voices*.

17. Personal telephone conversation, 20 November 2008.

18. <http://www.cleanclothes.org/component/content/article/8-urgent-appeals/64>, accessed 1 June 2009.

19. 'Lone unionist fights on and on and on...', *Hurriyet Daily News*, 22 November 2008, available at <www.hurriyet.com.tr/english/domestic/10416884.asp?scr=1>, accessed 25 November 2008.

20. <www.labourstart.org>, accessed 28 February 2009.

21. Personal telephone communication, 20 November 2008. On 24 December the court found that Emine Arslan and four workers from the Duzce factory had been illegally dismissed as a result of union activity, and that they should either be reinstated or properly compensated. Desa appealed these findings. On 20 January 2009, eight more workers won the same verdict. With the exception of the companies El Corte Ingles, Marks & Spencer and Debenham's, which have raised concerns with Desa, brands have taken no action, some of them referring to audits that had disclosed no irregularities. <http://www.cleanclothes.org/desa-renews-threats>, accessed 1 June 2009.

6. STRATEGIC DEVELOPMENTS

1. Personal conversation, Lisbon, 24 April 2008.
2. *ICF 2007 report*, CCC, November 2007, p. 38.
3. 'Textielwerknemers krijgen EU-geld', *NRC Handelsblad*, 19 September 2008.
4. Naomi Klein, *No Logo*, Harper Perennial, 2005, p. 327.
5. Ibid. p. 352.
6. Ibid. p. 328.
7. Julie Su, 'El Monte Thai Garment Workers: Slave Sweatshops', in Andrew Ross, ed., *No Sweat. Fashion: Free Trade and the Rights of Garment Workers*, Verso, 1997.
8. 'A code for Homeworkers: Australia's Fair Wair Campaign', *CC Newsletter* 11, August 1999, p. 9. See also the section in Chapter 7 titled 'The informal economy and migrant labour'.
9. *CC Newsletter* 4, March 1995, p. 5.
10. Personal conversation, Amsterdam, 30 December 2008.
11. Personal conversation, Brussels, 2 June 2008.
12. *CC Newsletter* 6, July 1996, p. 5.
13. Ibid., p. 8.
14. Ibid., p. 10.
15. Women Working Worldwide is an organisation supporting the rights of women working in international supply chains producing western consumer goods. Its ties with the Dutch CCC go back to the first CCC campaign against Philippine sweatshop labour, described in Chapter 1. Nead (Norfolk Education & Action for Development) is a locally based organisation that promotes awareness and action on global issues.
16. *CC Newsletter* 5, November 1995, p. 4.
17. Naomi Klein, *No Logo*, p. 393.
18. Ibid. pp. 395–6.
19. 'European Project', *CC Newsletter* 5, p. 5.
20. The companies are Hennes and Mauritz, Indiska, Lindex and KappAhl (<http://www.cleanclothes.org/component/content/article/3-codes-of-conduct/583-the-swedish-project-on-independent-monitoring>, accessed 1 June 2009). Hennes and Mauritz is the Swedish retail giant that conquered the market by means of its extremely fast turnaround of merchandise, and in 2008 operated in 29 countries with 1500 stores.
21. *CC Newsletter* 9, February 1998, p. 6.
22. Carole Crabbé and Isabelle Delforge, *Jouets de la Mondialisation*, Vista 2002; <www.vetementspropres.be/marques/jouetsdelamondialisation.pdf>, accessed 28 February 2009.
23. For more on public procurement, see section below on clean clothes communities. For more on the Fair Wear Foundation, see section below on codes and companies, and the relevant section of Chapter 10.
24. <www.helpdehema.nl>, accessed 28 February 2009. In 2007 Hema suffered a loss of 18.8 million euors, due to the high interest on the loans involved in its takeover by private equity firm Lion Capital. 'Schuldenlast drukt Hema in verliezen', *NRC Handelsblad*, 6 August 2008. In 2007, Hema started a line of textiles and clothes made from organically grown cotton.
25. <www.fashioninganethicalindustry.org>, accessed 28 February 2009.

26. <www.cleanupfashion.co.uk>, accessed 28 February 2009; LBL, *Who Pays for Cheap Clothes? 5 Questions the Low-Cost Retailer Must Answer*, 2006.

27. Bettina Musiolek, ed., *Ich bin chic und Du mußt schuften*, Brandes und Apsel, 1997; 'The Catch in Garment Production: Working Conditions in the Chinese and Philippine Garment Industries with Emphasis on Suppliers' Factories of German Companies', Südwind, 1997.

28. All campaign activities collected from *CC Newsletter* 7–24 , available at <www.cleanclothes.org>, accessed in the course of 2008.

29. *CC Newsletter* 12, May 2000, p. 3.

30. For a full version of the code and associated documents, see <http://www.cleanclothes.org/codes-of-conduct>, accessed 1 June 2009.

31. ICFTU, ITGLWF, ETUF/TCL.

32. Later, after the FWF had taken off and full compliance appeared to be even more complicated than presumed, the trademark was 'toned down' to a hang-tag in clothes that informed consumers about the company's FWF membership.

33. Trade union federations FNV and CNV, and industry organisations Mitex and Modint.

34. *CC Newsletter* 11, August 1999, p. 20.

35. *CC Newsletter* 22, October 2006, pp. 12–15. In 2009, the Jo-In project published its final report and decided to continue as a forum. It will focus on the formulation of a definitive common code, on collaboration regarding workers' complaints in factories from which several MSI members are sourcing, and on a common approach to freedom of association. For more information, see the section on the Fair Wear Foundation in Chapter 10.

36. In November 2005, CCC activists picketed the first major BSCI conference in Brussels. Detectives Thomson and Thompson, the sympathetic investigators featuring in Belgium's national comic Tintin, explained to passers-by that BSCI relied on weak auditing, was not accountable to the public, and did not involve local stakeholders (<http://www.cleanclothes.org/component/content/article/3-codes-of-conduct/467-clean-clothes-campaign-protest-at-bsci-qethical-sourcingq-conference>, accessed 1 June 2009).

37. Eileen Boris, 'Consumers of the World Unite! Campaigns Against Sweating, Past and Present', in Daniel E. Bender and Richard A. Greenwald, eds, *Sweatshop USA: The American Sweatshop in Historical and Global Perspective*, Routledge, 2003, pp. 214–215; Jeroen Merk, 'The Structural Crisis of Labour Flexibility: Strategies and Prospects for Transnational Labour Organising in the Garment And Sportswear Industry', CCC, 2008, p. 32, available at <http://www.cleanclothes.org/component/content/article/7-publications/116-the-structural-crisis-of-labour-flexibility>, accessed 1 June 2009.

38. <www.walmartstores.com/Files/2006ReportonEthicalSourcing.pdf>, accessed 15 March 2007.

39. Duncan Pruett, with Jeroen Merk, Ineke Zeldenrust and Esther de Haan, *Looking for a Quick Fix: How Weak Social Auditing is Keeping Workers in Sweatshops*, CCC, 2005. See also the section on audits in Chapter 10 of this volume.

40. <http://www.cleanclothes.org/documents/wearing_thin.PDF>, accessed 1 June 2009.

41. *CC Newsletter* 12, May 2000, p. 17.

42. *CC Newsletter* 13, November 2000, p. 22.

43. *CC Newsletter* 11, p. 17.

44. *CC Newsletter* 12, p. 5.
45. The Play Fair Olympic campaign of 2004 managed to convince Puma that it needed to do more. Together with other sportswear giants, Puma undertook steps to give its monitoring programmes more credibility, notably on freedom of association.
46. *CC Newsletter* 15, June 2002, p. 30.
47. *CC Newsletter* 13, p. 5.
48. <www.ethicaltrade.org/Z/lib/2006/09/impact-report/index.shtml>, accessed 28 February 2009.
49. Angela Hale and Jane Wills, eds, *Threads of Labour: Garment Industry Supply Chains from the Workers' Perspective*, Blackwell, 2005.
50. The reference section of the CCC website, <http://www.cleanclothes.org/codes-of-conduct>, presents an overview of CCC code–related work. Another valuable resource is the four-monthly *Codes Memo*, published on the internet by the Canadian Maquila Solidarity Network from 2000 onwards, in both Spanish and English. It compiles information on codes of conduct, government action on corporate social responsibility, and labour rights all over the world (<http://en.maquilasolidarity.org/resources/codesmemo>, accessed 28 February 2009).
51. The Permanent Peoples' Tribunal is an international opinion tribunal, independent from any state authority. Its verdicts adhere to international law and are delivered by high-level judges. It examines complaints regarding violations of human rights, submitted by their victims or groups representing them. The Tribunal was founded in 1979, inspired by the Russell Tribunals on the war crimes in Vietnam. After its first verdict on the conflict in Western Sahara, it tackled a range of issues, from the Armenian genocide to the rights of asylum seekers in Europe (<http://cpcabrisbane.org/Kasama/2007/V21n1/PermanentPeoplesTribunal.htm> and <http://upsidedownworld.org/main/content/view/1411/1/>, both accessed 2 January 2009).
52. Naomi Klein, *No Logo*, p. 391.
53. *CC Newsletter* 10, August 1998, p. 5.
54. Implementation of the monitoring programme was then stonewalled by the Bush administration, which rejected the request to allow the ILO to conduct the monitoring programme, and insisted that a private monitor be selected. Nikki F. Bas, Medea Benjamin, Joannie C. Chang, 'Saipan Sweatshop Lawsuit Ends with Important Gains for Workers and Lessons for Activists' (<http://www.cleanclothes.org/component/content/article/6/617-saipan-sweatshop-lawsuit-ends-with-important-ga>, accessed 1 June 2009).
55. *CC Newsletter* 10, August 1998, p. 5.
56. Personal conversation, Louvain-la-Neuve, 2 June 2008.
57. John Ruggie, special representative to the UN secretary-general for business and human rights, initiated and presides over the UN consultations. Chapter 9 will discuss the legal approach in more detail.
58. Eileen Boris, 'Consumers of the World Unite!', in Bender and Greenwald, eds, *Sweatshop USA*, p. 218. See also <www.studentsagainstsweatshops.org>, <www.workersrights.org>, both accessed 28 February 2009; <www.sweatshop-watch.org>, accessed 15 December 2007.
59. <www.sweatfree.org>, accessed 10 October 2008.
60. *CC Newsletter* 16, February 2003, p. 30.
61. <www.mvonederland.nl>, accessed 10 October 2008.

62. <http://SOMO.nl/html/paginas/pdf/Workwear_companies_2005_NL.pdf>, accessed 7 January 2009.

63. Personal conversation, Brussels, 2 June 2008.

64. Personal conversation, Louvain-la-Neuve, 2 June 2008. Other data on clean clothes communities from *CC Newsletter* 11, p. 18; *CC Newsletter* 17, December 2003, p. 16. For the CCCommunities model resolution, see *CC Newsletter* 19, July 2005, pp. 16–17.

65. The International Federation of Association Football (FIFA), together with international trade unions, drew up a comprehensive code of conduct in 1996. Immediately the World Federation of Sporting Goods Industry came up with its own, weaker code. Adidas and others then based their code on the WFSGI code. *CC Newsletter* 13, p. 9.

66. For the 2008 Beijing Olympic Games, the Dutch Olympic Committee provided athletes with an information kit put together by Amnesty International, a Tibet Support Group, the Clean Clothes Campaign, and the FNV trade union federation. A clean clothes logo to sew onto Olympic clothing and equipment was not an option: contracts allowed only the logos of sponsoring brands.

67. *CC Newsletter*, pp. 18–19.

68. 'Purchasing Practices can Undermine Workers' Rigths', in *CC Newsletter* 20, December 2005, pp. 10–11; Jeroen Merk, *The Play Fair at the Olympics Campaign: An Evaluation of the Company Responses,* CCC, ICFTU, Oxfam, June 2005.

69. *Tell The Sportswear Industry to Pay Fair!* (<http://playfair2008.org/>, accessed 18 June 2008).

70. Ibid.

71. *Play Fair 2008: No Medal for the Olympics on Labour Rights*, ITUC, ITGLWF, CCC (<www.playfair2008.org>, accessed 28 February 2009).

72. *Child Labour, Forced Labour and 'Work Experience' in China: The Blurred Lines of Illegality*, ITUC, GUF, HKCTU, HKTUC, Hong Kong Liaison Office, 2 August 2007, pp. 2–5 (<www.playfair.org>, accessed 28 February 2009).

73. <www.playfair2008.org/docs/Clearing_the_Hurdles.pdf>, accessed 10 January 2009.

74. *CC Newsletter* 14, July 2001.

75. 'North Sails, de schimmen achter het zeil', *Schoon Genoeg* 4, April 2005, p. 11; personal conversation with Christa de Bruin and Floris de Graad, Amsterdam, 4 June 2008; personal conversation with Tessel Pauli, Amsterdam, 10 December 2008. Tessel Pauli comments:

> It shows how slow the OECD and NCP procedures work. As a rule, the NCPs are reluctant to come right out and state that a company has violated OECD guidelines. The CCC considers this to be a result of weaknesses of the NCP procedures. They are slow and go for compromise behind closed doors. Truth-finding is less important than mediation.

76. Nina Ascoly and Chantal Finney, eds, *Made by Women: Gender, the Global Garment Industry and the Movement for Women Workers' Rights*, CCC 2005 (<www.cleanclothes.org/resources/1304-made-by-women>, accessed 1 June 2009).

77. Ibid.

78. See the section on Sri Lanka in Chapter 3.

79. ITGLWF, e-mail communication, 5 and 9 January 2009. The figures are a projection from a questionnaire that has been returned by a little over a quarter of affiliated unions.
80. Personal conversation, Bangkok, 28 November 2007.
81. E-mail communication, 31 December 2008.
82. Personal conversation, Bangkok, 27 November 2007.
83. Personal conversation, Bangkok, 30 November 2007.
84. CCC, *Organising the CCC International Network: A Framework for Partner Relationships*, June 2006 (<www.cleanclothes.org/the-principles-of-the-clean-clothes-campaign>, accessed 1 June 2009).
85. Personal conversation, Amsterdam, 20 May 2008. Since 2008, Marieke Eyskoot has been coordinator of the Dutch CCC.

INTERLUDE: THE EUROPEAN NETWORK UP-CLOSE

1. Personal conversation, Amsterdam, 19 February 2008.
2. Personal conversations, Brussels, 13 November 2006 and Louvain-la-Neuve 2 June 2008; e-mail communication, 15 September 2008.
3. Personal conversation, Amsterdam, 20 February 2008.
4. Personal conversation, Amsterdam, 20 February 2008.
5. Personal conversation, Brussels, 2 June 2008; e-mail communication, 26 August 2008.
6. Personal conversation, Lisbon, 21 April 2008.
7. Personal conversation, Amsterdam, 20 February 2008; e-mail communication, 20 November 2008.
8. E-mail communication, 6 August and 2 November 2008.
9. Personal conversation, Amsterdam, 20 February 2008.
10. Personal conversation, Amsterdam, 4 June 2008; e-mail communication, 20 October 2008.
11. 'Let's Clean Up Fashion: The State of Pay Behind the UK High Street', Labour Behind the Label, 2006; 'Who Pays for Cheap Clothes? Sweet FA? Football Associations, Workers' Rights, and the World Cup', TUC/LBL, 2006; War on Want, *Fashion Victims: The True Cost of Cheap Clothes at Primark, Asda and Tesco*, 2006. All reports available at <www.cleanclothes.org/pub.htm>, accessed 28 February 2009.
12. <http://fashioninganethicalindustry.org>, accessed 28 February 2009.
13. Personal conversation, Amsterdam, 21 February 2008.
14. Here and elsewhere in this chapter, where quotes are not preceded by a name, a common opinion is expressed; where a name is specified the text concerns individual experiences.
15. Personal conversation, Lisbon, 23 April 2008; e-mail communication, 12 October 2008.
16. Personal conversation, Brussels, 16 November 2006; Amsterdam, 21 February 2008; e-mail communication, 18 December 2008.
17. E-mail communication, 27 February 2009.

7. SUPPORT FOR WORKERS

1. Personal conversation, Bangkok, 27 November 2007.
2. Personal conversation, Bangkok, 25 November 2007.

3. *Strengthening the Urgent Appeals Network: Final Progress Report (March–July 2008) for the Sigrid Rausing Trust,* CCC, 2008.
4. Personal conversation, Amsterdam, 10 December 2008.
5. Kelly Dent, *Urgent Appeals Impact Assessment Study*, internal CCC document, July 2005, p. 67.
6. Personal conversation, Amsterdam, 20 February 2008.
7. Personal conversation, Brussels, 2 June 2008.
8. Personal conversation, Amsterdam, 21 February 2008.
9. Personal conversation, Lisbon, 22 April 2007.
10. Personal conversation, Amsterdam, 10 December 2008.
11. Personal conversation, Amsterdam, 10 January 2009.
12. *Sector-Wide Solutions for the Sports Shoe and Apparel Industry in Indonesia,* Oxfam Australia and the Clean Clothes Campaign, 2008 (<www.cleanclothes. org/documents/080320_Sector-Wide_Solutions_in_Indonesia.pdf >, accessed 1 June 2009).
13. *Decent Work and the Informal Economy, Report VI, International Labour Conference, 90th session,* ILO, Geneva, 2002, p. 5 (<www.ilo.org/public/ english/standards/relm/ilc/ilc90/pdf/rep-vi.pdf>, accessed 18 February 2009).
14. Nina Ascoly, *The Global Garment Industry and the Informal Economy: Critical Issues for Labor Rights Advocates,* IRENE/CCC discussion paper, 2004, p. 4 (<www.cleanclothes.org/documents/04-09-informal_labour_seminar_ discussion_paper_CCC.pdf>), accessed 1 June 2009.
15. Kristyne Peter, 'Organising Precarious Workers in Indonesia', *Metal World*, p. 15 (<www.imfmetal.org>, accessed 3 December 2008).
16. Ascoly, *Global Garment Industry*, pp. 12–16.
17. *Equality at Work: Tackling the Challenges, Global Report under the Follow-Up to the ILO Declaration on Fundamental Principles and Rights at Work, International Labour Conference, 96th Session, 2007, Report I (B),* Geneva: ILO, 2007, p. 33; ICFTU 2004 'Unions for Women, Women for Unions' campaign; 'The informal economy: women on the frontline', *Trade Union World Briefing* 2, 2 March 2008, p. 3.
18. E-mail conversation, 31 December 2008.
19. 'The Global Garment Industry and the Informal Economy', *CC Newsletter* 19, July 2005, pp. 8–11.
20. <www.sewa.org>, accessed 28 February 2009.
21. <www.irene-network.nl>, accessed 28 February 2009; Ascoly, *Global Garment Industry*, pp. 20–3.
22. Albania, Argentina, Finland, Ireland and the Netherlands (<www.ilo.org/ilolex/ english/newratframeE.htm>, accessed 4 February 2009).
23. *A Brief Report on the Conference Global Campaigning – Local Action, January 19–21, 2006,* CCC and CEC, internal document, pp. 51–3.
24. Kelly Dent, personal communication, Bangkok, 25 November 2007.
25. <www.tcfua.org.au/topics/2269.html>, accessed 11 February 2009.
26. Dent, *Urgent Appeals Impact Assessment Study*, July 2005, p. 26.
27. *Equality at Work: Tackling the Challenges, Report I (B),* pp. ix–x.
28. Anja K. Franck, *Key Feminist Concerns Regarding Core Labor Standards, Decent Work and Corporate Social Responsibility*, WIDE, Brussels, 2008, p. 26.
29. Ibid., pp. 20–1.
30. <www.ilo.org/public/english/gender.htm>, accessed 12 February 2009; Amelita King Dejardin, *Gender Dimensions of Globalisation*, ILO, September 2008

(<www.ilo.org/wcmsp5/groups/public/---dgreports/---integration/documents/
meetingdocument/wcms_100856.pdf>, accessed 12 February 2009); *Action
Programme on Achieving Gender Equality in Trade Unions* (<www.ituc-csi.org/
IMG/pdf/Gender_Equality_-_action_programme_E.pdf>, accessed 12 February
2009); e-mail communication with Doug Miller of ITGLWF, 31 December
2008.

31. For example, the Committee for Asian Women (<www.cawinfo.org>); Women
     in Informal Employment: Globalizing and Organizing (<www.wiego.org>);
     StreetNet (<www.streetnet.org.za>); and HomeNet (<www.newethic.org/
     homenet/home.html>), all accessed 28 February 2009.
32. Personal conversation, Amsterdam, 10 December 2008.
33. Personal conversation, Amsterdam, 10 January 2009.
34. Cha Mi Kyung, 'Who Built the South Korean Economic Miracle and Who
     are its Victims?' in Bettina Musiolek, ed., *Ich bin chic und Du mußt schuften*,
     Brandes und Apsel, 1997, pp. 45–55.
35. Private conversation, Bangkok, 28 November 2007.
36. Personal conversation, Brussels, 2 June 2008.
37. Personal conversation, Amsterdam, 3 September 2008.
38. Personal conversation, Amsterdam, 20 May 2008.
39. E-mail conversation, 31 December 2008 and 1 January 2009.
40. *A Brief Report on the Conference Global Campaigning – Local Action*,
     pp. 19–21.
41. Personal conversation, Bangkok, 27 November 2007.
42. *The Source: The Clothesource Digest of Sourcing Intelligence*, 2008, edn 12,
     p. 9; <www.betterfactories.org>, accessed 28 February 2009.
43. Personal conversation, Bangkok, 28 November 2007. Women Working
     Worldwide published a reader summarising experiences with action research
     in nine Asian and European countries: Jennifer Hurley, with Angela Hale and
     Joanne Smith, *Action Research on Garment Industry Supply Chains: Some
     Guidelines for Activists*, Women Working Worldwide, 2003.
44. Report of seminar, 'Workers' education and information on codes of conduct',
     December 1999 (<www.cleanclothes.org/component/content/article/3-codes-of-
     conduct/507-involving-workers-in-the-debate-on-company-codes>, accessed 1
     June 2009).
45. This dependency on companies may create a range of new obstacles. See section
     on China in Chapter 3.
46. *A Brief Report on the Conference Global Campaigning – Local Action*,
     p. 34.
47. Personal conversation, Amsterdam, 10 January 2009.
48. Personal conversation, Bangkok, 27 November 2007.
49. *CC Newsletter* 10, August 1998, p. 9.
50. Personal conversation, Amsterdam, 10 December 2008.

8.   CONSUMERS

1. Edna Bonacich and Richard P. Appelbaum, *Behind the Label: Inequality in the
    Los Angeles Apparel Industry*, Berkeley: University of California Press, 2000,
    p. 297.
2. Another cross-border fair trade organisation is the World Fair Trade Organisation
    (WFTO; formerly called International Fair Trade Association). Members of the

network include producer cooperatives, export companies, importers, retailers and individuals. Trading practices are monitored through self-assessment every two years. Members share their monitor reports for peer review, and each year a percentage are verified by an external inspector. Standards include working conditions, child labour and the environment. There are a number of WFTO members involved in selling clothing (<www.wfto.com/>, accessed 1 June 2009).

3. Personal conversation, Amsterdam, 19 February 2008.

4. Personal conversation, Amsterdam, 20 February 2008.

5. Cooperatives in the garment industry are usually initiated by workers who are locked out or dismissed for union activism, or because of factory closures. See, for example, the Thai Solidarity factory discussed in Chapter 3.

6. Personal conversation, Amsterdam, 6 November 2007.

7. Personal conversation, Amsterdam, 20 February 2008.

8. <www.fashioncheck.net>, accessed 28 February 2009. The following websites provide useful information about Fairtrade-labelled cotton clothes: <www.labourbehindthelabel.org/resources/reports/20/index.php> for LBL's view on Fairtrade; <www.cleanclothes.org/component/content/article/4-companies/106-background-to-fair-trade-initiatives> for information about Fairtrade cotton in the Swiss market; <www.fairtrade.org.uk/includes/documents/cm_docs/2008/c/cotton_qanda.pdf> for the Fairtrade Foundation's Q&A on cotton – all accessed 1 June 2009.

9. Personal conversation, Amsterdam, 6 November 2008.

10. Personal conversation, Amsterdam, 10 January 2009.

11. *Is Fair Trade a Good Fit for the Garment Industry?* Discussion paper 1, Maquila Solidarity Network, 2006, pp. 5–6 (<www.maquilasolidarity.org>, accessed 28 February 2009); personal conversation with Erica van Doorn (director, Fair Wear Foundation), Amsterdam, 3 September 2008. A hang-tag is a brand identification tag attached to a piece of clothing.

12. <www.nosweatapparel.com/sources/index.html>, accessed 28 February 2009.

13. Harvey Blume, 'Jeff Ballinger: Consumers, Workers, and the Internet', <www.nosweatapparel.com/news/interview3.html>, accessed 9 March 2008.

14. <www.nosweatapparel.com/sources/PT-Sepatu-Bata-DOCS/No-Sweat-Conclusions-re-Bata-Business-to-Fairwear.pdf>, accessed 28 February 2009. The CCC publishes an overview of 'ethical brands', including a claims evaluation, at <www.cleanclothes.org/faq/105>, accessed 1 June 2009.

15. Personal conversation, Bangkok, 29 November 2008.

16. Maquiladoras are factories in South and Central America that assemble parts into an end- or semi-manufactured product. With their unqualified, low-paid workforce, long hours and informal or no-contract work, they belong to the world of sweatshops.

17. <www.workersrights.org>, accessed 12 January 2009.

18. <www.solidaridad.nl>, accessed 28 February 2009.

19. Personal conversation, Utrecht, 20 November 2008.

20. Nico Roozen and Frans van der Hoff, *Fair Trade: Het verhaal achter Max Havelaar-koffie, Oké-bananen en Kuyichi-jeans*, van Gennep, 2001, p. 244.

21. <www.made-by.nl/merk_kuyichi_result.php?lg=nl>, accessed 28 November 2008.

22. A care label contains data about material, quality, and so on.

23. <www.made-by.nl>, accessed 24 November 2008.
24. E-mail communication, 1 January 2009.
25. <www.katefletcher.com/lifetimes>, accessed 28 February 2009.
26. The 'Better Bargain' campaign on giant retailers like Wal-Mart, Carrefour and Lidl was launched at the beginning of 2009.
27. Personal conversation, Louvain-la-Neuve, 2 June 2008.
28. *CC Newsletter* 14.
29. Personal conversation, Lisbon, 23 April 2008; e-mail communications, 12 October 2008 and 12 December 2008. For detailed information, see <www. made-in-no.com>, accessed 28 February 2009.

9. HARD LAW

1. Personal conversation, Bangkok, 27 November 2009.
2. World Bank, cited in *Corporate Social Responsibility at EU level: Proposals and Recommendations to the European Commission and the European Parliament*, ECCJ, November 2006, available at <www.corporatejustice.org/-ECCJ-.html>, accessed 28 January 2009.
3. Personal conversation, Louvain-la-Neuve, 2 June 2008.
4. See 'The legal angle' in Chapter 6.
5. 'Sweatshop Workers on Four Continents Sue Wal-Mart in California Court', Press Release, 13 September 2005, <www.laborrights.org>, accessed 15 March 2008.
6. Frieda de Koninck, 'Tussen droom en daad staan te weinig wetten en veel praktische bezwaren', in *Noordzuid Cahier* 4, Brussels: Wereldwijd Mediahuis, December 2000, p. 55.
7. *Controlling Corporate Wrongs: The Liability of Multinational Corporations. Legal Possibilities, Initiatives and Strategies for Civil Society*, report of international IRENE seminar, 20–21 March 2000 (<www.cleanclothes.org/component/content/article/1133>, accessed 1 June 2009).
8. Jennifer A. Zerk, *Corporate Abuse in 2007: A Discussion Paper on What Changes in the Law Need to Happen*, Core, November 2007, p. 27, available at <www.corporate-responsibility.org>, accessed 26 January 2009.
9. See section on China in Chapter 3.
10. Personal conversation, Bangkok, 28 November 2007.
11. <www.en.maquilasolidarity.org>, accessed 29 October 2008.
12. <www.schonekleren.be/wetgeving/Belgie.htm#Blabel>, accessed 1 February 2009.
13. Zerk, *Corporate Abuse*, pp. 25, 68.
14. Personal conversation, Louvain-la-Neuve, 2 June 2008.
15. *Act Now! A Campaigners' Guide to the Companies Act*, Core and Trade Justice Movement, 2007 (<www.corporate-responsibility.org/module_images/campaigners_guide_final.pdf>, accessed 29 January 2009).
16. <http://frwebgate.access.gpo.gov/cgi-bin/getdoc.cgi?dbname=110_cong_bills&docid=f:s367is.txt.pdf>, accessed 26 January 2009.
17. 'Reaction from the Clean Clothes Campaign to the European Commission Green Paper "Promoting a European Framework for Corporate Social Responsibility"', CCC, 21 December 2001 (<www.cleanclothes.org/component/content/article/1-news/148-reaction-from-the-clean-clothes-campaign-to-the-european-commission-green-paper>, accessed 1 June 2009).

18. Richard Howitt, *Update on Progress Towards a European Code of Conduct for European Enterprises Operating in Developing Countries*, 15 November 2000 (<www.cleanclothes.org/codes/howitt9.htm>, accessed 27 January 2009).

19. Speech by Richard Howitt MEP, introducing the debate on CSR, European parliament, Brussels, 30 May 2002 (<www.cleanclothes.org/component/content/article/9/553-campaigning-at-the-eu-level-for-corporate-social-responsibility-overview>, accessed 1 June 2009).

20. 'European Parliament votes to regulate multinational companies', press release, Richard Howitt, 31 May 2002 (<www.cleanclothes.org/component/content/article/9/553-campaigning-at-the-eu-level-for-corporate-social-responsibility-overview>, accessed 1 June 2009).

21. Letter of Richard Howitt, 16 July 2002 (<www.cleanclothes.org/component/content/article/9/553-campaigning-at-the-eu-level-for-corporate-social-respon-sibility-overview>, accessed 1 June 2009).

22. <www.corporatejustice.org>, accessed 28 February 2009.

23. 'Corporate Social Responsibility at EU Level: Proposals and Recommendations to the European Commission and the European Parliament', ECCJ, November 2006, p. 3 (<www.corporatejustice.org/-ECCJ-.html>, accessed 28 January 2009).

24. Press release, Richard Howitt, 13 March 2007 (<www.cleanclothes.org/component/content/article/9/553-campaigning-at-the-eu-level-for-corporate-social-responsibility-overview>, accessed 1 June 2009).

25. Filip Gregor and Hannah Ellis, *Fair Law: Legal Proposals to Improve Corporate Accountability for Environmental and Human Rights Abuses*, ECCJ, May 2008; Nina Ascoly and Joris Oldenziel, *With Power Comes Responsibility. Legislative Opportunities to Improve Corporate Accountability at EU Level* (<www.corporatejustice.org>, accessed 27 January 2009).

26. Speech of Richard Howitt MEP for Conference on Corporate Accountability, European parliament, Brussels, 29 May 2008 (<www.corporatejustice.org/IMG/doc/Speech_of_Richard_Howitt_MEP.doc>, accessed 28 February 2009).

27. Personal conversation, Amsterdam, 20 January 2009.

28. Christa de Bruin, coordinator, Dutch CCC – personal conversation, Amsterdam, 4 June 2008.

29. The Organisation for Economic Cooperation and Development unites 30 countries 'committed to democracy and the market economy' (<www.oecd.org>, accessed 28 February 2009).

30. The Trade Union Advisory Committee (TUAC) sees itself as an interface for labour unions with the OECD, and is actively involved in registering complaints under the OECD Guidelines (<www.tuac.org/en/public/index.phtml>, accessed 13 February 2009).

31. *Five Years On: A Review of the OECD Guidelines and National Contact Points*, OECD Watch, SOMO, 2005 (<www.oecdwatch.org>, accessed 28 February 2009); 'OECD Guidelines: Useful for Workers' Rights?' in *CC Newsletter* 21, May 2006, pp. 17–19; Anne Lally, *Freedom of Association and the Right to Collective Bargaining: A Clean Clothes Campaign Primer Focusing on the Global Apparel Industry*, CCC, September 2005, p. 16.

32. 'Outcome of OECD complaint case of German Clean Clothes Campaign against Adidas disappointing' (<www.cleanclothes.org/component/content/article/6/618-outcome-of-oecd-complaint-case-of-german-clean-clothes-campaign-against-adidas-disappointing>, accessed 1 June 2009).

33. OECD Watch, *Five Years On*, p. 11. Between 2000 and 2008, a total of 182 requests to consider 'specific instances' were filed; 136 were taken up, 86 of which had been concluded at the time of writing. *2008 Annual Meeting of the National Contact Points*, Report by the Chair, June 2008, p. 14 (<www.oecd.org/dataoecd/48/38/41721195.pdf>, accessed 27 January 2009).

34. OECD Watch, *Five Years On*, p. 5.

35. <www.milieudefensie.nl/globalisering/publicaties/ngotoolkit/TK_ENG_DEF.PDF>, accessed 3 February 2009.

36. Quoted in *Review of National Contact Points and the Implementation of the OECD Guidelines, Submission to the Annual Meeting of NCPs, June 2000*, OECD Watch 2008, p. 4.

37. OECD Watch, *Five Years On*, p. 43.

38. John G. Ruggie, *Protect, Respect and Remedy: A Framework for Business and Human Rights, Report of the Special Representative of the Secretary-General on the Issue of Human Rights and Transnational Corporations and Other Business Enterprises*, 7 April 2008 (<www.reports-and-materials.org/Ruggie-report-7-Apr-2008.pdf>, accessed 23 January 2009).

39. OECD Watch, *Five Years On*, pp. 48–9.

40. *Review of National Contact Points*, 2008, pp. 1–2.

41. Ruggie, *Protect, Respect and Remedy*, p. 24.

42. <www.ilo.org/ilolex/cgi-lex/ratifce.pl?C087>, accessed 27 January 2009.

43. John G. Ruggie, *Keynote Presentation*, Annual Meeting of National Contact Points, OECD, Paris, 24 June 2008, pp. 1–2 (<www.oecd.org/dataoecd/9/63/40933850.pdf>, accessed 27 January 2009).

44. *Controlling corporate wrongs.*

45. Letter from CCC International Secretariat to John Ruggie, 3 March 2007.

46. Letter from John G. Ruggie to Ineke Zeldenrust of the CCC, 17 April 2007.

47. Ruggie, *Protect, Respect and Remedy*, p. 9.

48. Ibid. pp. 5–6.

49. Ibid. p. 8.

50. In legal terms, due diligence is 'the diligence reasonably expected from, and ordinarily exercised by, a person who seeks to satisfy a legal requirement or discharge an obligation'. *Black's Law Dictionary*, 8th edn, 2006.

51. Ruggie, *Protect, Respect and Remedy*, p. 21.

52. Ibid. p. 22.

53. Ibid. pp. 23–7.

54. Ibid. p. 28.

55. 'Joint NGO Statement to the Eighth Session of the Human Rights Council', 19 May 2008 (<www.hrw.org/en/news/2008/05/19/joint-ngo-statement-eighth-session-human-rights-council>, accessed 23 January 2009).

56. Jennifer A. Zerk, *Filling the Gap: A New Body to Investigate, Sanction and Provide Remedies for Abuses Committed by UK Companies Abroad*, Core, December 2008, p. 13 (<www.corporate-responsibility.org>, accessed 26 January 2009).

10. COMPANIES

1. For the complete code, see <www.cleanclothes.org/codes/index.htm> (accessed 28 February 2009).

2. See the section on Bangladesh in Chapter 3.

3. Dr Martin Buttle, Dr. Alex Huges, Prof. Neil Wrigley, *Organising Ethical Trade: A UK–USA Comparison*, Newcastle University, University of Southampton, Economic & Social Research Council, 2007, pp. 15–16 (<www.cleanclothes.org>, accessed 20 January 2009).

4. *Codes Memo* 19, Maquila Solidarity Network, September 2005, pp. 1–10 (<www.maquilasolidarity.org>, accessed 28 February 2009). For the Nike *FY2004 Corporate Responsibility Report* and factory list, see <www.nikeresponsibility.com>; for the Gap *2004 Social Responsibility Report*, see <www.gapinc.com>; for the H&M *Corporate Social Responsibility Report 2004*, see <www.hm.com/ca_uk/hm/social/csr_rapport.jsp>. All accessed 28 February 2009.

5. Duncan Pruett, with Jeroen Merk, Ineke Zeldenrust and Esther de Haan, *Looking for a Quick Fix: How Weak Social Auditing is Keeping Workers in Sweatshops*, CCC 2005 (<www.cleanclothes.org/pub-archive.htm>, accessed 20 January 2009).

6. Ibid. pp. 14–15. Another report, called *Codes of Conduct Implementation and Monitoring in the Garment Industry Supply Chain*, commissioned by the Geneva-based Fondation des Droits de l'Homme au Travail and released in the same year, largely corroborates the CCC's findings. For a copy, contact the FDHT at <infos@fdht.org>.

7. Pruett et al., *Looking for a Quick Fix*, pp. 74–83.

8. Under the Suppliers Ethical Data Exchange (SEDEX) system, suppliers own the data and can choose which retailers can see it. Under the Fair Factories Clearinghouse (FFC) system, the retailers and brands at the top of the supply chain own the data and can choose whether to share audit results with other retailers. Buttle et al., *Organising Ethical Trade*, p. 16.

9. See <www.cleanclothes.org/codes-of-conduct>, accessed 1 June 2009, for more information on MSIs.

10. Quoted in *Codes Memo* 11, MSN, June 2002, p. 4 (<www.maquilasolidarity.org>, accessed 28 August 2008).

11. Ibid. pp. 3–4.

12. Personal conversations, Amsterdam, 3 September and 12 October 2008.

13. <www.jo-in.org>, accessed 28 February 2009.

14. *Interim Report, Reporting the Progress and Learning of the Jo-In Pilot Project in its First Phase of Implementation*, February 2003–September 2006, p. 18 (<www.jo-in.org>, accessed 28 February 2009).

15. Ibid., p. 19.

16. Personal conversations, Amsterdam, 3 September and 12 October 2008.

17. Ibid.

18. *Gap 2004 Social Responsibility Report* (<www.gapinc.com>, accessed 28 February 2009).

19. Dexter Roberts and Pete Engardio, with Aaron Bernstein in Washington, Stanley Holmes in Seattle, and Xiang Ji in Beijing, 'Secrets, Lies and Sweatshops' (<www.businessweek.com/mediacenter/podcasts/cover_stories/covercast_11_16_06.htm>, accessed 13 January 2009).

20. Buttle et al., *Organising Ethical Trade*, p. 19. The ETI, instead of monitoring and verifying code implementation, conducts pilot projects to arrive at a set of best practices. Sam Maher, working with the UK CCC Labour Behind the Label, reports that ETI has had some good results in the UK, including the

prohibition of the illegal use of migrant workers by gang-masters. 'ETI has also kept the BSCI at a distance in the UK', she says.

> But because there is no monitoring or verification, companies are allowed to stand still. So they do. And there is no transparency – you have to join ETI to get information. Its credibility rests on the fact that it includes all major UK retailers. We hope that internationalisation of the Fair Wear Foundation will challenge the ETI.

Personal conversation, Lisbon, 20 April 2008.

21. <www.fairolympics.org/countries/PLAYFAIRpress.pdf>, accessed 1 June 2009.
22. Jeroen Merk, *From Code Compliance to Fair Purchasing Practices: Some Issues for Discussion*, CCC, 2005, p. 6 (<www.cleanclothes.org/documents/05-05-Fair_Purchasing_Practices.pdf>, accessed 1 June 2009).
23. *Sportswear Industry Data and Company Profiles: Background Information for the Play Fair at the Olympics Campaign*, CCC, 1 March 2004, p. 13.
24. <www.forbes.com/lists/2007/37/biz_07fab50_Pou-Chen_O0QP.html>, accessed 20 December 2008. According to this site, Pou Chen moves production to China's interior to save money and opens factories outside China and Vietnam to circumvent European Union tariffs.
25. *The Source: The Clothessource Digest of Sourcing Intelligence*, 2008, edn 12, pp. 12–13.
26. Nina Ascoly and Ineke Zeldenrust, *East and South-East Asia Regional Labour Research Report*, CCC, December 2003, pp. 15–16 (<www.cleanclothes.org/component/content/article/9/7-publications-overview>, accessed 1 June 2009).
27. Jeroen Merk, 'Birnbaum's Global Guide to Winning the Great Garment War: A Critical Review', paper written for the seminar 'Pricing in the Global Garment Industry', Mulheim, Germany, 20–21 February 2003, pp. 9–10; Jeroen Merk, 'The structural crisis of labour flexibility: Strategies and prospects for transnational labour organising in the garment and sportswear industries', CCC, 2008, p. 11 (<www.cleanclothes.org/component/content/article/7-publications/116-the-structural-crisis-of-labour-flexibility>, accessed 1 June 2009).
28. See the section on Southern Africa in Chapter 4.
29. Gary Gereffi, at <www.pbs.org/wgbh/pages/frontline/shows/walmart/interviews/gereffi.html>, p. 11 (accessed 14 March 2008). The website contains a transcription of the interview with Gereffi.
30. Ibid., pp. 11–12.
31. Ibid., pp. 7–8.
32. *CC Newsletter* 25, May 2008, pp. 10–11.
33. A. Brenner, B. Eidlin and K. Candaele, 'Wal-Mart Stores, Inc.', 2006. Document prepared for the International Conference 'Global Companies – Global Unions – Global Research – Global Campaigns', quoted in Jeroen Merk, *Update on Global Social Compliance Programme*, CCC, December 2008 (<www.cleanclothes.org/documents/08-12-GSCP_update.pdf>, accessed 1 June 2009).
34. 'Who pays for our clothing from Lidl and KiK?' (<www.saubere kleidung.de/downloads/publikationen/2008-01_Brosch-Lidl-KiK_en.pdf>, accessed 28 February 2009); 'Aldi's clothing bargains: Discount buys discounting

standards? Working conditions in Aldi's suppliers in China and Indonesia: Suggestions for consumer and trade union action' (<www.suedwind-institut. de/downloads/ALDI-publ_engl_2007-08.pdf>, accessed 28 February 2009).

35. <www.tescopoly.org/index.php> (accessed 28 February 2009).
36. CC *Newsletter* 25, May 2008, pp. 10–11.
37. Merk, 'Structural Crisis'.
38. This is discussed in more detail in the section on urgent appeals in Chapter 7.
39. <www.asiafloorwage.org> (accessed 29 January 2009).
40. Ibid., pp. 29–30.
41. 'A Brief Report on the Conference "Global Campaigning – Local Action"', 19–21 January 2006, CCC internal document, p. 8.
42. E-mail communication, 31 December 2008.
43. 'Sector-wide solutions for the sports shoe and apparel industry in Indonesia', Oxfam Australia and CCC, 2008 (<www.cleanclothes.org/documents/080320_ Sector-Wide_Solutions_in_Indonesia.pdf>, accessed 1 June 2009).
44. Personal conversation, Amsterdam, 19 January 2009.

Bibliography

Ascoly, Nina and Chantal Finney, eds, *Made by Women. Gender, the Global Garment Industry and the Movement for Women Workers' Rights*, CCC, 2005.

Ascoly, Nina and Joris Oldenziel, *With Power Comes Responsibility: Legislative Opportunities to Improve Corporate Accountability at EU Level*, ECCJ, 2007.

Bender, Daniel E. and Richard A. Greenwald, eds, *Sweatshop USA: The American Sweatshop in Historical and Global Perspective*, Routledge, 2003.

Bieler, Andreas, Ingemar Lindberg and Devan Pillay, eds, *Labour and the Challenges of Globalization: What Prospects for Transnational Solidarity?* London: Pluto Press, 2008.

Bonacich, Edna and Richard P. Appelbaum, *Behind the Label: Inequality in the Los Angeles Apparel Industry*, Berkeley: University of California Press, 2000.

Burckhardt, Gisela, ed., *Who Pays for Our Clothing from Lidl and KiK?*, Kampagne für Saubere Kleidung, 2008.

China Labour Bulletin, 'Falling Through the Floor: Migrant Women Workers' Quest for Decent Work in Dongguan', *China*, Research Series 2, 2006.

——'Small Hands: A Survey Report on Child Labour in China', 2007.

Ching Yoon Louie, Miriam, *Sweatshop Warriors: Immigrant Women Workers Take On the Global Factory*, Cambridge, MA: South End Press, 2001.

Connor, Timothy, *We Are Not Machines*, Oxfam Community Aid Abroad, 2002.

Core/Trade Justice Movement, 'Act Now! A Campaigners' Guide to the Companies Act', 2007.

Crabbé, Carole, René De Schutter, Denis Lambert, Christophe Scohier and Benoit Théau, *De mode uit de doeken: 12 Vragen over werken in de textielconfectie*, Magasins du monde, Oxfam, 1999.

Crabbé, Carole and Isabelle Delforge, *Jouets de la Mondialisation*, Vista, 2002.

Dejardin, Amelita King, *Gender Dimensions of Globalisation*, ILO, 2008.

Duval, Chantal, ed., *Workers' Voices: The Situation of Women in the Eastern European and Turkish Garment Industries*, CCC and Evangelische Akademie Meissen, 2005.

Green, Duncan, *Fashion Victims: Together We Can Clean Up the Clothes Trade: The Asian Garment Industry and Globalisation*, Cafod, 1998.

de Haan, Esther and Gary Phillips, *Made in Southern Africa*, CCC, 2002.

Hale, Angela and Jane Wills, ed., *Threads of Labour: Garment Industry Supply Chains from the Workers' Perspective*, Blackwell, 2005.

ILO, 'Decent Work and the Informal Economy', Report VI, International Labour Conference, 90th session, 2002.

——'Equality at Work: Tackling the Challenges', Global Report under the follow-up to the ILO Declaration on Fundamental Principles and Rights at Work, International Labour Conference, 96th Session 2007, Report I (B), Geneva, 2007.

ITUC, 'Action Programme on Achieving Gender Equality in Trade Unions', 2007.

ITUC, GUF, HKCTU, HKTUC, 'Child Labour, Forced Labour and "Work Experience" in China – the Blurred Lines of Illegality', Hong Kong Liaison Office (IHLO), 2007.

ITUC, ITGLWF, CCC, 'Play Fair 2008. No Medal for the Olympics on Labour Rights', 2008.

Klein, Naomi, *No Logo*, Harper Perennial, 2005.

Labour Behind the Label, 'Let's Clean Up Fashion: The State of Pay Behind the UK High Street', 2006.

Labour Behind the Label, 'Who Pays for Cheap Clothes? Five Questions the Low-Cost Retailer Must Answer', 2006.

Loong-yu, A., N. Shan, and Z. Ping, *Women Migrant Workers under the Chinese Social Apartheid*, CAW, 2007.

Merk, Jeroen, *The Structural Crisis of Labour Flexibility: Strategies and Prospects for Transnational Labour Organising in the Garment and Sportswear Industry*, CCC, 2008.

Musiolek, Bettina, ed., *Ich bin chic und Du mußt schuften*, Brandes und Apsel, 1997.

Musiolek, Bettina, *Made in Eastern Europe: The New 'Fashion Colonies'*, Terre des Femmes E.V. Tübingen, 2004.

OECD Watch, 'Five Years On: A Review of the OECD Guidelines and National Contact Points', SOMO 2005.

Pruett, Duncan, *Looking for a Quick Fix: How Weak Social Auditing is Keeping Workers in Sweatshop*, CCC, 2005.

Roozen, Nico and Frans van der Hoff, *Fair Trade: Het verhaal achter Max Havelaar-koffie, Oké-bananen en Kuyichi-jeans*, van Gennep, 2001.

Rosen, Ellen Israel, *Making Sweatshops: The Globalization of the US Apparel Industry*, University of California Press, 2002.

Ross, Andrew, ed., *No Sweat: Fashion, Free Trade and the Rights of Garment Workers*, Verso, 1997.

Ruggie, John G., 'Protect, Respect and Remedy: A Framework for Business and Human Rights', Report of the special representative of the secretary-general on the issue of human rights and transnational corporations and other business enterprises, 2008.

Smit, Marijke and Lorette Jongejans, *C&A: De Stille Gigant, van kledingmultinational tot thuiswerkster*, Amsterdam: SOMO, 1989.

Stein, Leon, ed., *Out of the Sweatshop: The Struggle for Industrial Democracy*, Quadrangle/The New York Times Book Co., 1977.

War on Want, 'Fashion Victims: The True Cost of Cheap Clothes at Primark, Asda and Tesco', 2006.

Wick, Ingeborg, *Aldi's Clothing Bargains: Discount Buys Discounting Standards?*, Südwind, 2007.

Organisations in the CCC Network

The list below may serve those readers who want to know more about the CCC network and to get involved. It is not an exhaustive list, and the relationships between the CCC and the organisations represented differ widely in content and quantity. With some, the CCC collaborates on a daily basis; with others, less frequently. Some are research organisations; others are campaigns like the CCC; some only facilitate networking. Some local organisations in the network, like factory unions, are not included, since it would be of little use to a general reader to contact them, and vice versa. Their existence and importance is described in the book, and should anybody wish to contact them, the CCC International Secretariat may accommodate them. Similarly, national CCCs may accommodate requests for contacts in their own countries.

If any organisations are left out that should have been included, the author of this book is to blame.

AFRICA

AMDH	Association Marocaine des Droits Humains, www.amdh.org.ma
CSRSC	South African Civil Society Research and Support Collective, www.csrsc.org.za
FES Madagascar	www.fes-madagascar.org
KHRC	Kenya Human Rights Commission, www.khrc.or.ke
LRS	Labour Research Service South Africa, www.lrs.org.za
Streetnet	www.streetnet.org.za

ASIA

AMRF Society	Alternative Movement for Resources and Freedom Society, Bangladesh, P: 00880-2-8119260, F: 00880-2-9123718 E: amrf@dhaka.net
AMRC	Asia Monitor Resource Center, www.amrc.org.hk
ALE	Asia Labour Exchange, Indonesia, wulanbdg@gmail.com
AFWC	Asia Floor Wage Campaign, www.asiafloorwage.org
BIGUF	Independent Garment Workers' Union Federation, Bangladesh, T: +880 2 9346724, F: +880 2 8828403, E: biguf@dhaka.net, biguf@link3.net
CAW	Committee for Asian Women, www.cawinfo.org
CEC	Centre for Education and Communication, India, www.cec-india.org
Cividep India	Workers' rights and corporate accountability, www.cividep.org
CLB	China Labour Bulletin, www.china-labour.org.hk/en

CWWN	Chinese Working Women Network, www.cwwn.org
Dabindu	Sri Lanka, T: +94 4831365, F: +94 2233336, E: dabindu@stmail.lk
FTZ&GSEU	Free Trade Zones and General Services Employees Union, Sri Lanka, ftzunion@diamond.lanka.net
Garteks	Garment and Textiles Union Federation, Indonesia, T: +62 21 70987473, F: +62 21 8577646, E: garteks_sbsi@hotmail.com; fgarteks@ksbsi.or.id
GSBI	Federation of Independent Trade Unions, Indonesia. T: (62-21) 786 4203, F: (62-21) 786-4203.
GATWU	Garment and Textile Workers Union, gatwu@rediffmail.com
GM	Globalization Monitor, www.globalmon.org.hk/en/
HKCTU	Hong Kong Confederation of Trade Unions, www.hkctu.org.hk/english
IHLO	International Hong Kong Liaison Office of the international trade union movement, www.ihlo.org
Karmojibi Nari	Working women, Bangladesh, www.karmojibinari.org
KASBI	Kongres Aliansi Serikat Buruh Indonesia, kp_kasbi@yahoo.nl
KCTU	Korean Confederation of Trade Unions, http://kctu.org
KWWAU	Korean Women Workers' Association United, http://kwwa.tistory.com
LAC	Labour Action China, www.lac.org.hk/en/index.php
LBH Bandung	Bandung Legal Aid, Indonesia, www.lbhbandung.or.id
Munnade	Women Garment Workers' Front Bangalore, India, www.cividep.org/munn.htm
NGWF	National Garment Workers Federation, GPO Box No. 864 Dhaka, Bangladesh, T: 019 340268, a624831 (res.), F: 880 2 9562562, E: ngwf@aitlbd.net
SACOM	Students and Scholars Against Corporate Misbehaviour, Hong Kong, http://sacom.hk
SAVE	India, sare@mda.vsnl
SEWA	Self-Employed Women's Association, India, www.sewa.org
SPN	Serikat Pekerja Nasional, Indonesia, T: + 62 21 7981233, spn_dpp@yahoo.com
TIE Asia	Transnationals Information Exchange Asia, tieasia@streamyx.com
TLC	Thai Labour Campaign, www.thailabour.org
WAC	Workers Assistance Center, www.wacphilippines.com
WAC Cambodia	Women's Agenda for Change, www.womynsagenda.org
WE	Worker Empowerment, Hong Kong, www.workerempowerment.org
WRAWA	Women's Rights at Work Association, calisankadinlar@gmail.com

AUSTRALIA

AWW	Asian Women at Work, www.awatw.org.au

Fair Wear	FairWear Campaign Australia, www.fairwear.org.au
NikeWatch	www.oxfam.org.au/campaigns/labour-rights/nikewatch
Oxfam Australia	www.oxfam.org.au
TCFUA	Textile, Clothing and Footwear Union of Australia, www.tcfua.org.au
NSW	Working Women's Centres, www.wwc.org.au

EUROPE

AAI	www.agribusinessaccountability.org
Banana Link	www.bananalink.org.uk
CCC International	www.cleanclothes.org
CCC Austria	Clean Clothes Kampagne, www.cleanclothes.at
CCC Belgium (North.)	Schone Kleren Campagne, www.schonekleren.be
CCC Belgium (South)	Vêtements Propres, www.vetementspropres.be
CCC Denmark	Clean Clothes Campaign, www.cleanclothes.dk
CCC France	L'Ethique sur l'Etiquette, www.ethique-sur-etiquette.org
CCC Germany	Kampagne für Saubere Kleidung, www.sauberekleidung.de
CCC Italy	Campagna Abiti Puliti, www.abitipuliti.org
CCC Netherlands	Schone Kleren Campagne, www.schonekleren.nl
CCC Norway	Kampanjen Rene Klaer, www.reneklaer.no
CCC Spain	Campaña Ropa Limpia, www.ropalimpia.org
CCC Sweden	Kampanjen Rena Kläder, www.renaklader.org
CCC Switzerland	Clean Clothes Campaign, www.cleanclothes.ch
CCC UK	Labour Behind the Label, www.labourbehindthelabel.org
Changemaker	www.changemaker.no
Cidac	Portugal, www.cidac.pt
CFFB	Conseil des Femmes Francophones de Belgique, www.cffb.be
ECCJ	European Coalition for Corporate Justice, www.corporatejustice.org
ECRA	Ethical Consumer Research Association, www.ethicalconsumer.org
Erklärung von Bern	www.evb.ch
Eurocities	www.eurocities.eu/main.php
EFD	Evangelische Frauenarbeit Deutschland, www.evangelischefrauen-deutschland.de
FAIR	Societa Cooperativa Sociale www.faircoop.it
Fair Trade Center	www.fairtradecenter.se
FEI	Fashioning an Ethical Industry, http://fashioninganethicalindustry.org
Felicitas	Homeworkers Serbia and Montenegro, www.felicitas.org.rs
FNV (Mondiaal)	Federation Dutch Trade Unions, www.fnv.nl, www.fnv.nl/mondiaal
FPS	Femmes Prévoyantes Socialistes, www.mutsoc.be/fps
Frauensolidarität	www.frauensolidaritaet.org
Gaia	Portugal, http://gaia.org.pt

GoodElectronics network	www.goodelectronics.org
ICN	India Committee of the Netherlands, www.indianet.nl/english.html
KDF	Katholische Deutscher Frauenbund, www.frauenbund.de
KFB	Katholische Frauen Bewegung Austria, www.kfb.at
KARAT	Karat Coalition, www.karat.org
Le monde selon les femmes asbl	www.mondefemmes.org
LO TCO Bistandsnamd	secretariat, international Trade Union development cooperation, www.lotcobistand.org
MakeITfair	www.makeitfair.org
NEAD	Norfolk Education & Action for Development, www.nead.org.uk
NEWW	Network of East–West Women, Poland, www.neww.org.pl
No Sweat	www.nosweat.org.uk
ORG AUR	Decent Work, Romania, www.resurseumane-aur.ro
Permaculture and Peacebuilding centre Macedonië	www.ppc.org.mk/English/index.htm
Peuples Solidaires	www.peuples-solidaires.org
PHO	Polish Humanitarian Organisation, www.pah.org.pl
SASK	Trade Union Solidarity Centre Finland, www.sask.fi/English
SETEM	Federación SETEM, www.setem.org
SOMO	Centre for Research on Multinational Corporations, www.somo.nl
Südwind	Institut für Ökonomie und Ökumene, www.suedwind-institut.de, www.suedwind-agentur.at
Tropical Commodity Coalition	www.teacoffeecocoa.org
Terre des Femmes	www.frauenrechte.de/tdf/index.php
Tescopoly	Alliance concerned with the negative impacts of supermarket power, www.tescopoly.org
UFCS	Union Féminine Civique et Sociale, www.ufcs.org
Vie Féminine	www.viefeminine.be
WAD	Womens' organisation Bulgaria, www.women-bg.org
War on Want	www.waronwant.org
Wereldsolidariteit	www.wereldsolidariteit.be
WIDE	Women in Development Europe, www.wide-network.org
WO=MEN	Dutch gender platform, www.wo-men.nl
WWW	Women Working Worldwide, www.women-ww.org

LATIN AMERICA AND CARIBBEAN

ASEPROLA	Asociación Servicios de Promoción Laboral, Costa Rica, www.aseprola.org

CALDH	Centro para la Acción Legal para los Derechos Humanos, Guatemala, www.caldh.org
CAWN	Central America Womens' Network, www.cawn.org
MEC	Movimiento Mujeres Trabajadoras Desempleadas Maria Elena Cuadra, Nicaragua, www.mec.org.ni
STITCH	Women Organizing for Labor Justice, www.stitchonline.org
Other	Contact MSN: www.maquilasolidarity.org

NORTH AMERICA AND CANADA

AWID	Association for Women's Rights in Development, www.awid.org
CLR	Campaign for Labor Rights, www.clrlabor.org
ILRF	International Labor Rights Forum, www.laborrights.org
MSN	Maquila Solidarity Network, www.maquilasolidarity.org
NPEC	National Pay Equity Coalition, www.pay-equity.org
Solidarity Center	Support of independent unionising, allied to AFL/CIO, www.solidaritycenter.org
Sweatfree Communities	www.sweatfree.org
UNITE HERE!	Formerly Union of Needletrades, Industrial and Textile Employees and Hotel Employees and Restaurant Employees International Union, www.unitehere.org
USAS	United Students Against Sweatshops, http://studentsagainstsweatshops.org
US/LEAP	US Labor Education in the Americas Project, www.usleap.org
Wal-Mart Watch	http://walmartwatch.com
WRC	Workers Rights Consortium, www.workersrights.org

GLOBAL

Amnesty	Amnesty International, www.amnesty.org
BHRRC	Business and Human Rights Resource Centre, www.business-humanrights.org
CEGW	Corporate Ethics and Governance Watchdog, www.corp-ethics.com
CorpWatch	www.corpwatch.org
FLO	Fairtrade Labelling Organizations International, www.fairtrade.net
FOE	Friends of the Earth, www.foei.org
HomeNet	International network for home-based workers, www.newethic.org/homenet/home.html
Homeworkers Worldwide	www.homeworksww.org.uk
HRW	Human Rights Watch, www.hrw.org
ITGLWF	International Textile, Garment and Leather Workers' Federation, www.itglwf.org

IGTN	International Gender and Trade network, http://web.igtn.org
ITUC	International Trade Union Confederation, www.ituc-csi.org
LABOURSTART	www.labourstart.org
WIEGO	Women in Informal Employment: Globalizing and Organizing, www.wiego.org

Index